The
Rich & Famous
Money
Book

THE RICH & FAMOUS MONEY BOOK

Investment Strategies of Leading Celebrities

JEAN SHERMAN CHATZKY

John Wiley & Sons, Inc.

New York • Chichester • Weinheim • Brisbane • Singapore • Toronto

Copyright © 1997 by Jean Sherman Chatzky
Published by John Wiley & Sons, Inc.

ISBN: 0-471-18540-X

Printed in the United States of America

10 9 8 7 6 5 4 3 2 1

For Peter, whose love keeps me going,
whose humor keeps me sane,
and whose stunning grasp of Strunk & White
keeps me grammatically correct

Contents

Acknowledgments

Every book is a collaborative effort, and this one was literally the work of dozens of people—from the friends and colleagues whose brains I picked for profile ideas to the energetic publicists who worked diligently to drag their clients to the phone. I want to thank them all, but mention those who went above and beyond.

First, the financial experts who make my job a little easier each day: financial planners Dee Lee and Gary Schatsky, Keith Gumbinger at HSH Associates, Bernard Kleinman at Richard A. Eisner & Company, Don Phillips at Morningstar, Inc., Hrach Alexanian of OneSource, and credit card gurus Robert McKinley at Ram Research and Ruth Susswein of the Bankcard Holders of America.

Thanks also go to the publicists, agents, and business managers who helped orchestrate my subjects' participation: Jordan Berman, Cindy Bressler, Jim Bronner, John Calandro, David Hochberg, Judy Katz, Ginny Quirk, Kitty Thomas, Martha Wright, and Nicole Young. (I also owe a huge debt of gratitude to John Capozzi, who opened up his well-stocked Rolodex and let me have a peek.)

Many of my current and former colleagues at *SmartMoney* magazine were helpful at various stages of this project, notably Wally Konrad, Pete Finch, Nancy Better, Nellie Huang, Emily Harrison, Laura Holson, Bob Sabat, and Bob Safian. I especially want to thank *SmartMoney* editor-in-chief Steve Swartz and editor Stuart Emmrich, who gave me the time—and more importantly the skills—necessary to take on this book.

I want to thank my Today show family, Jeff Zucker, Michael

Bass, Linda Finnell, and particularly Janice DeRosa, for their support and encouragement, not only through this project, but in general.

My friends and relatives, who tirelessly offered up their favorite celebrities as possible profiles, will find that many of their suggestions made their way into this book. To that end, thanks go to: Diane and Ken Adler, Jonathan Birnbach, Audrey and Jerry Chatzky, John and Lucia Chatzky, Stefan Fatsis, Joan Gmora, Lisa Greene, Audrey Johnson, Susan Kleinman, Randall Lane, Amy and Frank Linde, Rosa and Bernie Meyers, Ilene and Steven Miller, Jane and John Nelson, Keith and Kim Oster, Evy and Brian Rosen, Gabrielle Roventini, David Sherman, Eric Sherman, and Ed Sussman.

I am hugely indebted to my agent, Robert Shepard, who knows just when to hold my hand; my able fact checker Gisela Williams; ace publicist Drew Kerr; Cape Cod Compositors for production; and of course the team at John Wiley who guided this book smoothly through the process, notably Myles Thompson, Peter Knapp, DeeDee DeBartlo, Laurie Thompson, Jack Savage, Bari Zahn, Michael Detweiler, and, mostly, my talented and unflappable editor Debby Englander, who was a pleasure to work with.

I want to thank my parents, Chuck and Elaine Sherman, for believing that I could write a book and encouraging me to do it, and my children, Jake, who wrote his own volume on a portable computer by my side, and Julia, who arrived just on time to allow me to meet my deadline.

Finally, I want to thank the 28 individuals who gave me a peek inside their financial lives. I hope you find their stories as fascinating as I did.

Introduction

I got hooked on celebrities' financial secrets back in 1994. It was March, and I had an appointment to interview Clinton campaign strategist James Carville about his investment and spending habits for my employer, *SmartMoney*, the *Wall Street Journal*'s magazine of personal business.

I remember being extremely nervous. *SmartMoney* was a new publication, and it was difficult to convince topnotch celebrities to agree to be profiled in our "Me & My Money" column. Carville, in truth, had acquiesced as a favor to a friend, Al Hunt, the *Journal*'s Washington editor. Now the interview was in my hands and I didn't want to blow it.

The weather came close to blowing it for me. Washington was hit by snow and Carville, delayed in Miami, had put off our interview until "sometime tomorrow." When he was finally ready, his assistant called me and said, "If you can get over here in 10 minutes, he'll squeeze you in." Great, I thought. Now all I need is for my tape recorder to die.

Thankfully, it didn't. And Carville, talking at his usual breakneck speed, had me caught up in his world of personal finance within minutes. He told a tale of financial woe—being practically penniless on the streets of DC following the first (unsuccessful) Gary Hart campaign—and I empathized (my first job in New York paid a whole $13,500 a year). He explained that he was nervous about retirement—"You see those charts that say if you put away $500 a year starting at age 20, by the time you're 50 you'd have a gazillion dollars. It makes you ill that you didn't do it."—and I felt anxious to get on the stick. And when he talked of holding onto his shares of Coca-Cola stock because he heard that Warren Buffett had just taken a large position, I found myself nodding right along.

What makes looking inside the investment world of an entertainer or sports star as compelling as learning about their romantic escapades? For one thing, it gives us a chance to see how we measure up. We can pat ourselves on the back for buying shares of Philip Morris along with football coach Mike Ditka, or funding our 401(k) to the limit as NBC's Matt Lauer does. We can roll our eyes at the celebrities' financial gaffes, telling ourselves that if we earned millions like NBA bad boy Dennis Rodman, we wouldn't fall behind on our Ferrari payments. And we can chuckle over their strange money habits, knowing that if we had a bank account the size of Helen Gurley Brown's, we'd never even *think* about taking the bus.

Perhaps even more compelling is the opportunity to learn from celebrities' money management habits. Let's face it: One way in which the rich *are* different is that they have access to the country's top financial minds. Ivana Trump's personal broker is Alan C. "Ace" Greenberg, the chairman of Bear, Stearns & Company. (Both are profiled in the coming pages.) Rodman's coterie of friends includes his agent, Dwight Manley, a proven financial whiz, as well as multimillionaire Jim Jennard, founder of Oakley sunglasses. And Mike Ditka has been known to hit the links with a CEO or two.

Another difference between *us* and *them* is that their account balances are fatter than ours. They can withstand an occasional loss, a fact that enables the wealthy to test the financial waters in ways many Americans would find too risky or controversial. But after hearing about their carefully honed strategies, we can now put them to use in our own portfolios. We may never have as many millions in the bank as Netscape founder Jim Clark or a Picasso on our office walls like divorce attorney Raoul Felder or as many different homes and properties as *The First Wives Club* author Olivia Goldsmith. But when Clark tells us he's made a small fortune buying quality stocks on negative news, that's a tactic we can use in our own investment dealings. When Felder explains he believes in buying the lesser works of great artists (not vice versa as conventional wisdom dictates), we might consider doing the same. And when Goldsmith—who's made a tidy profit in every piece of property she's flipped—says she looks for something beyond location, location, location in making her purchases, anyone who's ever considered buying real estate would be well advised to listen.

We can also cull a lot from their mistakes. Take stock tips from a well-meaning friend? Forget it, advises Matt Ditka, Mike's son and his stockbroker. His dad has seen 20 percent average returns on his portfolio the past few years; on the tips he's received from friends, he's been lucky not to incur a loss. How about cold calls? Steer clear, says sports agent Jim Bronner. "[Celebrities are] always being hit on by people who want to sell them investment products—and not very well thought out products at that," says Bronner, who counts Cecil Fielder among his clients. Fielder paid a bundle for whole life insurance, which carries a hefty commission, when what he really needed was cheaper second-to-die coverage. Many laypeople have done the same. What about ceding control of your finances to someone else? Never, says Olivia Goldsmith, who sunk $40,000 into the hole as a result of a nasty divorce.

In the pages that follow, you'll read about the investing, spending, and saving habits of more than two dozen celebrities. Their stories were not only surprising and candid, but heartwarming and a great relief. Some spoke about the financial lessons taught them by their parents. Others discussed what they want to teach their kids. Some confided how it felt to grow up without money. Others explained how they handled a financial setback. Just about every person described the feeling of losing a bundle on one truly insane investment (which of course didn't seem so crazy at the time).

Perhaps what makes their stories the most compelling is the fact that these people were willing to share their experiences. Radio psychologist Dr. Joy Browne often says that people are much more willing to talk about sex than they are to talk about money. Think about it from your own perspective. You probably don't want your colleagues knowing how much is in your weekly paycheck or how much you lost in the divorce. Perhaps you're not above bragging that you made a killing buying Intel, but when it comes to actually quantifying the gain, you'll pass. It's just not anyone's business that you've got a bundle stashed in Magellan—or that your retirement account falls way short of where you think it should be.

Celebrities, I can attest, share that sentiment. For every person profiled in the upcoming pages, there were a good half dozen who flatly refused my interview request. Many, from "Dilbert" scribe Scott Adams to actor Greg Kinnear, felt the information was just too personal. "[John Reed] values what privacy he can salvage from his job as chairman and chief executive officer of Citicorp and Citibank," wrote a bank spokesman in answer to my fax. "Steve [Young] is very private when it comes to his finances and his private life, so please do not take this personally," his agent replied. Even personal finance columnist Jane Bryant Quinn was reluctant to open the door on her finances. "I appreciate the offer," she said on my voice mail. "But I've always kept a very low profile in my personal life and I would just as soon continue that."

Others, from actress Sandra Bernhard to "Jeopardy's" Alex Trebek to writer Barbara Taylor Bradford (who canceled an interview at the last minute once she thought about what it would entail) said through their spokespeople they just didn't have a good enough handle on their money to sound intelligent talking about it. Still others couldn't imagine carrying on a conversation at length. "I'd be so boring!" was the message I received from humorist Al Franken. "I invest like a retired high school principal."

The truth is, he probably would have made many of us feel a lot less inadequate about our own investing strategies and spending habits. Those nagging self-doubts are what make us reach for *People* at the checkout counter when it features a cover line like "Financial Fiascoes of the Stars," a February 1997 report on how rapper M. C. Hammer went through $33 million and Kim Basinger had to sell her Georgia town. It's what makes us participate in cocktail party conversations about whether Michael Jordan is really worth $18 million a year, or the cast of "Seinfeld" a million—each—per episode.

The celebrities who sat down with me to discuss their financial lives did that and more. Each of the nine chapters that follow contains a few of their stories, organized by their investment style. You'll hear from the entrepreneurs like Lillian Vernon and Wendy's Dave Thomas about the fear involved in putting thousands to millions on the line for a dream business. From the stock junkies like astronaut

Jim Lovell and major league catcher Don Slaught you'll hear how they tell the difference between a highflier and a dog. And from couples like Ken and Daria Dolan and business partners like Mary Sue Milliken and Susan Feniger (the "Too Hot Tamales"), you'll hear how they handle differences in their money styles, ranging from the minor to the extreme.

At the end of each chapter, you'll find detailed advice on how to apply the celebrities' strategies to your own portfolios. That way you'll know just whose advice you want to take—and how far you want to take it.

THE
RICH & FAMOUS
MONEY
BOOK

Chapter 1

THE STOCK JUNKIES

Mike Ditka • Don Slaught
Jim Lovell

"I believe in companies. The people who run companies, the people who work for companies, the people who buy their products. Whether it's Pepsi or GE or Ford Motor."

—Mike Ditka

THESE DAYS, IT SEEMS THAT INVESTING IS SYNONYMOUS WITH mutual funds. You certainly get that impression from the business press, whether it's the "Superstar Funds" cover of *SmartMoney*, *BusinessWeek*'s "Mutual Funds Guide," or the weekly profile of a fund manager in the Money & Business section of the Sunday *New York Times*. After all, who wouldn't jump at the chance to have a seasoned professional investor to determine which stocks you should buy?

As it turns out, quite a number of people don't *ever* want that sort of input and even more prefer to go it alone occasionally. Count football coach Mike Ditka among the diehards. Apollo 13 captain Jim Lovell and major league catcher Don Slaught fall into the second category. All three like the challenge of stock picking the old fashioned way. They get a tip on the golf course or a call from their broker or money manager, or take notice of a new product or service that seems to be catching on. They follow it up with a little homework like reading the 10K, glancing at the Value Line report, or calling up earnings estimates on their home computer. They are not traders, but long-term investors. Slaught has been known to buy more of a company he believes in when it takes a dive. Lovell held onto his stakes in Exxon and Merck—against the advice of his brokers—and both have been winners. And Ditka explains: "If you get into a stock with a good track record, you're not going to lose it. Chances are you're going to get 10 to 15 percent over time."

The allure of individual stocks for these three—as well as for David Brown (page 160), Nicole Miller (page 28), and many others you'll read about in the chapters ahead—is the feeling of being closer to the action. Choose wisely, they've learned, and you'll beat the pros at their own game.

Mike Ditka

MIKE DITKA, 58, the newly-installed coach of the New Orleans Saints, is best known for his 11-year stint as "Da Coach" of the Chicago Bears. Ditka was named coach of the year in 1988 and took the Super Bowl in 1989 before being released during a tough 1992 season. After leaving the Bears, he became a broadcaster, hosting a thrice weekly radio show in Chicago and providing football analysis for NBC. He recently opened a restaurant in Chicago called Iron Mike's.

HALL OF FAME FOOTBALL COACH MIKE DITKA LIKES TO TELL THE world that he has mellowed. That infamous end-of-game explosion at Jim Harbaugh in Minnesota after the Bears had blown a 20-point lead and lost to the Vikings, 21–20? It would never happen today. The reports from his gin-playing buddies that they had to tote along extra cards, because if Ditka lost he'd tear up the pack? That was a long time ago. The blowups on the golf course, putters twisted and whacked in two? Been there, done that.

Today, according to Ditka, he's a kinder, gentler version of his former self. He's no longer angry about being fired in the midst of a losing season in 1992, and after years of blustering that he would never return to professional coaching, he took the helm at the New Orleans Saints, tearing up on the podium when the announcement was made: "I'm an idealistic guy," he shrugs.

However, one place Ditka's new attitude is conspicuously absent is in his investments. Whether Ditka is choosing stocks, investing in a new business, or gambling with his buddies on the golf course, *mellow* is about the last word you'd use to describe his strategy.

HOLDING ON TO GOOD COMPANIES

Take a look at his portfolio. At his age, 58, you'd expect his stock investments to be balanced with substantial holdings in both fixed-income securities and even lower risk investments like CDs—insurance to weather whatever choppy waters the market brings. Not Da Coach. He's got well over 90 percent of his money in the markets in individual stocks. The one comforting factor is that most of his portfolio is in large companies like General Electric, Pfizer, Merck, Walt Disney and Colgate-Palmolive, not small, riskier start-ups. This past year he bought AT&T, which he believes is a solid long-term holding. He also recently added to his position in Philip Morris, a company he loves not only for its products but also for its $4.80 dividend, which enables him to keep income rolling in as he watches hopefully for the price to appreciate.

Ditka gets his stock ideas from two primary sources: his buddies on the golf course (many of whom are top-level corporate executives) and his broker, who happens to be his son Matt, 30, who works for Milwaukee-headquartered Robert Baird & Company. Ditka's about even on the recommendations he's gotten from friends. Some have gone up with the market, but a company called SoftNet Systems he purchased on the recommendation of a friend has since released a few sorry earnings reports and tanked. Ditka was able to sell part of his investment at a respectable $16, but it was recently trading at around $5.

Fortunately, his son's suggestions (many of which come out of the research department at Baird) have done considerably better. They've enabled Ditka to pull in a 20 percent annual return in both 1995 and 1996. Matt Ditka's biggest winner has been Intel purchased at both $59 and $69, recently trading around $130. "We thought it was a good company that had been hit too hard," Matt Ditka says. He's also done well by Dad with Ford Motor, which has risen 28 percent since Ditka bought it. Cobra Golf was a two-time winner. Matt got his father in at $30, and sold at $36. The stock then dropped back to $30 and Matt, who had started hearing rumors that it was a takeover target, bought it back. The rumor mill paid off; his shares were bought out at $36.

That's not to say father and son are always on the same page. Matt Ditka lobbied his father to buy more Motorola throughout 1996 despite a couple of dismal earnings reports (one of which many investors believe was responsible for the market's rough period in the summer of that year). "It hasn't been outstanding lately," admits Matt, "but I still love it." The mellow Ditka took the loss on the chin. He didn't even pick up the phone to rant and rave at his son. "He's pretty calm about [losing money] as long as we did it for the right reasons," says Matt, clearly relieved.

There have also been times when the son made the correct call but his father didn't listen. Matt suggested selling U.S. Robotics at $82, after almost a 100 percent gain, but his dad continued to believe in the company's potential, so they've stuck with it. It has since dropped to $75 and Mike Ditka still isn't ready to let go. "His philosophy is pretty much—very much—buy and hold," says Matt. In other words, a large fundamental change has to occur in order to convince Mike Ditka to change course.

"I believe in companies," Mike Ditka says. "The people who run companies, the people who work for companies, the people who buy their products. Whether it's Pepsi or GE or Ford Motor." This is why, Ditka explains, he hasn't bought into the mutual fund craze of the past few years. He has a few funds, remnants from his relationships with previous brokers, including a small number of shares in GT Global, Kemper Small Cap, and Van Kampen American, and two bond funds in his IRA, Franklin Tax Free and Salomon Brothers Closed End Bond Fund. Upon signing up with his son's firm, he instructed Matt just to hold the existing funds for the sake of diversification, but not to take any new positions. In his mind, they're too far from the source. They're also not as much fun.

A DOG OF AN INVESTMENT

Funds and individual stocks have proven more lucrative than some of Ditka's more ambitious investments. His worst play was a dog— literally. It was a hot dog stand called Ditka Dogs, that served up foot-longs dripping with mustard, sauerkraut, onions, chili, the works. The Coach had visions of franchising Ditka Dogs in every food court, highway rest stop, and airport corridor, but it didn't quite work out that way. The original stand, right in the heart of Chicago, was a bit too glitzy for its product. Overhead was out of control, the management team was unprepared, and Ditka was too busy coaching to keep a finger in the pot. For three years, Ditka continued to dump money into the place—after all, the hot dogs tasted pretty good—but finally he wised up and pulled the plug. "We had no chance of getting our money out," he says with 20/20 hindsight. He was out $400,000.

Still Ditka hadn't given up on the restaurant business. A successful joint bearing his name—like a Rusty Staub's or Mickey Mantle's in New York—was still one of his dreams. An early $40,000 investment in five Chicago-based Burger Kings that has earned him his money back 10 times over has convinced him there's profit to be made in the food world. So he tried again. In January 1997, Iron Mike's, an upscale steak, fish, and chop house, opened its doors in Chicago's Tremont Hotel. Its decor? Chicago Bears memorabilia, of course. It's no Charlie Trotter's (see page 102), but Ditka hopes this concept will take off and spread through the country. (A New Orleans location, perhaps?)

FIVE MILLION OVER THREE YEARS

For the past several years, the bulk of Ditka's income has come from NBC, where he worked as an analyst for NFL games beside Greg Gumbel, Chris Collinsworth, and Joe Gibbs. (For the 1994 Super Bowl, he even traded quips with O. J. Simpson.) Many high-profile coaches have sat out their game for a while in the booths, waiting for their next shot at a championship to materialize. The skeptical Chicago press has speculated that if Ditka's tenure proves as short as his predecessors' (the Saints have had 10 coaches in 30 years), he'll go running back to the booth, his tail between his legs.

Yet, after pulling in a cool $5 million over the next three years, Ditka could just as easily slow the pace. He could return to radio (during his coaching hiatus, he cohosted a show in Chicago three times a week for an hour a shot). He could make the occasional cameo, such as his recent appearance on the sitcom "Third Rock from the Sun." Or he could just play golf.

Anyone who knows Ditka will tell you that golf has become his life. He hits the course twice a day except in the dead of winter. He belongs to a slew of country clubs—two in Chicago, one in Indiana, another in South Carolina, one in Scotland. And he is part owner of one in Naples, Florida, called Olde Florida. The latter course is private, with a $100,000 admission ticket. Ditka and his buddies built the place primarily for their own enjoyment, but ownership will eventually revert to the members once enough people sign up to pay back the original investment. Will it make Ditka money? It should, although Ditka was more concerned with playing a good round. "We didn't want people messing around for five hours," Ditka gripes. "Here you get off on time. You finish on time. The people who play our course enjoy it a lot more than any other course."

One reason Ditka is able to be so cavalier about his investments is that money doesn't drive him. "I don't respect money," he says a bit flippantly. "It's not my god. If I have it, I'm very generous—I give to people on the street. A hundred-dollar bill means a lot more to some guy down on his luck that it does to me." Without it, Ditka says, life would go on, just as it did when he was a child—the son of a blue-collar steel-mill worker in Carnegie, Pennsylvania.

HARD WORK AND HARD PLAY

It's not as if he doesn't put in a solid day's work anyway. Even Ditka's critics agree: The man toils. In the Bears, he took a team he had inherited and won more than 100 games in the 11 regular seasons, something only five pro coaches have ever accomplished. He was named coach of the year in 1988 and took the Super Bowl in 1989, and even Harbaugh, the player Ditka chewed out on the sidelines, later said: "It was an honor to play for Mike Ditka." Despite the fact that his new job pays extremely well, there has been great speculation that for Ditka taking it not only means a pay cut—it means working even harder.

"My parents raised four kids. We never had anything, but we never needed anything—we had clean clothes, a pair of shoes, enough to eat, my parents had a car. And everybody else was the same. The only people who had more were kids whose fathers were doctors or lawyers." Ditka learned from his father that "you get out of life what you put into it. If you expect something for nothing you're not going to get it, but if you're willing to put in a hard day's work, you'll get something back."

As hard as he works, Ditka also plays—and spends. The hand-rolled cigars he covets don't come cheap. Nor do the old cars that line his garages. Ditka has been collecting classic vehicles since he was an assistant coach for the Dallas Cowboys. Today he's got four in his garages: a Jaguar XK120, an Auburn roadster, a 1961 Bentley purchased in London, and his current favorite—a 1948 Packard that was rebuilt over the past six years with all-new mechanics. "It takes me back to my childhood, though it's something I certainly didn't have when I was a kid," Ditka says. Between the cars and his two substantial homes, one outside Chicago, the other in Naples, Florida, Ditka isn't lacking for niceties. "If I have a desire to go to Florida, I go to Florida," he shrugs. "If I can't get a plane at a decent time, I'm liable to lease one."

He's tried to give his four children—all from his first marriage—a taste of the good life as well. All have country-club memberships they wouldn't be able to afford on their incomes. Not only does that allow them to enjoy a more-than-occasional day on the links, but also, as Ditka points out, they can meet people who might be able to help them get ahead in business.

The get-ahead mentality that drives Ditka, however, isn't always in his best interest. Matt Ditka recently sat his dad down and tried to talk him into scaling back his investment risk. Someday, the son argued, this bull market is going to end. Some of his other clients were selling stocks as a hedge. His dad would have none of it. Matt tried another tactic: "You'll have to retire eventually," he said to his dad. Mike Ditka waved his son off.

"I plan on living to be 150 and I'm not worried about outliving my money, either," Da Coach says matter-of-factly. "I'm way ahead of where I was supposed to be in this life so, I figure, the sky's the limit."

Don Slaught

DON SLAUGHT, 39, known as "Sluggo" since his college days, is the backup catcher for the San Diego Padres. Born and raised in California, he began his athletic career at UCLA. Out of college he played for a number of years for the Texas Rangers before being traded to the Pittsburgh Pirates, Chicago White Sox, and, most recently, the Padres. He and his wife, Sandy, spend the off-season at their home in Texas. They are the parents of four.

ALL STOCK INVESTORS—AND CERTAINLY ALL ATHLETES—DON'T fly by the seat of their pants as Ditka often does. Major league baseball player Don Slaught, for one, has had just as much success as Ditka in the market. But his approach is much more methodical and, occasionally, contrarian.

It was late 1987, not long after Black Monday, and Slaught, a young catcher with the Texas Rangers, was at an impasse with his investments. His value investments, stocks like Ford Motor and mutual funds including Nicholson and several from Fidelity, were in the tank. Slaught sank down in the couch in the Dallas office of his financial adviser, John Calandro, and asked: "What do I do?"

Calandro sized up his client. He knew he was going to offer the same piece of advice to this twentysomething ball player that he'd been giving seasoned investors twice Slaught's age. He just wasn't sure how Slaught was going to take it. "We put more money in the account," said Calandro. "We double our investment. We buy more."

Slaught sat silently for 10 seconds, then looked Calandro straight in the eye. "Okay," he said. "Let's do it."

It was, of course, the right move. The mutual funds, including the Janus Fund, that Slaught got into at the time, have been solid performers. Nonetheless, Calandro was floored. It was his first indication that his young client possessed a maturity well beyond his years. "I would have bet money that he—like the other athletes I work with—wouldn't do it," he remembers. "Most athletes are rear window investors. They go by yesterday's hot *Money* magazine tip. That's not how Don makes choices. He understands that his age gives him the ability to bail out of any early decisions he makes."

After a series of trades, Slaught now plays for the San Diego Padres. Like Kevin Costner's wizened catcher in *Bull Durham*, his managers count on him to be a coach on the field and keep inexperienced players in line. It is one of the reasons his playing time has extended years beyond his—and others'—expectations. This same levelheadedness continues to serve him well in his finances. For example, Slaught has believed that the market was a bit overheated over the past year or so. But he didn't panic and get out; he held on and prospered. "I think a lot about what I'd lose if I pulled some back now," said Slaught in late February. "But the truth is I feel pretty comfortable. Most of the money I have invested now, I won't need to touch for 10 years. If the market tanks, I'll probably add to my positions."

AN ASTUTE INVESTOR

Don Slaught's firm grasp on his finances comes to him naturally. An economics major at UCLA, he sailed through required courses in statistics and accounting. He reads the *Wall Street Journal* daily, sifts through every issue of *Money* and *Forbes*, and gets a number of financial newsletters. His most recent asset allocation chart is usually within reach.

Currently, Slaught's assets are divided as many financial planners would recommend for a man of his age, especially one in the prime of his earning life. He has 70 percent of his assets in equities (about 40 percent large-cap, 10 percent small-cap, and 20 percent international), 20 percent in fixed income, 5 percent in cash, and the remaining 5 percent in riskier, hit-or-miss ventures. He's even analytical about what he spends. On cars, for example. "The cars I own are a '67 Corvette and a '71 Volvo P1800," Slaught explains. "They're cheaper to own over the long run than if I bought new. I paid $45,000 for them. I put in about $1,000 a year fixing them up. Insurance is cheaper because they're registered as antiques. And I drive them. But when I'm ready to sell, I'll be able to get my $45,000 out. If I bought a new Mercedes, I could have paid $50,000, but five years later, I'd only get $20,000 out."

Slaught didn't always have it all figured out. Fresh out of college in 1980, he signed with the Kansas City Royals. One of the first things he did with his relatively small paycheck was open an account at a local brokerage firm. His first stock pick was a winner and Slaught flipped it. In hindsight, Slaught realizes, that was actually a curse. It sent him on a hunt for other flashes in the pan. There were times he would sit on a stock for nine months while it sat stagnant. Frustrated, he'd sell and of course it would start to rise. "I made a lot of mistakes by trading too fast," he recalls. "I was losing on the upside. I was losing on the downside. I was playing all the rumors. Most of those things, if I had just stuck with them, I'd have made money."

Finally, after a number of years investing with little success, Slaught made a concerted effort to settle down. His failures had taught him two important lessons: First, buying for the long term is almost always better. And second, he didn't have enough time to do the necessary research to invest on his own. "Being a baseball player, I was either at practice or on the road," says Slaught. "I didn't have the luxury of being right on top of things. I had to invest more in people."

GETTING THE RIGHT ADVICE

Beginning in the mid-eighties, Slaught began building his "team" of investment advisers. "I don't think one person can pick both real estate and stocks, or one investment firm can be good at both growth investments and value plays," he says. "I diversify by using people for what they're good at." First on board was Calandro, an estate-planning attorney, whom Slaught went to see about a will. They were introduced by a mutual friend, a practice pitcher for the Texas team, on the day after Slaught was hit in the face by a fast ball thrown by Oil Can Boyd. "Another quarter of an inch and he would have died," Calandro says. "I doubt he even remembers that first meeting." In fact, what Slaught remembered was that Calandro seemed to have a knack for making very complicated estate planning concepts, like insurance trusts and charitable remainder trusts, understandable. In no time, Calandro was supervising his client's entire financial picture.

Next on the roster was the California firm of Van Deventer & Hoch, hired to build a low-risk value stock portfolio. "We picked a beta that we thought Don could handle, then after his contracts started kicking in, increased his risk," Calandro explains. They did that by hiring Pasadena-based money manager Roger Engemann to build a second portfolio in growth stocks. Slaught's cousin, a real estate syndicator, and his father, a developer, handle his investments in land and property, and also watch the performance of the other advisers.

Once a quarter, Slaught and Calandro sit down and go over the professionals' performance. In between, they leave well enough alone. Engemann doesn't call to ask if he can sell NationsBank. Van Deventer doesn't check in before selling Ford. "Don doesn't ask how to build the watch, he wants to know what time it is," Calandro explains. Should performance lag the market, a bad quarter isn't going to get one of his managers fired. But, six months to a year of underperformance would call for some serious rethinking.

Slaught has other holdings as well. On the fixed income side, he has bond mutual funds with Fortis and Fidelity. His baseball retirement plan—into which he contributes the maximum each year, partially matched by his team's contribution of $7,500—is sitting in Vanguard's well-regarded Windsor II. He also has a SEP-IRA (simplified employee pension plan) to which he contributes the maximum allowable. There are a couple of real estate deals, which have fared only so-so. And on a much riskier front, he's socked money into a few partnerships with venture investor

Russell Cleveland. Cleveland pools $20 million from assorted investors and then divides the money among 10 different start-up companies—in some instances simultaneously assuming a seat on a company's board. "The hope is that out of the 10 you get two big winners," Slaught explains. "It's risky, but with the potential for very high returns."

DOING YOUR HOMEWORK

One thing all of Slaught's many financial holdings have in common is that they are well analyzed. He brings his father and cousin along to many business meetings. He scours all the literature before coming to the bottom line. "I like to get three, four, even five different opinions from different people—and not just brokers—before I make an investment. I listen to my father, I listen to my wife; mostly I ask, does this investment feel good to my heart? That's saved me several times.

"I remember one in particular," he says. "It was a partnership deal in a start-up company and it looked great on paper. I was tempted—I saw the big dollar signs; I thought about the profit that could be made. But something was making me feel uncomfortable. So I'll tell you what kept me out of it. I asked myself: 'If I did make the large dollars, would it change my lifestyle?' And the answer was no. So I figured, why take the risk?"

Slaught is quite proud of the fact that he could retire today knowing that his wife, Sandy, and his four children—three girls and a boy—would be taken care of. School is paid for. Weddings are done. "If I died, they'd be able to lose their first fortune, then have a second and third chance before the money ran out," says Slaught. "It's much easier to make financial decisions once you know that your family is taken care of, and your house is paid for. The rest is gravy.

"I'm a big believer in financial moves you can't lose on like trusts and charitable foundations," says Slaught. When I contribute $100,000 each year to my foundation, I know that's money I don't have to dole out.

"The living trusts afford my estate privacy and ease of transition to my children. The irrevocable trust provides financial security and some estate protection for my children. The charitable remainder trust gives me the ability to donate the principal of an investment but retain some rights to the interest earned. And the charitable foundation enables me to make larger gifts in high-earning years that are distributed out over several years."

In fact, one of the first things Calandro helped Slaught do was to set up a charitable foundation. His biggest winners in the stock market aren't sold, leaving him with capital gains taxes to pay. Instead, they're funneled into the foundation via a charitable remainder trust that will provide income for a number of years to the Slaught children before the principal is given to a variety of Christian and children's charities including the Make-A-Wish Foundation. "I know that someday when I die, my family will get more of my money than the government will," says Slaught, whose Adi Foundation is named after his mother, who passed away a few years ago.

Today, having played years longer than anyone believed he would, Slaught is looking at playing just another year or two. Retiring will bring on two major life decisions. Slaught will have to pick a place to live—Texas has the benefit of no state income tax, but Slaught and Sandy are both a bit homesick for their native California. He also has to choose a second career. Slaught lists three tempting alternatives: There's real estate development, perhaps in partnership with his father and cousin. There's a job in baseball as a coach or a manager, which he'd love, though he notes the months away from home are really rough. Or, he could purchase and run a small business, perhaps an electronics or sporting goods store, and spend time with his kids.

But Calandro has a fourth. "I think he could be a financial adviser," he says. "He'd have to take a step back, go through the whole learning process, get the right credentials. But I know he'd have an immediate clientele in sports. And I know he'd be good at it." Calandro pauses. "He has great intuition."

Jim Lovell

JIM LOVELL, 69, captained Apollo 13, the 1970 space flight that captured the world's attention because of a nearly catastrophic midspace explosion. He retired from NASA in 1973 and had several careers, first in the shipping industry, then in telephones, before chronicling his memories of the flight in Lost Moon: The Perilous Voyage of Apollo 13 *(Houghton Mifflin, 1994). Since the book and the 1995 hit film based upon it were released, Lovell has had a lucrative speaking career. He and his wife Marilyn split their time between Horseshoe Bay, Texas, and Lake Forest, Illinois.*

UNLIKE DON SLAUGHT, WHO WILL LIKELY EARN MOST OF HIS LIFETIME income before he hits 40, astronaut Jim Lovell has had to be exceedingly patient. That was especially hard for four days in 1970.

From April 13, 1970—when a midspace explosion altered Apollo 13's mission from a peaceful moon expedition to a desperate attempt to return safely to earth—until April 17, when the craft successfully splashed down, Captain James R. Lovell, Jr., recalls two themes that played over and over in his mind. First, of course: How do we get home? A close second: Does my family have enough money to survive?

Back then NASA's astronauts, even the standouts like Lovell, were paid about as well as college professors. In 1952, Lovell's first year out of naval training at Annapolis, he took home around $7,000. In 1968, when he became one of the first people to orbit the moon, he was earning nearly $20,000. And when he retired from NASA as a captain in 1973, he was bringing in $26,000. Today's astronauts earn somewhere between $50,000 and $70,000, a fortune to Lovell's ears.

But huddled in the lunar module, which served as lifeboat for the three Apollo 13 passengers during the aborted mission, Lovell didn't think much about how grateful he was to his employer. Instead he dwelled on the modest life insurance policy he'd taken out for his family. If he returned home to earth, he swore, he'd make sure his wife Marilyn and his children would be taken care of financially.

FINDING A NEW CAREER (OR TWO)

In the two-and-a-half decades that followed, Lovell has done just that. How? He worked in one industry, then another, investing his take-home—aggressively, but wisely—along the way. "I guess you could say I've had three careers," the longtime Texan fairly drawls from his office in the Chicago suburbs where he now lives half of the year. "Maybe four." Following the fated Apollo flight, Lovell watched other astronauts walk the moon from his new post at Mission Control in Houston. Two years later, he retired from both NASA and the Navy, began what he likes to call his "second career" in the tugboat industry, and embarked on the beginning of his quest for a no-worry financial scenario.

Back in the 1970s, two family-owned and -operated tugboat companies had a monopoly on docking ships in the Houston area. As Lovell prepared to leave NASA, one of the companies, Bay-Houston, was looking for a leader. The grandfather who had long run the company was getting too old to be the hands-on manager. "I was the bridge," Lovell explains. "I ran the company until the grandson was ready to take over." Although he earned a fair salary—easily topping his astronaut's pay—the family offered him no stake in the company's future. Certain that ownership was one of the keys to financial stability, Lovell left in search of a position with an equity stake.

He found it in telephones. In January, 1977 Lovell joined a friend in business selling phone systems for a company called Fisk Telephone. This was a new venture, a result of a Supreme Court decision allowing companies to own phone equipment that marked the beginnings of deregulation. Lovell's 8 percent of Fisk became more valuable as annual sales leapfrogged from $6 million to $40 million. Fisk was then purchased by a larger player in the business called Centel. Lovell stayed with Centel—and held onto his Centel stock—until he retired in 1991. A few years later, his Centel shares were swapped for shares of Sprint in yet another acquisition. "To a great degree, that was the Lovell family fortune, such as it is," he says. "Over the years Sprint has done very, very well indeed."

Before retiring, Lovell had the forethought to negotiate for use of his office and his secretary for a year to ease his way into the slow lane. ("I did it," he quips, "so the culture shock wouldn't be so great on my wife.") Lovell's plan was to fund his retirement by making speeches about his Apollo 13 experience; he'd already been doing so occasionally and had always received more requests than he could handle. Now that he had a free calendar, he figured, he'd simply start accepting more invitations. As luck would have it, the Gulf War began, and the corporations that hired him to highlight their events scaled back on corporate symposia. Suddenly, Lovell had an empty calendar and less than $50,000 in speaking income for the year, less than he'd earned in some time.

WRITING HIS MEMOIRS

It was Lovell's longtime secretary who suggested he put his Apollo 13 experiences down on paper. The three astronauts who shared the capsule had wanted to start writing that immediately upon their return to earth, but other engagements intervened. Fred Haise stuck with the space program for a number of years before heading into the aerospace industry; he's now retired from Grumman Technical Services. And Jack Swigert left NASA for politics; he was elected to Congress from his home state of Colorado, though he died of cancer before taking office. "Despite the best intentions of all of us, we never got around to it," Lovell shrugs.

Serendipitously, it was right around this time Lovell received a letter of introduction from Jeff Kluger, a writer, who was also interested in telling the story of Apollo 13. They met, connected, and embarked on what eventually became a two-and-a-half-year writing project. It didn't take that long, however, to figure out that they were onto something big. With just one chapter and an outline on paper, the pair's agent at William Morris sparked a bidding war for U.S. and foreign rights to the book and even for screen rights. The six-figure advance for *Lost Moon: The Perilous Voyage of Apollo 13* (Houghton Mifflin, 1994) was followed by a six-figure option from Ron Howard's company, Imagine Films Entertainment. And in 1995 when the movie came out with America's hottest actor, Tom Hanks, in the Lovell role, the astronaut's speaking career (his fourth, if you're counting) took on new life. Last year, Lovell gave 149 speeches at $25,000 a pop ($20,000 after agent's fees). Add it up. His seven-figure income is astounding even to Lovell himself—who points out that he grew up, after all, in a one-room apartment that didn't even have its own bath.

FOUR INVESTMENT PORTFOLIOS

Having finally made his fortune, Lovell has been working hard to find smart places to invest it. Along with his four careers, he now has four investment portfolios. One contains the remainder of his Centel—now Sprint—stock. A second consists of what began as his Centel 401(k), which has been rolled over into an IRA, as well as a defined benefit plan for his self-employment income. That is invested in stock mutual funds. A third is loaded with municipal bonds and bond funds.

Then there's the Lovells' primary stock portfolio, which, for estate planning purposes, is in Marilyn Lovell's name. It is run day-to-day by Donaldson, Lufkin, Jenrette, though Lovell says he watches the performance of the brokers like a hawk. "As we're talking I have the trade confirmations of the things they're doing right in front of me," he says. "Whenever I get one, I look up the commission, the profit or loss. Periodically, I get updates with the rate of return." His speaking engagements, which are mostly corporate, also provide him with a number of stock ideas. After giving a speech to executives of Sun Microsystems, for example, Lovell instructed his brokers to buy that stock as he did with Microsoft. His brokers wanted to unload both Exxon and Merck, but experiences on the road convinced Lovell to hold—both have been winners.

But he has still had his share of dogs. In his younger days, Lovell bought into various land partnerships in the Houston area, many of which are barely above water. "I've kept the faith," says Lovell. "Hopefully they'll come back." Back in the late seventies and early eighties, he also made what he calls "very foolish" plays in tax shelters. The worst of the lot: Liberian lumber. "I was very naive in those days," he shrugs.

Lovell's traditional real estate investments, which are considerable, have done much better. He and his wife have residences in both Horseshoe Bay, Texas, and Lake Forest, Illinois, and hold the mortgages on their children's homes as well. "I'm the banker, but I've made sure it's an arm's-length transaction," Lovell says. "I set up an account with DLJ, and I'm charging them regular rates. In fact, one of the boys was complaining about his 8 percent [mortgage]. He said he can get a cheaper rate elsewhere." Still, Lovell says he prefers doing business with his children this way, rather than simply giving his children the deeds to their homes. "They have to know the value of money," he says. "At least this way, if they crash, they have a friendly banker they can fall back on."

ESTATE AND TAX PLANNING

While Lovell's not eager to give his kids a handout today, he and Marilyn have made certain that their estate will pass smoothly when the time comes. They've established what are known as A-B or marital trusts so that if he predeceases her, the income from his assets in trust flows to her and vice versa, though the underlying stocks, bonds, and real estate remain in trust to be passed along to the eventual beneficiaries—their children—at the death of the second spouse. This move saves the heirs hundreds of thousands in federal estate taxes, which seems to be the one type of taxes Lovell is reluctant to cough up.

Ask him if he believes the federal government is swiping too much of his current income, and he'll give you an earful. Forget those tax shelters of the seventies; today he's singing a different tune. "I'm a flat tax advocate," he says defiantly. Not in the sense that Steve Forbes is a flat tax advocate; Lovell doesn't believe one rate will work for everybody. He favors a somewhat regressive flat tax. If he were in the White House, Americans would be taxed at whatever rate it took to pay for the government's budget each year (one year 18 percent, the next 20) on income over $50,000. Income below that level would be taxed on a sliding scale, which would zero out when if you weren't earning more than a designated level of sustenance. There would be no deductions. And the sole job of the IRS would be to oversee the process to make sure everyone is paying a fair share.

Accountants would hate this plan, Lovell is quick to admit, because it would put a lot of them out of business. "I couldn't do my taxes now," he says. "My 1040s, they're fairly simple, because that's just earned income. But the forms for investments and land deals are too much. I would be more than happy to figure out all the income I have and just pay a percentage."

The other government program that Lovell would love to overhaul? Social Security. When he turned 65 four years ago, before his speaking career took off, he went to his local Social Security office to get information on the entire system. "Let's take a look at how much you'll be getting from us each month," said the woman behind the counter.

"I have a Navy pension," Lovell offered, in an attempt to make sure the government didn't overpay him.

"Oh, don't worry, that doesn't count," she said.

"I get a pension from Centel too; that should put me over the limit," said Lovell.

The woman pooh-poohed that as well.

"And I have some investments that are making money also."

"Those don't count either," she said.

"Well, what does count?" Lovell asked incredulously.

"Just earned income."

"You mean," he said, "if I made a million a year in just investments and pensions, I could still pick up Social Security? No wonder we're going broke. If I was running things, all of your income would apply to Social Security. That way the only people who'd get it are the ones who really need it."

Lovell laughs, knowing he sounds like he's about to announce his candidacy for Congress. In fact, he'd love to run for office. But today that's not the fifth career he has in mind. Lovell's son, Jay, has been a chef in the Chicago area for many years, but has always wanted to open a restaurant of his own. His father is about to make that possible by entering the food business, as the money man. They're working toward opening an eatery in Chicago's North Side. It'll be an elegantly casual theme restaurant, Lovell says, with the artifacts and awards he collected in the space program discreetly on display. The backdrop for the restaurant's design: a huge mural, 20 feet long and 8 feet high, that was the basis for the patch for Apollo 13.

"They say the restaurant business is the most difficult to be a success in," says Lovell. "Perhaps this will be my most dangerous career . . . in a different sort of way."

WHEN IT'S *YOUR* MONEY . . .

YOU MAY NOT HAVE A STOCKBROKER IN THE FAMILY LIKE MIKE Ditka. You probably don't have his paycheck either. Or that of Don Slaught or Jim Lovell. But that doesn't mean you need to steer clear of individual stocks. Many experts believe that the mutual fund craze has done individual investors a disservice by convincing them that they can't pick stocks as well as the pros.

In fact, most equity funds underperform the market each year. That's why David Gardner, coauthor of *The Motley Fool Investment Guide* (Simon & Schuster, 1995), says bluntly: "We think individual stocks are where everyone should be. Sure, there are some great funds, with good long-term performance records. But by the time you get into them, some have lost their managers, others have attracted so much money they end up *being* the market—they're invested in every stock that makes up an index—and then you have to take out expenses. Customers would have been better off in an index fund."

That said, picking stocks takes work. Whether you adhere to the stock picking strategies of Warren Buffett or Peter Lynch, develop your own methodology, or utilize one of the stock selection methods our experts suggest below, you'll need both time and confidence in your convictions. Says Gardner: "We're speaking to people who feel comfortable in this exploration, and have the patience and savvy that it takes to manage one's own money."

If this describes you, there are a few basic guidelines to follow in building a stock portfolio. First, invest for the long term. "One problem is that most people who want to buy individual stocks don't have the prudence and patience of mutual fund investors," says Media, Pennsylvania financial planner Howard Rothwell. "You're better off assuming you *won't* make a killing in everything you buy, but having a reasonable return objective—say, 10 percent annually—for every position. After all, you may want to hold GE for the rest of your life." Besides, if you trade too often even discounted commissions will quickly eat away at your returns. (Assume you invest $1,000 in a stock. The average discount broker will charge you $40 to make your purchase, another $40 to sell. That's 8 percent of your initial investment down the drain.)

Second, diversify. Eventually, you'll want to have 10 to 20 different stocks, depending on how many you can monitor. Fewer than 10 and you've got too many eggs in one basket. More than 20 are tough to keep tabs on. But be wary of diversifying too quickly with too little capital—if you put less than $1,000 into a stock, you'll wind up throwing too much of your return away in commissions. You're better off diversifying slowly as you stockpile the additional cash.

Third, select or develop a methodology. You could go the fundamental route, using your computer to screen for companies of a certain size, in certain sectors, with specific earnings growth rates or a limited amount of debt on their balance sheets. "There are thousands and thousands of different corporations; you have to have some way of narrowing the field," points out Bernard Kleinman, a financial planner and CPA with Richard A. Eisner & Company in New York. Next, you'll want to examine the Securities and Exchange Commission (SEC) documents (like the annual report and proxy statement) for the companies that rise to the top of your lists. These, unfortunately, contain not only a great deal of pertinent information but also a lot of junk. Read the annual report from back to front, Kleinman suggests, starting with the footnotes. There you'll get a brief description of what the company does, as well as unusual accounting procedures or outstanding litigation. The proxy statement, which contains information about a company's officers, is also especially important. "If it turns out that the chairman is 93, and his son, the vice chairman, is 70, that company may not have much of a future," says Kleinman. "On the other hand, it may be a good target for a takeover."

These days, you can also gain a lot of information about particular stocks in cyberspace. Gardner's Motley Fool site on America Online, for example, is flush with individual investors discussing specific stocks. Internet newsgroups like misc.invest are also chock-full of participants, though they're not as well organized as the Motley Fool boards. If you're interested in technology stocks, you should also check out the tech forums on CompuServe. This is where computer types congregate to talk about problems in the latest versions of their favorite software or hardware. Their impressions often foreshadow a company's struggles or successes for the next couple of quarters.

If you're not confident about your ability to go it alone, you could also follow someone else's methodology. Gardner, for example, has two to suggest. First is his Dow Dividend model. This involves examining the 30 companies that make up the Dow Jones Industrial Average to isolate the two to five that have the highest dividend yield and have been beaten down the most during the past year. You purchase equal amounts of those stocks (whether you buy two, three, four, or five depends on how much cash you have; Gardner advises putting at least $2,000 a year into each company). This process takes about 30 minutes. Once you buy the stocks, you hold them a full year before evaluating their performance. "Don't follow them. Don't look at them. And certainly don't trade them," he says emphatically. Over the past 30 years, Gardner notes, this strategy has almost always beaten the market.

If you want to take a more active role, Gardner advocates a second approach: buy shares of "great" companies through a direct purchase plan (it'll save you the commission). Look for large companies with a solid profit margin (within their industry) and that sell directly to consumers. "A company making a product like Coke is ingrained in basic life, but a company making a gidget that goes into another company's machine is much more vulnerable to the whims of business," he explains. "We feel when we buy Nike or Coke, there's some guarantee of safety." Again, he suggests starting with a $2,000 investment. Once you're in the plan, you can send off checks for $30, $50, whatever you can afford each month, and over time, move into a second company, then a third. "This works for people who are a little more relaxed with money and their overall view of the world," he says. "They aren't going to panic if the media says that tech stocks are overvalued." And again, they aren't going to sell unless they need the money for something, or they see a fundamental change in the business. "If Goodyear announced a new theme park, you might want to take a real hard look at that," he says. "It could be a coup. But it's more likely a mistake. But the idea is to never sell completely out of the market. And not to worry that the professionals have too great an advantage."

Kleinman agrees. "Someone asked my son Joe, a commodities trader: 'How do you make money in the market?' And a wiseguy from across the room said, 'Buy low, and sell high.' But Joe said: 'That's not what I do. I buy high and sell higher. If a company is selling low, it may be for a good, fundamental reason. But a company moving up may have a lot of opportunity for growth. You may have missed the first few points of the movement, but you can take advantage of the last 10 to 15.'"

LAST WORD: SHOULD YOU BE USING A DISCOUNT BROKER?

THERE ARE TODAY FOUR DIFFERENT KINDS OF STOCKBRO-
kers. Traditional brokers, like those with Merrill Lynch
and Dean Witter, provide you with investment ideas and charge
you with high commissions for that information. Discount brokerage firms, like Charles Schwab, provide many of the services that the traditional firms offer, such as administering
your IRA, but they don't employ large Wall Street–style
research departments, so you'll pay much less to trade
through them. Deep discounters like National Discount Brokers
have even more bare-bones offerings, so their prices are lower
still. And, when you use an electronic brokerage firm like
E*Trade, you typically don't even talk to a person but make
your transaction using a computer or telephone. Here are a
few considerations when you're deciding which type of firm is
right for you:

- **Price.** To buy the same 100 shares of a $50 over-the-
  counter stock will cost you about $105 through Merrill
  Lynch, $55 through discount broker Charles Schwab, $25
  through deep discounter National Discount Brokers, and
  $19.95 through E*Trade.

- **Product availability.** While a traditional broker offers a full
  menu of products and services, those offered by the discounters vary widely. Some will trade products like futures,
  options, even collateralized mortgage obligations (CMOs).
  Others stick to stocks and mutual funds. Typically, the
  deeper the discount, the fewer the available products. Make
  sure the firm you select serves all your needs before you
  open an account.

- **Mutual fund menu.** For many people these days, a
  discount broker is simply a mutual fund supermarket, pro-

viding the ability to choose—with no transaction fee—
among hundreds of mutual funds. Fund selection varies
widely, however. Take a look at each broker's list of no-
transaction-fee funds before making your decision.

- **Electronic trading.** Some firms provide quotes for free on
  a 15- to 20-minute delay; others charge a monthly fee for
  real-time quotes. Some charge for their software and others give it away when you open your account. You'll always
  want to evaluate your options before filling out the paperwork.

Chapter 2

THE RISK- AVERSE

Nicole Miller • *Matt Lauer*
Alan Dershowitz

"I don't look for the home runs. I'm satisfied with a ground rule double. It helps that my guy has good criteria. He says he'll call me the morning I lost any sleep."

—Alan Dershowitz

IF YOU'RE LIKE MOST PEOPLE, TAKING TOO MUCH RISK PROBABLY makes you uncomfortable. Some folks become uneasy when they think about attempting something physically dangerous such as boarding a tiny commuter aircraft or walking over a shaky bridge. Others feel the fear rise in their throats when crossing emotional milestones like getting married or having a baby. Still others dread taking a flier on a stock.

In fact, it makes sense that so many people are fearful of investing. After all, you're taking your hard-earned, hard-saved money and putting it into a stock or mutual fund over which you have very little control. But, the alternative is even more frightening. You know that if you stick it in a bank account yielding two to three percent, you're going to lose big after taxes and inflation. What can you do about it?

As you'll see in the coming pages, a fiscally conservative bent is not necessarily innate. NBC "Today" show coanchor Matt Lauer and attorney Alan Dershowitz have always been careful with their money, but fashion designer Nicole Miller went through nearly a decade when her investment habits were as daring as the designs she puts on her ties. Nor does watching your pennies necessarily lead to fear of finance. Lauer recalls a time, not too many years back, when he didn't know if he'd be able to pay his rent. But Dershowitz's and Miller's pockets haven't been empty in decades.

Of course, now all three of these wildly successful individuals can count themselves among the well-to-do. And they're taking steps to making sure they forge ahead in this world of financial security. In Lauer's case, that means being a little more adventurous; in Miller's it means scaling back. At the end of this chapter, you'll find steps to help build your own portfolio with just the right amount of risk for your particular stage of the game.

Nicole Miller

NICOLE MILLER, 47, the designer and co-owner of Nicole Miller, Inc., is the patron saint of cocktail party attire. Her chic little-black-dresses and novelty ties have been adorning fashion-forward women and men for more than a decade. Miller hit the Manhattan design scene in 1974 as head dress designer at P. J. Walsh, a small manufacturer. In 1982, she started her own firm. Today, her company has licensing agreements with two dozen vendors and a number of freestanding boutiques. Recently married, she is the mother of a one-year-old son, Palmer.

WHEN I FIRST SAT DOWN WITH FASHION DESIGNER NICOLE Miller, back in the fall of 1993, she slipped into the profile of the aggressive investor like one of her figure-fitting party dresses. Miller had close to 100 percent of her assets in the stock market. Her favorite—and best performing—domestic issues were the companies she featured on her famous novelty ties. Philip Morris (which she'd purchased after creating a Miller Beer tie) was up more than 80 percent. Comic book publisher Marvel Entertainment (Spider-man, the Incredible Hulk, and Captain America had all been immortalized in silk) had more than doubled. And motorcycle manufacturer Harley-Davidson was up 250 percent and still rising.

Nearly a third of Miller's holdings were in international markets, yielding similarly good results. Foreign phone companies in particular, like Petersburg Long Distance and Telecom Argentina, had proven to be big winners. And Miller was all for keeping the heat on. She had three brokers at three New York houses competing for the best monthly return, not just in her head, but on paper. "I always pit the brokers against each other," Miller said for the interview, which ran in *SmartMoney* magazine. "I say, 'So-and-so is doing better than you are. So-and-so is 10 percent ahead each month.'"

Her private life, too, was chock-full of risks. Then 42, Miller was a veritable advertisement for the pleasures of single life. She went away most weekends with friends, windsurfed in the summer, skied in the winter, and scuba dived when she could manage a few extra days on some remote island. *People* magazine featured her in its pages, making her way through her large TriBeCa loft on Rollerblades. And the tabloids had a field day with her fortieth birthday—which also happened to be St. Patrick's Day—when she and friends from the New York City Ballet danced atop the bar at Punsch, a hot new restaurant.

By the end of 1996, Punsch and Miller's go-go days were both long gone. She married a former Lazard Freres investment banker named Kim Taipale in 1995 (he is now the managing partner of a private investment firm and heads the Center for Advanced Media Studies at Columbia University's Institute for Learning Technologies). In late March 1996, their son Palmer was born. And so was Miller's desire to preserve some of what she was earning for his future. She instructed her money managers to tone it way down. From a bold asset allocation of 100 percent equities, Miller's portfolio underwent a dramatic shift. She now has 35 percent in domestic stocks, 15 percent in foreign stocks, 10 percent in money market funds, and the remainder in bonds. Most financial planners would deem her mix downright risk-averse for a woman her age, especially one who's not planning on retiring anytime soon.

A MORE CONSERVATIVE APPROACH

"When you go through changes like I've gone through in my life you get a little more conservative," shrugs the designer, now 47. She's seated in her corner office, high atop Manhattan's fashion avenue, a picture of the beaming baby front and center on her desk. "I'm not a free-wheeling single person anymore. I don't want to take as many risks." She now funds her individual retirement accounts to the maximum. She had her estate plan completely revamped. Prior to her marriage and her son's birth, her will specified that all her assets go to her parents and siblings. Now that they're being left to her husband and child, Miller explains, it seems more crucial to preserve them, rather than just to grow them.

In addition to finding that she has a lower threshold for the ups and downs of the market, Miller, who in earlier years was instrumental in selecting her investments, says she simply has less time for it. She was an avid reader of the *Wall Street Journal* as well as many of the business publications. *Forbes* magazine once even featured her in an advertisement. Now the publications she receives sit in a pile waiting weeks if not months to be read, and she has canceled her subscriptions to others. Once in a while, however, she will offer a directive to one of her money managers, proving she keeps at least one eye on the market. These days, it's less demanding financial television like CNBC, Miller says, that fits more neatly into her new lifestyle.

MONITORING SELECTED INDUSTRIES

In recent years, she's been watching two industries closely. The first, of course, is fashion. Many apparel companies went public in the last financing wave, and Miller is a fan of at least a couple. She believes Tommy Hilfiger will do well long-term, she explains, because "the company has a lot of momentum, they're moving into a lot of new businesses, and I see that continuing." Gucci, which created quite a sensation with its initial public offering (IPO), is also high on her list. "That's a solid organization with a lot of talent and expertise. They're very professionally run, and they got a new life with [designer] Tom Ford. The combination they have going is kind of magical," she says. "Plus, they back up their lines with really good advertising. And they keep getting a good strong reaction from the press."

Miller also keeps tabs on Wal-Mart, Kmart, and many of the other stocks in the food and drug sectors. She considers it part of her role as a director of Smith's Food & Drug Centers, a Salt Lake City company in which she also holds a sizable position. Miller believed Wal-Mart had a good grip on the market for a while, but has since soured on the stock. "Unfortunately, Wal-Mart has made a lot of enemies by squeezing a lot of people out of the market," she says. "That's not even good for the customer. You need at least some competition in the marketplace to make for a better product."

Of course, Miller points out, she still keeps close tabs on the folks managing her money. But as her company has grown since 1993, expanding sales from an estimated $35 million a year in sales to an estimated $50 million, Miller has become a wealthier woman. That, it seems, has thrown her for a bit of a loop as well. "There are some sums of money that you feel comfortable managing," she explains. "But there are certain sums that I'm not comfortable with. That's when it's time to put it in someone else's hands." The market is making her uncomfortable as well. "In 1995, it felt like it was much easier to get ahead. You could put your money anywhere and win. This year [1996] has been a trickier market to read. Even though a lot of people have done well, it hasn't been so universal. This year, you really had to call it right."

A SAVING MENTALITY

One look at Nicole Miller, with her bright-red hair, her of-the-moment leggings and flats, and you'd think this burst of conservatism had come out of left field. But in fact, that's not true. She grew up in the quaint town of Lenox, Massachusetts, the daughter of an engineer who spent his entire career at General Electric, and her French-born mother, a homemaker. Her parents saved every cent they could, putting their nest egg into savings bonds and Treasuries.

Never a big spender, Miller helped pay her way through the Rhode Island School of Design and—by winning a schoolwide competition with her design of a red velvet dress—into business. Her $1,000 prize was seed money for a clothing boutique she opened in Stockbridge, Massachusetts, when she graduated in 1973. Moving to New York the next year to pursue her own design career, Miller didn't have a lot of pocket change to live it up in the city those first few "miserable" years.

"Somebody asked me, 'What did you buy when you felt like you had money?'," Miller recounted the first time we talked. "And I said, 'Well, nothing.' To me it seems like the more money you have, the less money you feel like you have. When you make your first $10,000, you feel like that's a lot of money. That seems like more than your first $2 million does."

When she landed in the city in 1974, Miller beat out nearly 200 other applicants for a job as head dress designer at P. J. Walsh, a small manufacturer. By 1982, that company was out of business but Miller and its former president, Bud Konheim, had formed their own venture—Nicole Miller, Inc. The company slowly built to $2 million in sales until 1990 when Konheim suggested she turn some leftover printed silk into ties. Practically overnight, the ties—which featured everything from soccer players to kick off the World Cup games to Bordeaux paraphernalia, a mainstay for the *Wine Enthusiast* catalog—became a $7-million business. Chevy Chase wore them, as did James Woods, and soon every trendy man (and some women) in America wanted a piece of the $60 neckwear. Even Miller's mistakes, though few and far between, sold. An early basketball-themed tie that featured a basketball player sporting a Celtics uniform with Larry Bird's number (33) had just one simple faux pas: The player was black. The company was flooded with offers of up to $1,000 per piece.

From ties Miller progressed to boxer shorts, then to men's fashions and children's. Sales of her primary line—well-priced dresses, many for cocktails and black-tie events—took off as they appeared on fans like Demi Moore and Meryl Streep. Today, the company has licensing agreements with close to two dozen vendors. Across the country, 30 boutiques bear her name (four are company-owned), but the company is aiming at 50. They'll be located, preferably, near hot trendy restaurants. Miller and Konheim believe that's where their typical customer hangs out. There are also eight in-store shops in Bloomingdale branches around the country.

MINDING THE COMPANY AND THE MARKET

Today, Miller and Konheim each own 50 percent of the company. In addition to running the company together, they are close friends. Konheim wanders into her office early one afternoon to shoot the breeze about a difficult customer who's having trouble finding six of the same Nicole Miller dresses for her daughter's bridesmaids to wear. Konheim is an avid investor and—Miller says—and excellent stock picker. She recently asked him for a list of the issues he liked and, though she only bought one, she watched as seven out of seven quickly doubled. When Miller had a little more time and a little more confidence, they used to frequently take fliers together. But it's apparent he's still trying to bring her into the fold.

She pauses to explain that, in fact, she misses playing the market. She still maintains little charts at home to keep track of her investments; she just has no time to look at them. After all, she is a natural with numbers. Through high school her strengths were physics and calculus. When it comes to phone numbers, her memory is her Rolodex. "It's fun," she says of picking stocks. "It's a challenge. Maybe in another year or so I'll get back on track."

Perhaps with her own public offering. Back in 1993, Miller rejected out of hand the possibility of taking her company public. Now, however, she says she's considering it, though she'll definitely wait until the next IPO wave. "We're not structured like your typical corporation," she says. "We're very family-oriented. And I certainly wouldn't want stockholders to start forcing me to make cheaper clothes." She glances around the room at her cluttered empire. "I'd think about it," she says. "But only if I was sure they wouldn't ruin our fun."

Matt Lauer

MATT LAUER, 39, became the coanchor of NBC's "Today," the nation's top-rated morning show, early this year after three years at the show's news desk. Prior on-air stints took him to Huntington, West Virginia, Boston, Massachusetts, and Secaucus, New Jersey, before he settled in as the early-morning man at WNBC in New York. An avid skier and golfer, the divorced Lauer remains single to the delight of many viewers outside "Today's window each morning. He gets up at 4:15 A.M. to make it to the office on time.

MATT LAUER DOESN'T HAVE NICOLE MILLER'S GUMPTION WHEN IT comes to his investments. A peek at his recent past explains why.

It's 1991 and Lauer is considering taking up residence on a friend's couch. The prior year he'd lost his fourth consecutive job when the three-hour morning marathon he was anchoring for a Secaucus, New Jersey, station was unceremoniously canceled. Lauer consoled himself with the knowledge that he'd find something. He always did. At least this time, he didn't have to read about his firing in a local newspaper (as happened two jobs before in Boston). The producers told him face-to-face.

For the first few months, Lauer looked for a job by day, hung out with his friends at night. "There were times when I was sitting home watching baseball games making $200,000 a year, which was fine," he remembers. "The weird thing about television is they pay you a ridiculous amount of money but then they can pull it away from you. They sign you to a contract and it might be for $200,000 a year over three years, and then they cancel your show. Well they basically have to pay you." At least for a while. Six months went by. Then a year. And Lauer's bank balances were moving into the red zone. "It got really ugly," he says. "I got to the point where I was about a month away from not making the rent."

Lauer had already applied for a job as a landscaper when WNBC, New York City's Channel 4, called offering him the coanchor spot on its early-morning show. His career was relaunched, his bank balances repadded. (A good thing, too, because the landscaping company never called.) But like Scarlett O'Hara, Lauer has never forgotten.

Even after five years of full employment, Lauer is still very careful with his money.

BLUER THAN BLUE CHIPS

A good chunk of cash, for example, sits in the 401(k) plan provided by his employer. For a long time those 401(k) dollars were completely invested in straight-arrow mutual funds—S&P 500 index funds and intermediate-term bond funds. Then a couple of years ago, he started to stretch his wings a bit, putting a slice of those dollars into individual stocks. "My stocks are blue chips to the point that they are bright blue," he said at the end of 1996, about holdings like General Electric (which owns his employer, NBC), IBM, and AT&T. "I don't believe I've got a stock that is less than 30 years old," he explains. No Gap. No Home Depot. "And no Microsoft," he shrugs. "Which is stupid. I should have Microsoft, except that—I don't know—there is a phobia in me of new technology. I report every day about the new technology companies that missed the one opportunity and are left behind by their competition and watch their stock prices drop.

"My dalliance with the stock market is what most people would consider an absolute sure thing," he continues. "I'm also not the kind of guy that goes to play blackjack in Atlantic City." Lauer's 401(k), in which his contributions are partially matched by his employer, is about as close to a sure thing as one can get. "I don't know why anybody who's offered [a 401(k)] doesn't fund it with the maximum amount they can without it being painful to their weekly living," he says. In fact, Lauer has made retirement saving such a habit that at times he's forgotten he's doing it.

A few years back, for example, Lauer signed a contract that boosted his income considerably. He began to spend more freely— leasing a pricier apartment, skiing for a few extra days each winter. A year later, he sat down to take a detailed look at his bank balances and he panicked. The sum in his primary savings account hadn't moved. "You idiot," Lauer chastised himself. "You're making all this extra money and you're spending it all." Then he remembered that when his salary leapfrogged, he had voluntarily boosted his 401(k) contribution. "In that one year of sitting there and doing nothing, I had put aside a substantial amount of money," he laughs. "It's out of your mind, so you don't tend to think you're making this great investment, but to me it is the smartest, safest investment you can make."

Many of Lauer's other investments are similarly cautious. For many years now, the anchor has shouldered financial responsibility for his mother. To make sure that the money for her needs never runs out, he has built a portfolio of bonds which are "laddered" to mature at various intervals over the next 15 years. They will keep his mother comfortable even if his income shrinks dramatically. Plus, there's a modest life insurance policy with his mother as beneficiary.

For a long time, the rest of Lauer's money was—unapologetically—in cash. He kept a good six figures in a checking account and even more in linked savings. Despite the fact that the money didn't earn enough to keep him ahead of taxes and inflation, he slept better knowing it was there. "There's a nagging thing in my personality that I almost need to be able to pop into my ATM machine and see that—very, very liquid—I have a certain amount of money at my disposal," he says thoughtfully, chin in hand. "It's even more than a rainy day. I like to know that if I want to really splurge, if I want to go out and buy a great car tomorrow, I can do so without transferring funds or other administrative hassles."

Still, there were times, especially as the Dow moved past 5,000, then 6,000, then higher—when he reported on an IPO that had shot through the roof, or how retail stocks had skyrocketed— when Lauer felt he was missing something.

"I have this dream," he explains. "I'm at a cocktail party and Mort Zuckerman and Rupert Murdoch are there—which could happen; I come into casual contact with people like that all the time." In his dream, Lauer strolls over to the two media moguls. "I've got $100,000," he says to them. "Mort, if I was to give you, say, $20,000 of it today, where would be the first place you'd put it? Rupert, if I gave you that $20,000 what would you do?" Murdoch purses his lips and opens his mouth to reveal his answer. Zuckerman clears his throat, his best financial advice on the tip of his tongue. And of course Lauer— who hasn't gathered his nerve to ask the question in real life—snaps out of it.

Making a bundle on a hot tip is something many of the subjects in this book have actually accomplished. Others, like Helen Gurley Brown (see Chapter 8), have taken a piece of whispered advice and lost. Matt Lauer hasn't quite stepped up to the plate. For one thing, he believes three out of five people would tell him they wanted nothing to do with his little investment fling. He also isn't sure he has the confidence to follow through.

"I am not creative," he says. "And at times in my life I have said, 'I really need to get someone who is very creative and who can really work on this.' But, I will say, a lot of my friends who make the same kind of money that I do, when we talk on the golf course, a lot of them are very disappointed and you hear horror stories. I don't want to be the guy who ever tells the horror story. I'd just rather be safe and know that when I'm 75 years old, I'll still have a terrific income and terrific reserves. I'm not looking to become somebody on the top wealth list. I'm just not."

GETTING HIS ACT TOGETHER

Finally, as 1996 rolled into 1997 and Lauer got both the coanchor job at "Today" and a sizable hike in salary, the need for someone who could "really work on" his money won out over the fear of a horror story. Lauer combed his friends and colleagues for recommendations and hired a full-service money manager whose job it is to design and execute an investment strategy as well as to do some detailed tax, estate, *and* insurance planning.

Slowly but surely, the newsman's assets are taking shape. The 401(k), with its core component of GE stock, remains intact, but much of the money Lauer had in individual stocks has been shifted into mutual funds invested for growth and income. The cash has been yanked out of checking and invested in higher-yielding-but-still-accessible money market funds. The results aren't in quite yet, but Lauer's feeling pretty good about his decision. "I talked to a number of people and a got a sense that this guy had the same goals that I did," he explains. "He wanted to make the most of what I had, and keep the most possible out of taxes, but he wasn't trying to get rich quick in risky ways."

The new manager is also in charge of paying Lauer's bills, which means keeping tabs on his spending. The anchor just purchased what he described as his first truly fabulous car, a Jaguar, but his other expenses are fairly modest. A meal in one of New York's three- or four-star restaurants is always balanced by a few nights of cheap take-out. He still rents his apartment on Manhattan's Upper East Side, a two-bedroom that's comfortable but a far cry from lavish. And he's just put himself in the market for a vacation home.

Lauer's friends and colleagues have been harping that the Hamptons—the towns on the eastern tip of Long Island, the chic summer residence of Steven Spielberg, Martha Stewart, Ralph Lauren, and others—are the place to be because properties in such high demand are more likely to hold their value. Not interested, says Lauer, who has set his cap for a remote location in Upper Upper Westchester County or Connecticut. "Maybe I'll have a more difficult time selling it because location is not a plus like East Hampton would be," he says. "But it's where I want to be and I think that especially for a vacation house that's the most important thing. I'm not buying it as an investment. I'm buying it as peace of mind."

CLOSET SPLURGES

The anchor's only other real splurge is—you guessed it—his clothing. He grew up, the son of an insurance salesman who later went into retail, in a solidly middle-class environment where extravagant purchases—like the Mustang his father bought in 1962—were so few and far between they're permanently etched in his memory. Another thing he remembers from his childhood is that both his father and stepfather were extraordinarily generous and giving. "I remember, when I was thirteen, maybe fourteen years old, one of the biggest thrills my stepfather ever had was bringing me into the city, where he worked, taking me out to dinner, and taking me to Barneys for a great navy blazer." He smiles. "He didn't want to just go to some store out in Greenwich or in Westport, he wanted to take me to Barneys and he wanted me to get *the* great navy blazer. And it didn't matter to him that I was still growing and a year later, I was going to need another navy blazer. He just wanted me to have the feeling of knowing that I had something great. And as a result of that, I do get a big kick out of buying great things, especially clothing."

Which doesn't mean that Lauer has the ability to drop a big chunk of change without a second thought. "I have a couple of close friends," he explains, "and there was a time in the late 1980s and early 1990s when we made a lot of money and lived pretty fast, and the feeling was that we were going to enjoy ourselves first and then become responsible human beings." Over the past four years, that's exactly what has happened. And as Lauer looks toward his fortieth birthday in December, he approaches it with a newfound financial maturity. "Just a few years ago I didn't have a will, and I didn't have life insurance. I thought, first of all, I don't own anything—what am I going to leave someone except my baseball cap collection? But now I realize that a will not only protects your money from the government, it protects your family from expenses."

Having his financial act together is a big relief. Even if his time at NBC proves to be relatively brief—which Lauer doesn't see as an "outrageous possibility"—he won't have to worry about the rent again. "This is an enormously fickle business," he explains. "Anybody who comes to this business gung ho and full of cockiness and confidence usually gets slapped down and learns an important lesson. I know that while today I am the quote-unquote up-and-comer, when I get to where they expect me to go there will be someone else who will be labeled the up-and-comer. Cycles being what they are in television, if this show hits a cycle where one of our competitors becomes more popular, the changes that will be made will not be with the format of the show. They'll be made with the hosts and the talent. I understand that."

He also knows that he can handle it. "I have the history that tells me I won't lose sight of who I am or what I am, and I probably won't crumble up on the floor and cry," he shrugs. "And hopefully at that point I'll have gotten a lot smarter with my investments and will be able to laugh at everybody."

Alan Dershowitz

ALAN DERSHOWITZ, 59, is the country's foremost civil liberties attorney. A longtime professor at Harvard Law School, Dershowitz has handled hundreds of top-drawer cases including the appeals of Michael Milken, Leona Helmsley, and Claus von Bülow. He was a member of O. J. Simpson's "dream team," and has written a number of best-sellers including Chutzpah, Reversal of Fortune: Inside the von Bülow Case, *and* Reasonable Doubts. *Brooklyn-born and -bred, Dershowitz and his family now reside in Cambridge, Massachusetts.*

UNLIKE MATT LAUER, ALAN DERSHOWITZ HAS FEW CAREER doubts. Why should he? After all, he's the attorney who got the nod for the O. J. Simpson criminal appeal, should it have been necessary. His books regularly shoot to the top of the best-seller lists. And he's represented some of the heaviest hitters in business and finance. Junk-bond king Mike Milken. Hotel queen Leona Helmsley. Newspaper heiress Patty Hearst.

You would think that along the way he'd pick up a hot stock tip, a morsel of advice on how to boost the returns in his personal portfolio. Never, scoffs the Harvard law professor known as much for his quick tongue and cynicism as for his representation of Claus von Bülow and Mike Tyson. "I would never ask a client for advice," says the mustachioed Dershowitz, clearly horrified. "I would never even enter the discussion. I think a lawyer-client relationship should be a one-way street."

Instead, Dershowitz used to needle his family, his friends, and particularly his colleagues at Harvard Business School for recommendations. He'd buy stocks on their advice, occasionally picking companies because they were located in Harvard's neck of the woods. Many took him on a stock market roller-coaster. The one he remembers most vividly, Thinking Machines, quickly went belly-up.

For Dershowitz, making money in the market was quickly becoming more gut-wrenching than earning it in the first place. He hated it. "I don't find the stock market fun," he rails. "I don't enjoy money. I don't enjoy billing. I don't like that aspect of my life at all. I think of the money I make as a by-product of the fun I'm having, of teaching, and writing and defending people."

RELY ON A PROFESSIONAL

In fact, the one financial lesson hammered home by representing Milken (who Dershowitz continues to believe will be vindicated by history), and dozens of other moneyed types is this: There is absolutely no way for an individual investor to compete with Wall Street. Rumors about corporate earnings and management shake-ups may move quickly from the mouths of top analysts through the brokerage firms to the ears of institutional investors. But there's a definite information lag before the scuttlebutt makes its way to individual shareholders. As the recipient (and often disseminator) of the earliest and juiciest pieces of information in legal circles, it was especially difficult for Dershowitz to settle for a place on the second tier.

So he shifted strategy. He hired a financial planner to handle his day-to-day accounting and reconnoitering. And he cut back on his purchases of individual stocks and bonds and upped his position in mutual funds, where the presence of a manager on call to evaluate the rumors and make studied purchase decisions allows him to sleep better at night. "I've learned to go to people who are experts," Dershowitz gladly admits. "I make no micro decisions about which particular stocks I'm in anymore."

Today, the 59-year-old has an entire portfolio of mutual funds—a wide array from the most conservative of bond funds to the more aggressive Scudder Capital Growth to some very aggressive small-cap, high-tech growth funds and even a little bit of junk. His retirement portfolio from his years at Harvard is invested with TIAA—CREF (the Teachers Insurance and Annuity Association—College Retirement Equities Fund), which he noted proudly did very well during the market's brief correction in the summer of 1996. When it comes to fund selection, Dershowitz's only restrictions are loosely imposed moral ones. He doesn't want to own cigarette companies and won't knowingly buy gambling stocks, though he admits he can't monitor all of his funds closely enough to know if they've recently picked up a company he wouldn't buy on his own.

NOT REACHING FOR HOME RUNS

Even though he's taken a step back from the purchasing process, Dershowitz still tries to monitor most of his investments carefully. He examines the share prices of all his holdings at least once a month, more when the market is rocky. In July of 1996, for example, when both the S&P and NASDAQ took substantial hits, Dershowitz was on the line to his advisers every day, sometimes twice. He knew he was driving them up the wall, but he didn't care. Dershowitz wanted to sell some of his more aggressive holdings; his advisers recommended weathering the storm. Until he and they reached a decision, he was going to call all he wanted. In the end, they split the difference. "I don't look for the home runs. I'm satisfied with a ground rule double," he says. "It helps that my guy has good criteria. He says he'll call me the morning I lost any sleep."

Not surprisingly, the attorney describes himself as conservative. His portfolio is balanced with about 25 percent in fixed income securities, which he describes as a "hedge." Even his real estate holdings—a small home on Martha's Vineyard and his primary residence, a modern home within walking distance of the university—were selected in part because he believed they'd hold their price in practically any real estate environment. "I figure it's a parachute, something I could borrow off if I need to," he explains. "After all, real estate within a mile of Harvard has to maintain some value."

Most people nearing 60, as Dershowitz is, would be thinking ahead to the next stage, their own retirement. But with a second family underway—his daughter from his second marriage is now seven—Dershowitz isn't quite ready to start shifting the balance. "I still have seven years of private elementary school, four years of private high school, four to eight years of college and graduate school to pay for," he hopes. "My goals remain long-term." The big ones: Nest eggs for his two children from his first marriage, a college fund for his seven-year-old, and a cushion large enough to sustain his style of living as he eases his way into retirement, a decade or two down the road.

A MODEST LIFESTYLE

It helps that his lifestyle is fairly modest, a remnant of his childhood. The Dershowitz family—his father owned a small dry goods store on the Lower East Side—wasn't poverty-stricken. In fact, Dershowitz says he didn't realize until he arrived among the blue bloods at Harvard Law that he grew up working-class. What he did understand was that he grew up working. Before he graduated from high school, his resume sported no fewer than five jobs: baby-sitter, delivery boy, counterman at a local delicatessen, busboy, waiter. "In those days, if you wanted to go out on a date, you had to earn money," he explains. "I would ask a young woman out three weeks in advance so that I could save." The cheapest tickets to the theater were $2.90, a hefty sum back then. So Dershowitz and his date would always sit in the last row, in the back of the second balcony, where he'd explain matter-of-factly that he wasn't comfortable having anyone sitting behind him. Taxis weren't in the budget either. When the young Dershowitz saw one in his Borough Park neighborhood, it meant someone was either lost or dead. "The streets were empty; on one long block with two sides, there might be four cars," he says. "Today there might be 80 or 90. But life was pretty good."

To this day, he's a man of few splurges. With his first legal fee, earned from working for F. Lee Bailey, the newly minted attorney made his first big purchase, a Volvo. Dershowitz was 29 years old, and he paid $3,000 for the car. He drove it out of the showroom, four miles down the road, and the engine gurgled and died. "They hadn't put any gas in it," he laughs. To this day, all the Dershowitzes still drive only Volvos, and they run them into the ground. The attorney doesn't have a taste for expensive sports like boating or skiing or golf. Once a year, he and his wife Carolyn go on a romantic vacation for a couple of days, most recently to Florence. He loves walking, and going to basketball games, and does admit to dropping a bundle on Celtics season tickets each year. But as for real extravagances, unless you count the swimming pool he and his wife recently had built in the backyard (his neighbors call it the O.J. pool), there aren't many.

Save for several thousand books. "I grew up in the milieu where the public library was the temple. For me, the day I got a library card was the day I was an adult," he remembers. Every week, he and his brother would take the subway to the Brooklyn Public Library, right next to the Botanic Gardens, where they were allowed to take out four books for the week. "I remember the first day I was wealthy enough to buy hardcover books," Dershowitz recalls. "It was when I started doing some outside [of teaching] work, I was able to have a little more expendable cash, and the first thing I did was to buy books. Now at home I have a nice library, a functional research library, full of law books, books on politics and economics. I'm writing a book on the Jewish future and I have 100 Jewish books that I can look at."

A GOOD LIVING

Today, of course, he makes a mighty good living. His books, most notably *Reversal of Fortune*, about the Claus von Bülow case, and *Chutzpah*, held their own on the best-seller lists. During 1996 and 1997, he had a deal to appear nightly on CNBC discussing the Simpson case, and made frequent appearances on other programs as well.

And of course there's the appeals business, in which Alan Dershowitz seems to be the top name on most every wish list. His hourly fee slides with the wealth of his clients, though he typically bills at a rate he calls "fair" for a person of his age and experience, around the $400 to $500 a senior partner in a large firm would charge. "In my class on legal ethics, I tell my students: 'Always go up to the line when you're representing someone else, but be more conservative on your own behalf,'" he says. "'Err on the side of charging less. Err on the side of paying more taxes. When it comes to your own financial security, be zealous. Sometimes it's hard [to know exactly where the line is]; you may not be able to define it, but you know it when you see it.'" Of course, Dershowitz admits, there are certain clients who would be willing to pay him anything. "But I didn't charge Mike Milken more than a person who'd have a million in the bank," he defends, "though obviously I charged him more than someone with $50,000."

He cherry-picks his cases from the more than 5,000 requests for counsel that flood his Cambridge office each year, taking what he calls "the most interesting ones," those that might make good material for his classes, and especially those that might make a good book after the record is closed. He tells his students that they should never allow money to be a factor in whom they represent, holding up his own pro bono work—a full 50 percent of his cases—as evidence that some of the most interesting cases will come without remuneration. Recently, for example, he signed on to handle the appeal of the photography student who was threatened with charges of child abuse for photographing her four-year-old son while he was urinating. No fee. "It's a very important case for me," he says.

Dershowitz tries to refer many of the cases he doesn't have time for to other qualified attorneys, many his former students. And he'll try his hardest to dissuade those he must turn away from representing themselves. That, he believes, should be the last resort. "Lawyers provide a very important service," he says. "They don't make mistakes that laypersons make." And he should know. A few years back, Dershowitz and his son both got speeding tickets and decided to fight them. His son, Elon, walked into the Cambridge court prepared. He had charts helping him to demonstrate that there was no possible way he could have been speeding. Dershowitz, on the other hand, tried to wing it. Guess who lost?

Despite dispensing more than his share of free advice, there are still times when the money coming in is too much for Dershowitz's conscience. For those, he has established a small charitable fund. "My wife calls it my guilt fund," he shrugs. "Whenever I earn a fee that I don't feel comfortable with, I put it in the fund." Once a year, that money gets turned over to various Jewish charities and universities, Amnesty International, the American Civil Liberties Union (ACLU), and the other organizations high on Dershowitz's support list.

Which money went in there? The Mike Tyson funds? The fees from the Jim Bakker case? Dershowitz shies away from the question. "My job is depressing," he shrugs. "I'm working with people, quite often, who have unlimited amounts of one thing—money—but limited amounts of something else—freedom, or life, or time. And they're willing to risk what they have limited amounts of in order to get more money. In the Leona [Helmsley] case, what could have motivated someone who had all this to even get close to the line? What did she need? An extra car? An extra rec room in the house?"

He stops. "I try my best not to come close to any lines at all."

WHEN IT'S *YOUR* MONEY . . .

DO YOU SEE YOURSELF IN NICOLE MILLER'S LEOPARD-SPOTTED shoes? Are you just wary enough? Or, perhaps, a little more conservative than you ought to be?

"Part of the problem with the bull market we have had for the past couple of years is that people's fears have been allayed," notes Andrew M. Hudick, a Roanoke, Virginia financial adviser and former president of the National Association of Personal Financial Advisors. "All investments should involve some degree of fear because there's some degree of risk. That's the whole idea behind diversifying your portfolio. If one or two investments don't work out, you hope that the others will."

At every stage of your financial life cycle, you want the risk you're taking to be appropriate—not an easy balance to strike. When you're young, in your 20s, 30s, and early 40s, you can afford to be more aggressive with your investments, because you have considerable time before college tuition bills and the cost of retirement stare you in the face. During those years your long-term funds—that pool of money you won't be using for at least five to 10 years—should be invested primarily in stocks. Why? First, you'll likely need a 6 percent return on your money just to keep ahead of inflation and taxes. These days, a money market account isn't going to do that; neither are most short-term Treasuries or certificates of deposit. Second, statistics show stocks will provide the best return over the long term—with this portion of your portfolio, at least you have the time to ride through the market's ups and downs (and yes, as the crash of 1987 showed, you'll be better off riding through those downs).

Your short-term funds—those that you're planning to use within the next five years, to put a down payment on a house, for example, or to pay for your son's bar mitzvah—are better off in safer harbors like Treasury securities, balanced mutual funds, or even certificates of deposit that you've chosen to maximize yield. (*Money* magazine publishes a list of the best-paying CDs in the United States each month, as do many local newspapers.)

You should have a firm grasp on your goals. Ask yourself: Short-term, am I saving for a week on the beach or for a down payment on a three-bedroom colonial? Long-term, do I want to retire when I'm 50 or do I plan on working until 65 or 70? Then figure out how much money you'll need to get there.

By far the best way to begin is to follow Matt Lauer's example: Participate in your employer's retirement savings plan. In most medium-to-large companies, and these days, more and more smaller ones, this is likely to be a 401(k), a program with several compelling advantages. Employers often match some or all of the contribution that you make to the plan each year, giving you an instantaneous return on your investment. If your company contributes one dollar for every two dollars that you ante up, for example, you've already made 50 percent on your money. Plus, money in the plan grows, tax-deferred, until retirement—so interest racks up more quickly than if Uncle Sam's take was skimmed off the top.

If your company doesn't offer a 401(k) or similar plan, you want to be certain to open an IRA. The most you can contribute is $2,000 annually, and you should try to contribute the maximum. Unfortunately, no one is going to match your IRA deposit, but like a 401(k) you don't pay taxes on the money you put into the plan until withdrawal so your dollars add up faster than in taxable vehicles.

Putting your money in an IRA or 401(k) is just step one. You then have the job of allocating those assets, deciding what portion to invest in stocks, in bonds, and in cashlike securities. The goals you set will give you a solid indication of just how aggressive you need to be. The greater return you're striving for, the larger the portion to invest in stocks. (If you're getting a late start, however, you may want to modify your goals rather than take unnecessary risks.) But, cautions Hudick, boosting your savings rate, especially in the early years, can be much more lucrative than striving for yield: "One thing people need to understand, especially if they don't have a ton of money, is that they're going to save a lot more than their investments will earn," he says. "Increasing your savings from 3 percent to 6 percent of your $34,000 salary can mean the difference between putting away $1,000 and $2,000 a year. That means a lot more to your bottom line than trying to make an above-average 10 percent on your money, rather than an average eight."

Most people in their 20s and 30s should begin with an asset allocation of 70 to 80 percent in stocks or stock mutual funds, 15 to 20 percent in bonds, and the rest in cash or liquid securities like money market funds, certificates of deposit, or Treasury securities. As you move through your 40s and into your 50s, you should moderate your risk, lowering your stock allocation to around 60 percent (the bulk of the assets coming out of stocks should move into bonds, a smaller share into cash), and by the time you're in your 60s, your bond portfolio should equal or outweigh the money you have in stocks.

For many people, the fear of investing is directly related to selecting individual stocks. The good news is that with 8,000 available mutual funds, you can build a diversified portfolio without investing in a single individual stock. The bad new is that with 8,000 available mutual funds, it's become just as tough to select a decent fund as an individual stock. That's why, particularly for beginners, the best first purchase is an index fund. Unlike an actively managed mutual fund in which a manager selects the stocks or bonds that make up a fund's portfolio, an index fund invests in nearly every stock that is part of a particular index. There are 125 different index funds, according to Morningstar, a company that rates mutual funds. The vast majority track the S&P 500, an index of the largest publicly-traded companies, but there are also funds that track small company indexes like the Russell 2000 and broader indexes like the Russell 3000—a mix of large and small companies. And there are bond index funds as well.

You'll be best off starting with a fund that parallels the S&P 500, says Morningstar president Don Phillips: "It's fairly easy to track, because the results are widely reported. That's important at this stage of the game, because you never know how you're going to react to the market until you get your feet wet. If you purchase a fund that tracks the Russell 2000, you're not going to get information on your holdings from watching the local news."

To choose an index fund, Phillips notes, you really need to know the answers to only three questions: What does the fund index, how well do they index it ("All the major shops—Vanguard, Fidelity, Dreyfus—seem to be quite capable when it comes to indexing," Phillips says), and what will you have to pay in sales charges? The answer to the last question should be "not a cent"; the vast majority of index funds are no-load.

In 1996 the S&P 500 index returned 22.95 percent, outperforming the average U.S. equity fund at 19.3 percent and trouncing the returns of the smaller-cap Russell 2000. But in other years the picture has been quite the opposite. That's why Phillips suggests a good second addition to your fund portfolio would be a smaller-cap index fund, and then perhaps an international index fund. Once you gain your footing in the market, you can begin to move into managed mutual funds— a carefully selected growth fund or two, followed by a small-cap fund, and eventually an international fund to round out your holdings.

In bonds, again, a good place to begin is with a no-load index fund like Vanguard's Intermediate Term Bond Index, which invests in securities that will mature in 4 to 10 years. A short-term bond fund is too similar to your savings account, while long-term is more speculative than most new investors are ready for. As you diversify this part of your portfolio, you'll round out the mix by adding a longer-term bond fund or two as well as some tax-free municipal bonds if they make sense at your income level, and perhaps a high-yield (junk) bond fund down the line. In both stocks and bonds, look for funds that have a track record of at least three to five years. Good bets are funds that have earned five stars from Morningstar, which can be found in most local libraries as well as on America Online and more recently on the Internet at www.Morningstar.net.

If you don't feel confident enough to take these few steps yourself, a financial planner can take you by the hand. ("Once people write me a check, it seems to spur them into action," Hudick quips.) I recommend fee-only financial planners—those that charge a flat fee, rather than taking a commission on shares of stock or funds that you purchase—because I believe they're more likely to evaluate an investment on its own merits, rather than on the chunk of change it'll put in their pockets. The Consumer Federation of America recently issued a report noting that many commission-based financial planners are masquerading as part of the fee-only world. Your best bet is to call the National Association of Personal Financial Advisors (the fee-only planners association) at (888) 333-6659, for the names of several advisers in your area. Then, of course, you'll want to check references.

LAST WORD: RETIREMENT SAVINGS PLANS

No MATTER HOW RISK-AVERSE YOU ARE, ONE INVESTMENT you'll definitely want to make—and you should start sooner rather than later—is for your own retirement. Say you want to have $500,000 when you retire at age 65. Begin funding your retirement account when you're 25, and you only have to put away $75 a month (assuming a 10 percent return) to reach your goal. Wait until you're 45, however, and you have to put away 10 times that amount, or $750 each month. A 55-year-old playing catch-up has to round up $2,250 each month. Get the picture?

There are other advantages as well. The tax advantages of funding accounts like 401(k)s and IRAs translate into an instant return, and if your company matches any portion of your contribution you're well ahead of the game. Here's a brief look at how the different retirement savings plans operate:

- **401(k)s.** For 1997, employees can sock as much as $9,500 into their company's 401(k). These contributions aren't taxed until you withdraw the money, which allows interest to accrue at a more rapid pace, and many companies also match the funds you put in, if not dollar for dollar, then perhaps 50 cents on the dollar. You won't be able to withdraw your money without facing a 10 percent penalty until you reach age 59½, but you may be able to borrow from the account. While borrowing isn't recommended, in an emergency it can be a better bet than taking out a cash advance on your credit card or borrowing from your bank. The rates are typically lower than average and you pay the interest back to yourself.

- **IRAs.** Each year the government allows working people not covered by an employer-sponsored retirement plan to contribute up to $2,000 a year, tax-deferred, to an IRA. This year, for the first time, couples in which one spouse doesn't earn income, or earns very little, can make the same $2,000 contribution for the nonworking spouse (a big improvement over the $250 nonworking spouses were formerly allowed to deposit). As with a 401(k), if you need your money before you reach age 59½, you'll usually face a 10 percent penalty for early withdrawal; a change in the tax laws for this year eliminates the penalty if you're using the money to pay unreimbursed medical expenses that are more than 7.5 percent of your adjusted gross income or health insurance premiums following a layoff.

- **SEP-IRA.** An IRA under a simplified employee pension plan for the self-employed may give you the opportunity to contribute and deduct far more than the $2,000 at which an IRA is capped. Again, you're subject to a 10 percent penalty for withdrawals before age 59½.

Chapter 3

THE REAL ESTATE MOGULS

Dave Barry • Jeff Blake

M ANY PEOPLE PROFILED IN THIS BOOK MIGHT HAVE BEEN included in this chapter on real estate investors. Ivana Trump (see page 146), for example, has a full portfolio of homes and apartments that she expects will rise in value simply because she lives in them. ("I improve on places with my name," she shrugs.) Author Olivia Goldsmith (see page 140) seems to have a golden touch. And Mary Sue Milliken (see page 172) of "Too Hot Tamales" fame has taken some spare cash and formed a real estate partnership with her sister, a broker.

For Dave Barry and Jeff Blake, investing in real estate was their first foray into investing.

Barry got into the business in the 1970s. He was living outside Philadelphia, working for a small daily newspaper and making next to nothing, when he and a couple of his longtime chums hit on the notion that real estate was a gold mine. They bought one unit, then a few more, and soon they were making, if not a fortune, then at least a tidy profit, though Barry notes the process did have its drawbacks: "The stock market doesn't have clogged toilets at four A.M.," he laments.

Although Blake didn't start investing until the early 1990s, real estate was already second nature to him. As a teen in Florida, he spent summers working for his grandfather, a contractor, doing hard labor putting up single-family and duplex homes. A few years later at East Carolina University, he majored in construction management. His overall impression: As long as you choose your ventures carefully, investing in real estate is a no-lose proposition. Blake's first couple of deals have shown that to be the case.

In the pages that follow, you'll find the lessons that these two now-quite-seasoned investors have picked up along the way, along with some advice from real estate professionals about how to select quality investments in today's shaky and regional markets. One thing is for certain: If you're looking for a famous landlord, you've come to the right place.

Dave Barry

DAVE BARRY, age 50, is the Pulitzer prizewinning humor colum-
nist of the Miami Herald. *The author of 13 books, most recently*
Dave Barry in Cyberspace, *he also contributed the first chapter to*
the recently published novel Naked Came the Manatee. *The CBS*
television series "Dave's World" starring Harry Anderson was
loosely based on his life. Barry is the father of one and makes his
home in the Miami area.

PULITZER PRIZEWINNING HUMOR WRITER DAVE BARRY IS NOT
exactly comfortable with home repair. That much is clear from
the cover of *Dave Barry's Homes and Other Black Holes* (Fawcett,
1988), in which Barry sits perched on an out-of-commission commode,
clutching a hammer in his grasp. But that hasn't kept him from buying
real estate.

Inside the pithy volume (which begins with a chapter on "Why It
Was Probably a Mistake to Buy This Book") Barry weighs in on everything from choosing a broker ("The best place to obtain a broker is at
a junior high school, where you'll find that virtually all the teachers
obtained real estate licenses once they realized what a tragic mistake they had made, selecting a profession that requires them to
spend entire days confined in small rooms with adolescent children")
to do-it-yourself renovations ("WARNING: ANY MONEY YOU SAVE BY
DOING HOMEOWNER PROJECTS YOURSELF WILL BE OFFSET BY THE
COST OF HIRING COMPETENT PROFESSIONALS TO COME AND REMOVE
THEM SO YOU CAN SELL YOUR HOUSE") to the hidden meaning of "location, location, location" ("If you have school-age children, by far
the most important factor in selecting a neighborhood is, of course,
the proximity of the nearest Toys Backwards "R" Us store").

What Barry does not acknowledge in this, one of his many best-
sellers, is that he has some actual experience in the world of real estate. Not only has he owned several houses as he moved from
Pennsylvania to the Miami area, where his homes grew in size with his
success, but he's also tried his hand at real estate from an investor's
perspective as well. Back in 1979, when Barry wrote a column for a
daily paper in West Chester, Pennsylvania, he read a book that told its
audience how to make millions by borrowing money with practically no
collateral and buying real estate. Barry shared the concept with his

buddies, Joe DiGiacinto—a friend he's known since the two were born in the same hospital, five days apart—and Buzz Burger, a college chum, and they agreed: It was a no-brainer.

A few days later, the threesome trotted off to a local bank, Barry explained when we spoke several years ago for a profile in *Smart-Money*. He said at the time: "[The bankers] thought this was the funniest thing they'd ever heard."

Being laughed at—by bankers no less—took some of the wind out of the trio's sails, but still they forged ahead. They scraped together $10,000 of their own money to use as a down payment, borrowed $30,000 from the bank, and bought a two-family row house in West Chester. Early on, they shared the pleasantries of management—shopping for new appliances to replace the ones the tenants shorted out, answering phone calls about plumbing disasters that always seemed to occur in the middle of the night. "When we started out, we were such nice guys," Barry remembered over lunch in a Miami bar. "We were unaware of the fact that people will look you right in the eye and really lie to you."

It must not have been that bad. Eventually the one row house became six, and though Barry and DiGiacinto moved out of the area, leaving Burger (who has never quite forgiven them) to landlord solo, they still have two properties today.

STAYING AWAY FROM STOCKS

To Barry, real estate has one important factor on its side: It's not the stock market. His view of that venerable institution is even more sharp-tongued: "You find yourself a reputable stockbroker (defined as 'a stockbroker who hasn't been indicted yet') and you give him some money," he once wrote. "He keeps some for himself and uses the rest to buy you a stock that he got on a Hot Tip and Recommends Highly, although of course he keeps his own personal money in a mayonnaise jar. Eventually you start to notice that your 'can't miss' stock is not performing up to expectations, as evidenced by the fact that the newspaper is now listing it on the comics page. Finally, you tell the broker to sell it, which he does, taking another chunk of the proceeds for himself and paying the balance to you out of one of those bus-driver-style change dispensers. Then he's off to the golf course, to pick up some more Hot Tips for you."

That, all jokes aside, is why Barry is largely hands-off with his portfolio. "My investment philosophy is that I send my money to Joe," Barry says of the aforementioned DiGiacinto, who grew up to be a lawyer in Westchester County, New York, specializing in estate planning. In particular, Barry values the fact that his old chum is not only extremely conservative but "relentlessly meticulous."

DiGiacinto handles Barry's investment portfolio, a Keogh for retirement started with Barry's publishing fees, and the trust-fund account for Barry's son Robert, now 16. The basic portfolio is invested with income as the primary goal, with 60 percent in fixed-income investments and the remaining 40 percent in equities—of that, a slim 7 or 8 percent in foreign stocks. In fact, as conservative as DiGiacinto happens to be, he's not quite as conservative as Barry himself. For the past few years, the attorney believed that Barry should increase his equities allocation and tried to steer him in that direction. But his client stuck his ground. "Time has proven me right and him wrong," DiGiacinto shrugs.

Both the Keogh and Robert's trust are invested much more aggressively, with a mix of approximately 75 percent equities and 25 percent fixed-income investments. All three accounts are primarily in mutual funds—many from the Twentieth Century family of funds as well as Fidelity. The latter's Contra fund has done especially well by Barry, DiGiacinto notes. With all of the investments, Barry takes a long-term stance. "We don't buy and sell a lot," says DiGiacinto. Even the money in trust, which was originally intended to fund college for Rob, may end up staying there. "I generally tell my clients that if you can afford to use your own funds by the time college rolls around, you should go ahead and do that," says DiGiacinto. "Rob's trust has already grown substantially, and it will continue to grow so it's there for other purposes."

Though Barry gets plenty of stock tips—from his readers, his buddies at the *Miami Herald*, even on the Internet—he says he's never taken one. He's only picked one stock in his life and that was nearly a decade ago when he was spending a ton of money each year taking Rob and his motley crew of friends to Disney World. "If we weren't actually in Disney World, we were standing outside the fence," Barry said when we originally spoke. "If the lines were too long we just threw money over." He figured that since the company must be making money on his contribution alone, he might as well get something in return, so he instructed DiGiacinto to take a position in Walt Disney stock. It was a smart move.

As far as Barry's investments are concerned, that's about it. He doesn't buy into the concept of venture capital, or collecting cars (he's still driving a Ford Explorer purchased in 1993). And he doesn't consider the three-bedroom house in South Miami he bought just a few months ago with his second wife, a sportswriter, to be an investment.

WATCHING PENNIES

But as his readers well know, Barry is concerned with how much things cost. He was especially happy to bid adieu to 1996 because never again would he have to read about insanely wealthy people bidding hundreds of thousands of dollars for a piece of Jacqueline Kennedy Onassis' old junk. He believes that restaurant checks should be split down the middle (no matter who had the Sprite and who had the glass of wine that cost a few cents more). And he has said his latest book, *Dave Barry in Cyberspace* (Crown, 1996), was just a ploy to enable him to write off his many computers on his tax return.

Taxes are particularly high on Barry's hit list. According to DiGiacinto, Barry has never liked paying taxes. He has issues with the IRS, issues with the capital gains tax, issues even with sales tax. Every year he devotes at least one of his columns to nailing the government where taxes are concerned. Why? He believes it's ridiculous that ordinary, everyday citizens can't make sense of the tax code, much less file their own returns. (In Barry's case, he might give it a shot if he didn't have those real estate investments complicating matters.)

This year, his wit was directed at the notion of a flat tax, which in Barry's mind might actually make some sense: "It's income-tax time again, Americans: time to gather up those receipts, get out those tax forms, sharpen up that pencil, and stab yourself in the aorta," he wrote in a column devoted largely to answering common tax questions like: "Q: I understand that Congress is considering a so-called 'flat' tax system. How would this work? A: If Congress were to pass a 'flat' tax, you'd simply pay a fixed percentage of your income and you wouldn't have to fill out any complicated forms and there would be no loopholes for politically connected groups, and normal people would actually understand the tax laws, and giant talking broccoli stalks would come around and mow your lawn free, because Congress is not going to pass a flat tax, you pathetic fool."

"I consider myself an intelligent person, and I don't have a clue about how you would know you've really done the right thing as far as taxes are concerned," said Barry back in 1993. "Nobody else seems to have a clue either. In fact, the IRS says if you ask them a question and they give you the wrong answer it's not their fault." When Barry ran for President in 1996—which he has done every four years going back to Reagan's days—he said he'd like to devote a greater percentage of the budget to relocating the prostate gland so that doctors could access it more easily. Other than that, Barry explains, he sees no good reason for collecting taxes.

The Prostate Platform was indicative not only of Barry's hatred of taxes, but also of the fact that this year he turned the big 5-0. Still boyish of face, he's a long way away from thinking about retirement; in fact, a long way from slowing down. This year alone, in addition to the cyberspace volume, he hit the best-seller list with Chapter 1 of *Naked Came the Manatee*, a mystery that was a joint effort among a dozen Florida-based writers (and from which all proceeds are going to charity). Thankfully, DiGiacinto notes, he left behind his financial worries about retirement many years ago.

In part, that was because Barry never became a big spender. He was one of four children of a Presbyterian minister, and there wasn't a lot of extra cash to go around during childhood. After Haverford College, he chose the life of a struggling writer, supplementing his reported pieces with an occasional humor column and sustaining himself on bar food.

ONLY AN OCCASIONAL SPLURGE

Even after he landed his gig at the *Miami Herald* in 1983, Barry kept his spending in check. The mainstays of his wardrobe are still polo shirts and Docksiders; the thought of trading in his Levi's for an Armani suit and tie makes him laugh. Through the eighties and into the nineties, his income continued to skyrocket, supplemented with speaking fees and even—for a short few years—fees he earned as his life became the fodder for the network sitcom "Dave's World," starring Harry Anderson. He's left scratching his head to remember a major splurge. There was a Gibson Les Paul guitar, shrugs Barry. Its hefty price tag: $800.

It all comes back to the fact that Barry is still quite a regular guy. The kind who will one day kick back with his first grandchild and explain why Tonya Harding was bad, Bob Dylan was good, and Pez is still one of the great inventions of all time. Then, in all likelihood, Barry will recount one of his favorite tales of his youth—not the one about how he had to walk 12 miles to school in the freezing cold, but the one about how, after working as a struggling young writer for some time, he broke into the more lucrative end of the business.

It was 1981 and Barry had just become a father. The ever-observant Barry turned the story of his son's birth into a humor article that he sold to the *Philadelphia Inquirer Magazine* for $250. A few days later, he received a call from an editor at the *Chicago Tribune* asking how much Barry would charge him to reprint the piece.

"Uh—$50?" Barry said cautiously, not wanting to price himself out of the market.

The editor laughed: "How about $500?"

"Well," said Barry, breathing a sigh of relief, "you drive a hard bargain but . . . ."

Jeff Blake

JEFF BLAKE, age 26, quarterback for the Cincinnati Bengals, is currently playing his sixth season in the NFL. During his 1995 season, he passed for more than 3,800 yards and 28 touchdowns, set a Bengals record for pass completions, and was named AFC Pro Bowl Quarterback (an honor he nearly mirrored in 1996 by being tagged as alternate quarterback for the game). Blake came out of East Carolina University, where during his senior year he led the football team to its highest-ever ranking in the polls. He and his wife Lawanna split their time between Miami and Cincinnati. They are the parents of three.

LIKE DAVE BARRY, JEFF BLAKE GOT OFF TO A SLOW START IN HIS field. For a few years early on in his football career, it looked like the quarterback was going to have to fall back on his college degree—a

BA in construction management from East Carolina University—in order to support his wife, Lawanna, and their three young kids. He had a stellar season in his senior year in college, during which he led the team to its best-ever record and a berth in the Peach Bowl, earning himself a few Heisman Trophy votes along the way. Once he made it into the NFL, however, he hardly got onto the field. The New York Jets, who claimed him in the sixth round of the 1992 draft, let him watch the action on the sidelines for a full two years.

When the Cincinnati Bengals picked him up on waivers just before the start of the 1994 season, he again hoped he'd see some playing time. But as the third-string quarterback, behind David Klingler and Don Hollas, Blake started to think about looking for a day job. Maybe he'd head home to Florida. The Disney company was still overtaking Orlando. Surely a former NFL player could find work on some development project down South.

Then came midseason and a game against the Super Bowl champion Dallas Cowboys. Klingler and Hollas both went down early with injuries and Blake came off the bench with enough force to give Troy Aikman and his boys a scare. While Klingler and Hollas nursed their wounds, Blake took the next two games, passing for a solid 300 yards each. By the time the 1995 season rolled around, he no longer needed to think about sending out his resume.

His football aspirations may have been realized, but Blake still had every intention of using his college degree. After three years of making the league minimum (around $110,000), when the money finally started to roll in, Blake knew he wanted to invest at least part of it in real estate. His philosophy is straightforward. "If you make a reasonable real estate investment you can always break even because it's always there," Blake explains. "I have a friend and teammate, Lee Johnson, who carries one of those stock market calculators wherever he goes. He tells me that he wins some and he loses some. I'm not up for that yet."

LOCATION, LOCATION, LOCATION

For Blake, real estate has the benefit of being familiar. In school, he was taught that the best properties had access to good schools, restaurants, branches of popular banks, and grocery stores. In life, he learned proximity to Disney World doesn't hurt either. His first foray into real estate was purchasing his own house, a new five-bedroom, in Orlando not far from the theme park. Blake befriended the developer on the project, who later offered him the opportunity to buy land in another subdivision he was developing—this one even closer to Fantasyland. "I bought a lot that's a little over an acre for $350,000," says Blake. "People have already offered me $600,000 to take it off my hands." He's holding out, though. "I'm waiting to sell until someone builds a million-dollar house on one of the adjacent lots. If you can show that you can put a million-dollar house on it, you can sell it for a lot more than [just the land is] worth."

Blake has yet to see the profits from one even larger real estate deal, but he has high hopes. He and nine other football players are the majority investors in a golf/condo development in Knoxville, Tennessee, called Royal Oaks. The plan is to put two championship-level courses (three nines are complete, and the fourth is underway) as well as 1,200 residential units on the 600-acre property. It's already 25 percent sold out and the investors—including former Chicago Bear Jay Hilgenberg, who provides hands-on management, and Jim McMahon—have started gathering each Memorial Day for a two-day tournament to promote the complex. Last year, 30 football players, including all of the investors, were on hand. "A golf investment is a good marriage for football players," explains Blake's business manager, Michael Weisberg, who handles the day-to-day financial affairs for two dozen football players. "Baseball players are busy throughout the golf season. Football players are done with their seasons by January, so they can be available to show their support over the spring and summer."

"I know my return will be good," Blake says emphatically. "The demographics of the area are strong—it's growing well, a commercial center is going up nearby, the next thing to come will be a mall. The bigger it gets, the bigger we can go. The only problem is, with so many other guys in the deal, your percentage isn't as large as you want it to be. I'm hoping that some other guy might want to sell some of his shares, or all of his shares, as we go on." Right now, all of the money the community is making is being plowed back into the next phase of development. But Blake figures that by the time he retires, the community will provide a hefty boost to his annual income.

INVESTING FOR RETIREMENT

Retirement is not as far away as you might think. At age 26, Blake figures he's got about 10 years left to play. That's a long time in the NFL, but unlike a lawyer or businessman who'll hit his peak earning years in his forties or early fifties, Blake is in his right now. The solid seven figures he pulls in as one of the league's leading quarterbacks has to last him and his family well beyond the next decade.

That's definitely possible, says Weisberg, who runs his business from the North Chicago suburbs. Making it happen takes two things. The first is a preference for ultraconservative investments. Blake's financial heart may be in real estate, but 70 percent of his dollars are in bonds. "Real estate is for growth and that's okay," Weisberg explains. "But the majority of his assets will always be invested in fixed income. As he gets older and the money piles up, and when he can meet his annual income needs from the bonds we put him in, then he can move into other investments—stocks, real estate, and other things—in a bigger way. Right now, we've got to do all the planning so that he is set by the time he's thirty-two or thirty-three years old."

Blake's entire bond portfolio is comprised of highly rated—AA or AAA—tax-free municipal bonds. Since he lives in Florida, where state taxes aren't an issue, there's no need to limit his purchases to triple tax-frees. Weisberg selects the holdings on a weekly basis from a list provided by Blake's brokers at Robert Baird & Company. "If you see AAA tax-free bonds paying 5.5 percent on this day or that day, that's what he's buying," says Weisberg. "If they're paying less, so be it. The way I work is that if a guy knows that $2 million invested conservatively can bring him $10,000 of disposable income each month, and that'll do the trick, then that's what we concentrate on first. Stocks may do better. They may do much better. But nobody can guarantee it."

Weisberg and Blake aren't ignoring the market altogether—a tougher challenge in this fast-forward climate than at most times. The stocks that comprise 20 percent of Blake's portfolio are mostly large-cap, New York Stock Exchange, story stocks, with an occasional over-the-counter play thrown in. Recently, for example, he's been a holder of Spiegel, the catalog company, and he has been in and out of Starbucks Coffee a number of times over the past few years.

Another way he's working toward his accumulation goal is by

participating in the National Football League's 401(k) plan. Each of the last four years, he's kicked in the full amount he's allowed to contribute tax-free. His teams have matched his contributions one dollar for three dollars. Because this money is designated as long-term, it's invested more aggressively than the rest of Blake's portfolio: 50 percent is in growth stocks, 25 percent in international, and 25 percent invested for income. "I've got almost a hundred grand in the thing!" Blake says excitedly. "I've got at least another 10 years in the league. That'll be sitting nice when I'm ready to retire."

THE KEY TO BUDGETING: JUST SAY NO

If maintaining a solid, conservative investment strategy gets Blake 50 percent of the way to sealing his financial future, the other half of the equation is smart budgeting. It's Weisberg's job to say no—quickly and decisively—to the dozens of requests for investment funding and loans that pour in each month. "My clients say that 'no' is my favorite word," Weisberg laughs.

It falls to Blake not to blow the program by spending every free dollar he has. This, Weisberg admits, has been less of a problem for Jeff Blake than for many of the other players he deals with. "I'm a necessity type of guy," explains Blake. "Even when I was a kid, my dad could put $20 on the dresser and it might sit a whole week before I'd even notice it was there. I was playing sports, not thinking about new pants or new shoes. I was wearing football shoes or baseball shoes most of the time anyway."

It helped that money was never really that tight. From the age of six, when his mother drowned in a swimming accident, Blake was raised by his father, a former Canadian Football League player who became a high school coach in Stanford, Florida. Though he held summer jobs working for his grandfather, a contractor, his father wouldn't allow him to work during the school year. "He wanted me to devote my time to doing well in school and playing ball," Blake says. "For that I'm thankful."

Father and son had hopes for a scholarship to one of the Florida's great football schools. But Blake, at 6 foot 0 and 202 pounds, was considered small for a quarterback, and the only offer that came through was from little-known East Carolina. His first two years were largely wasted, as the coach stuck to a running offense, making little use of Blake's best asset: his passing arm. But by his senior year, the coach decided to play the game Blake's way and ended up with a winning record as a result.

A MODEST LIFESTYLE

Still, as the draft rolled around, Blake's size kept him back in the salary department. In his first year with the Jets, his after-tax income was a mere $75,000. Much of that went to rent an apartment on New York's Long Island ($1,200 a month) and a few hundred more to paying off his Isuzu Rodeo. Most athletes were living considerably better; Blake saw this firsthand, particularly because he spent many of his off-the-field hours at the home of his godfather, New York Yankees outfielder Tim Raines. "Now, he had very long money," Blake remembers. "His wife had like 30 tennis bracelets." But even once Blake's salary kicked in at top levels, he kept his spending down. "I have a nice house and three cars, but I don't really splurge like the other guys," he says. "I don't have seven or eight cars. My wife has some jewelry, but not close to what my godmother has."

As his professional future became more secure over the last couple of years, he has loosened the purse strings a bit. Blake recently bought himself his first truly flashy car, a Porsche 911 Cabriolet. And he decided to invest $100,000 in a movie called *51 Runner*, about blacks in the NFL during the fifties and sixties. As a bonus, the director promised him a small role.

Perhaps the truest sign that he's feeling solid financially came last November—after six years of marriage and the birth of three children—when he and his wife Lawanna finally made out a will. Underlying the document are trusts for the three children that give them access to their funds starting at age 21, with the final payout at 30. "I don't want to give them too much too fast because I want them to have the opportunity to try to make it on their own," says Blake. "And I want them to be mature enough so that they don't blow it."

The fact that he's talking about a time when his children will, in fact, be older than he is right now makes Blake smile. "That's just the breaks," he shrugs. "When you have to work your way up from the bottom to get to the top, you learn to appreciate it more."

WHEN IT'S *YOUR* MONEY . . .

ACCORDING TO THE LOS ANGELES–BASED CENTER FOR REAL Estate Studies, 7 out of 10 millionaires got started by making money in real estate. It's no wonder the concept is so appealing. But is it a cakewalk? Far from it. Whether you get into real estate by buying a charming-but-dilapidated bungalow and putting in sweat equity to bring it up to shape, or by buying a few shares in a real estate investment trust (REIT), there are a number of factors to consider.

For the most part, people take their first steps in real estate investing in one of two ways: They either remain in their primary residence and buy another property to rent out, or buy a second property to move into and rent out their original residence. The latter is the better move, says Peter G. Miller, author of *Buy Your First Home Now* (HarperCollins, 1996) and the originator of America Online's real estate site. "When you move out you can get residential financing," he explains. "It isn't as easy to get investor financing. You might have to put more money down, accept a slightly higher interest rate, and it may be harder to qualify for." Indeed, if you need income from the property in order to make the mortgage payments, many lenders are going to want to see a fairly long-term leasing arrangement—at least a full year. That's not going to be easy to finesse if you're planning to convert your new property into a rental *after* you sign the papers.

There also are a number of financial issues to consider before making your decision: Are you going to rent the property out yourself or hire someone to do it? As an owner, you'll be responsible for insuring the dwelling (though your tenants should have renter's insurance as well). And if you've decided to assume the landlord duties, rather than pass them along to a management company (which will cost you a good 10 to 15 percent of the rental income), understand that your phone is going to ring at 4 A.M. when a pipe bursts—and you'll have to drag an unhappy plumber out of bed.

The final key to success is finding a decent property. A growing job base, good schools, and reasonable climate are all baseline criteria, but it's still up to you to find a property that will not only escalate in value, but also grow faster than the rate of inflation. Jane Garvey, founder of Chicago Creative Investors Association, a real estate investment group, suggests looking for properties in need of simple fixes (cleaning, painting, landscaping, carpeting, and countertops, for example) while steering clear of those with problems that are either too expensive to fix (crumbling foundations, major plumbing repairs) or not solvable (busy locations and poor layouts).

How do you find such hidden gems? "There's no one secret," Garvey admits. "Basically, you've got to keep your eyes open all the time. Drive around neighborhoods and look for places that need work on the outside. Keep an eye out for homes where when a windstorm hits nobody picks up the sticks." In Garvey's organization, the members buy properties in foreclosure and at auction. Some read legal publications for news of divorces and deaths. Others have brokers call them when a deal looks right. "When you find a property that goes months and months on the market, there's more opportunity for investors to get a deal."

One good piece of news is that mortgage rates, which stuck in the 8 percent range during 1996, look to remain stable through 1997 and possibly beyond. HSH Associates, the nation's largest publisher of mortgage information, is forecasting rates for 1997 between 7.3 percent and 8.5 percent for a basic 30-year fixed-rate loan.

When you're buying investment property, shopping around for a mortgage is even more important than when buying residential property, HSH vice president Keith Gumbinger notes. The secondary market is much smaller for investment property than for residential property, which means varying underwriting requirements from company to company and rates that may be all over the board. Heading straight to a mortgage broker's office to find the best deal may sound like the perfect solution, but you still want to get a ballpark idea of what's out there yourself. "That way," Gumbinger notes, "you can go into the broker's office and say, 'Here's what I found. If you want to work with me, find me something better.' "

A second home may be the way most beginning investors go, but others prefer to start with commercial property, raw land, or even time-shares. Again, you have to understand that each of these comes with its own set of rules: Financing rules are different, as is tax treatment, and what separates a good investment from a lousy one varies greatly. On the commercial side, if landlords in your area are beginning to offer free rent or pay for expensive building modifications, that's one sure sign that the market is going down, says Frank Linde, a New York real estate developer. If they're willing to cut these kinds of deals, you know it's a tighter market and a better time to buy. Raw land can be a good deal if you hit upon an up-and-coming area, but it's not depreciable and typically not income-producing. And time-shares have such a dodgy history, you're probably best off steering clear of them altogether. (If you've got your heart set on one, don't make the mistake of buying new. There are too many second-hand time-shares available at huge discounts to make that a smart move.)

Finally, if you like the idea of real estate but don't particularly want to get your hands dirty, consider a real estate investment trust or REIT. These are publicly-traded securities that use investor capital to acquire property and/or create mortgages. They typically specialize in one area of real estate investing—hotels, health-care properties, shopping centers, or office complexes, for example. Before you buy, Peter Miller notes, it's important to look very carefully at the future projections for the properties a REIT owns. "For example, will changes in technology empty out major office towers?" he asks. "Think about it this way: If each office worker needs 230 to 250 square feet of office space, if one person decides to telecommute that's 230 to 250 feet of office space not needed. But what if 400 decide to work from home? You have to look at the trends around the country."

That's why many experts agree that if you're going to buy REITs you should buy several different kinds and immediately diversify your holdings. An easy way to accomplish the same goal is to purchase shares in a REIT mutual fund, such as Fidelity Real Estate Investment, which holds over 80 issues, or the Vanguard REIT Index, which holds even more issues and sports the lowest expense ratios available. Of course, as with any investment, you'll want to call for a prospectus and check the fund's track record before you make a purchase.

LAST WORD: MORTGAGE MANIA

WHETHER YOU'RE BUYING YOUR FIRST HOME OR A SECOND to renovate and flip, one of the biggest mistakes people make is not shopping around for a mortgage as carefully as they do for a house. The differences in the rates you're offered—even within a single market—can be a percentage point or more, which translates into thousands of dollars over the life of your loan. The good news is, with rates abnormally stable, according to Keith Gumbinger, vice president of HSH Associates, you're sitting in a borrower's market. There's plenty of room to dicker on points. And lenders are so eager for business, they'll be happy to push your paperwork through, even to stretch the financial ratios, to make sure your application passes muster. Now all you need to do is make sure you're applying for the right mortgage in the first place: a loan that not only serves your cash-flow needs now, but for years to come. Here's a look at a few of the more popular loan products:

- **Fixed-Rate Loans** are best for customers who know they won't be moving anytime in the near future. The 30-year fixed-rate loan is, far and away, the most popular product, with a market share of about 50 percent; 15-year fixed-rate loans capture another 10 percent of customers. If you can take the 15-year without feeling strapped, it'll save you on interest; but if you're unsure, go with the 30-year and pay it off more quickly by making additional payments to principal when you're feeling flush.

- **One-Year Adjustables** make sense if you know you'll be transferred in a few years, or if you're buying a starter house. Notes Gumbinger: "The difference in rates between a 30-year fixed and a one-year ARM [adjustable rate mortgage] has to be at least 2.5 percentage points to really start drawing folks in." Otherwise the risk of your rate jumping the full 6 points it's allowed makes these loans too expensive.

- **Hybrid Adjustables**, also called 5-1s or 7-1s, are fixed for the first five or seven years of their terms, then they convert to one-year ARMs. Because of their adjustable component, they're a lower risk for the bank; thus you save on your rate for the first portion of the term. Typically, a 5-1 hybrid—one of the most popular products on the market today—runs $3/8$ to $1/2$ point cheaper than a 30-year fixed. If you're buying a starter house and plan to move up in 5 to 10 years, this is the loan for you.

- **No-Cost Loans** are all the rage these days. In the past, mortgage seekers would routinely cough up two points plus closing costs to seal their deals. Today, accepting a slightly higher interest rate—say, $8^{3}/4$ percent instead of 8 percent on a 30-year fixed—means you can make it through the transaction without paying either points or closing costs. If you're strapped for cash at signing, a no-cost loan is an extremely appealing option.

- **B, C, and D Loans** are mortgages for folks with a blemish or two on their credit reports. In the past, people with faulty credit histories were out of luck; but recently lenders realized too many people were in that boat to eliminate them out of hand. Instead, a growing group of lenders is serving this community, though at significantly higher rates. Most good mortgage brokers keep lists of the lenders that will underwrite these loans.

Chapter 4

THE GURUS

Alan C. "Ace" Greenberg
Lou Dobbs • Charles Schwab

"I used to be, in my youth, clairvoyant. I had this perfect ability to call market turns. But as I got older I found that long-term investing is the way to go."

—Charles Schwab

DURING THE PAST 10 YEARS, PERSONAL FINANCE HAS BEEN transformed from cottage industry into big business. Back in the early 1980s, a quick thumb through *Money* magazine, a few minutes with Jane Bryant Quinn, or a sleepy Saturday morning watching "Wall Street Week" was all it took to bring you up to date. No more. Now there are more investment resources than you can easily count—from magazines like *Worth* and *Individual Investor* to finance-oriented cable channels like CNBC and CNNfn to Internet sites like the Motley Fool and TheStreet.com. It's enough to make your head spin.

The money gurus you're going to read about in this chapter stand out because of their ability to separate smart financial moves from the, well, not so smart ones. Alan C. "Ace" Greenberg has taken the money of hundreds of America's wealthiest individuals and parlayed it into more. As his client Ivana Trump (page 146) notes: "They don't call him Ace for nothing." Lou Dobbs saw that financial stories were as fascinating, if not more so, as any other piece of a news broadcast. The success of Dobbs's "Moneyline"—the country's first daily financial news program—is the reason we have channels like CNBC today. Before anyone else, Charles Schwab saw that individual investors would want to make their own investment decisions rather than relying on costly full-service brokers. Today he owns the largest discount brokerage firm in the world.

It's rare that you can catch a glimpse of these folks' personal money styles. When Ace Greenberg writes in his corporate memos about how he encourages his firm's employees to give generously to one cause or another, you can be sure he's doing the same with his own money. And Chuck Schwab, as you'd expect, uses a discount broker. But reports don't often get more detailed than that. Lou Dobbs, in particular, feels that in order to maintain his journalistic integrity, it's crucial to keep his opinions off the air.

Yet these folks have learned many important lessons in their decades of work in the financial industry. Their personal portfolios have long been the beneficiaries. Now, perhaps, yours can too.

Alan C. "Ace" Greenberg

ALAN C. "ACE" GREENBERG, 70, is the chairman of the board of Bear, Stearns & Company. A career stock trader, Greenberg joined Bear, Stearns as a clerk, following his graduation from the University of Missouri, and worked his way up the ranks, becoming CEO in 1978. He is the author of Memos from the Chairman *(Workman, 1996), a collection of actual memos he sent to the firm's employees through the years. Greenberg is also one of New York City's most notable philanthropists.*

TO GAIN AN AUDIENCE WITH BEAR, STEARNS CHAIRMAN ALAN C. "Ace" Greenberg, you have to clear a couple of obstacles. First there's his assistant, who greets your request for 45 minutes with The Chairman with a knowing chuckle. "He says he wouldn't give his own mother 45 minutes," she says, phoning back. "But you can have five to 10." Then, there's the walk to his desk—through a locked door in the lobby so inconspicuous it might be a broom closet, up a private elevator, into a trading area on the second floor.

You wind your way through a maze of Quotrons, a sea of multi-line phones, an army of bespectacled traders. And there at the end of the corridor is Greenberg, 70, his bald head distinguishing him from the masses a few decades his junior. He's not holding court in some leather-bound office, but is seated in the fray, on a raised platform at the back of the floor, where no intimidating doors keep institutional salesmen from peppering him with their queries at whim. He does have a plush office elsewhere in the building, but this clearly is the environment he prefers. His favorite tombstones (announcements of public offerings, like the one from the recent Planet Hollywood deal) and press clippings (from *Fortune* and *Business Week*), are crammed onto a window ledge behind his seat, along with a caricature of Greenberg reading—what else?—the financial pages.

It's a Monday morning in early January. On Friday, the market broke yet another record, closing over 6,700. Not surprisingly, Greenberg, still the primary broker for 131 active accounts, is already hard at work. Even when the market takes a breather, Greenberg has his eyes on the screen in front of him that keeps tabs on the dozens of issues in which he holds large positions. This morning he is focused on KSF—Quaker State Corporation. "Sell 5,000 KSF," he orders. Then a few minutes later: "Sell 25,000 KSF."

BUYING COMPANIES, NOT INDUSTRIES

Donald Trump once said of Greenberg: "He has the best trading ability I've ever seen." Greenberg says that his method—at least the one he follows for his own account—is nothing if not straightforward. "I like big companies with big capitalizations that are listed on the New York Stock Exchange," he says. What about those on the AMEX, or the big companies NASDAQ has roped in like Microsoft and MCI? "Those are okay for other people," Greenberg says. "They're just not for me."

He picks companies rather than sectors, focusing on two factors. "I look for companies that are earning big money," he says. "And I like those where the management is brilliant and honest. Smart, honest management—you can't beat it." The simplicity of those messages exemplifies Greenberg's approach to both business and life. He derides such modern-day management tools as TQM (total quality management) and BPR (business process reengineering), and would rather focus on the CS (common sense) lessons he learned from his father, who owned a chain of ready-to-wear stores. "Tell the truth, people," Greenberg remembers his father saying, along with about "100 other" examples of common sense wisdom. But perhaps the most useful in Greenberg's later life was this pearl: "If you own something bad, sell, because tomorrow it's going to be worse."

It's become Ace Greenberg's secret weapon. "I must keep [my investments] when the market's going up," he says. But when it's headed down, Greenberg limits his losses by getting out of any investment after it has dropped 10 to 15 percent. He's made plenty of bad buys but he never gives himself a chance to lose his shirt. Despite a lifetime of sticking to these rules, in recent years selling from his own portfolio has become especially difficult. Greenberg has made such big gains in his favorite holdings that he's not sure he'll ever be able to unload them. "If you're a citizen of New York City, it's very hard to sell, because you're facing capital gains [taxes] of close to 40 percent," he explains. Unless the market takes a stunning drop, Greenberg will most likely pass along his biggest winners as part of his estate. The beneficiaries will receive a step-up-in-basis—they'll inherit the assets at their current value—and be able to then get out (if they so choose) without taking a big tax hit.

A FOCUS ON LIQUIDITY

A portfolio of well-managed New York Stock Exchange issues is about it as far as Greenberg's investments are concerned. He has no slice of a high-flying venture capital firm. No tax shelters. No limited partnerships. Save for his apartment on Manhattan's Upper East Side and his summer house in the Hamptons, he doesn't even have real estate, and, as Greenberg says: "Those aren't investments; I *live* there." Besides, he raises an eyebrow: "I like liquidity. Being able to get out at a moment's notice."

Atop that list is stock in Bear, Stearns, which Greenberg took public (on the New York Stock Exchange, of course) in 1985. The SEC, he says, wouldn't look kindly on him discussing his stock, or for that matter stocks in the brokerage industry, but his holdings show he's a big believer. The 1996 proxy statement says Greenberg holds close to a million shares—1.23 percent—of the firm, which analysts still regard as one of the standouts on the Street.

An Oklahoma boy, Greenberg came to Bear, Stearns in 1949, following his graduation from the University of Missouri. He'd known for many years he wanted to work on Wall Street, but in those years if you didn't have a diploma from one of the Ivies it was tough to even get an interview at certain firms. Bear, Stearns was not as discriminating. Greenberg began as a clerk earning $32 a week, $1,664 a year, but soon talked his way into a spot on the arbitrage desk and a raise. Four years later, Greenberg was running the desk, bringing home $25,000 a year in salary and another $50,000 in bonus money. (The gains he was pulling in, many people believe, are what earned Greenberg the nickname Ace, but in fact it's a remnant of his college days. When a dismal male-to-female ratio made it tough to get dates at school, Greenberg's roommate suggested he might have an easier go if he had a flashier moniker. Willing to try anything, Alan Greenberg became Ace Gainsboro. Only the Ace part stuck.)

When Greenberg was 29, the trading position next to Bear, Stearns chairman Salim "Cy" Lewis opened up and Greenberg, though a bit nervous (Lewis was known for his temper) slid in beside him. Two years later he was made a partner and when Lewis died of a heart attack in 1978, he became CEO.

Under Greenberg's leadership, the company saw its total capital explode. It was $46 million when he assumed the helm, $517 million when he took the company public, and over $10 billion at last count. During the 1980s, the company came up with an innovative options strategy to allow corporate raiders like Carl Icahn and Donald Trump to secretly accumulate blocks of stock in companies they were interested in taking over. But perhaps what earned him the most attention was his take on expenses and keeping them under control.

COST-CUTTING AT THE OFFICE

As documented in a series of memos he wrote to the company's general partners from the time he took over in 1978—and recently published to considerable acclaim in *Memos from the Chairman* (Workman, 1996)—Greenberg isn't one to tolerate waste.

"I have just informed the purchasing department that they should no longer purchase paper clips. All of us receive documents every day with paper clips on them. If we save these paper clips, not only will we have enough for our own use, but we will also, in a short time, be awash in the little critters. Periodically, we will collect excess paper clips and sell them (since the cost to us is zero, the Arbitrage Department tells me the return on capital will be above average)," he wrote, then went on a similar tear about memo pads and his firm's sky-high Federal Express tab.

Such cost-cutting measures have helped drive Bear, Stearns' stock price from a split-adjusted $6.71 upon its opening in 1985 to $25.71 at the beginning of 1997, and have nicely padded Greenberg's own pocket. He has been a mainstay on *Business Week*'s list of the most highly compensated executives, topping out at $19 million in 1996. In fact, the *Wall Street Journal* devoted an entire article to the fact that the top five earners at Bear, Stearns last year took home more than $81 million, well over the $58 million the NBA champion Chicago Bulls were to be paid for the next season.

SPENDING MONEY—FOR THE BENEFIT OF OTHERS

Greenberg allows that he spends his own money much more freely. But, in fact, there are not a lot of high-ticket items on his Visa each month. "I have a lot of hobbies," he says, leaning back in his chair. "But none of them are really expensive." Yo-yos certainly aren't going to break the bank. Neither is Greenberg's repertoire of magic tricks (mostly done with cards). And though Macunudo cigars have gone up in price recently, they're not burning a hole in Greenberg's deep pockets. Even Greenberg's bridge habit—a daily trip after the close of trading to the Regency Whist Club on Manhattan's East Side, where he's been known to wager $1,000 or more on one rubber—isn't going to break a man of his means. "I'm not into expensive art," he continues, determined he'll think of *some* high-priced habit. "I'm not into expensive cars. I'm not into . . . I guess I just give my money away. I enjoy giving money away.

"When I was in college," Greenberg explains, "I decided to become a philanthropist, because philanthropists always seemed to have a lot of money." The list of charities Greenberg supports, from the New York Public Library to the Police and Fire Widows' and Children's Benefit Fund, is long and impressive. He is said to be New York City's largest contributor to the United Jewish Appeal. Immediately following Bear, Stearns IPO he gave away stock and cash worth $4 million, and he insists Bear, Stearns' managing directors follow his example. They must give at least 4 percent of their compensation to charity each year (tax returns are checked to make sure everyone toes the line).

The appearance of strong-arming his associates doesn't bother him in the least. While Greenberg sat trading and chatting that Monday morning in early January, one young associate approached him about an invitation to a upcoming benefit. Invited to sit with some 40 other prominent folks on the dais, Greenberg could not attend. "I'll just send a nice note," the associate said helpfully, but Greenberg shook his head. "You've gotta send him something," he said, referring to the issuer of the invitation. "Isn't he chairing the event? If he's the chairman you've got to give him something. Otherwise it's insulting. It doesn't have to be $25,000. I'd suggest $5,000." It wasn't clear from whose account that $5,000 would be withdrawn.

Twenty-five minutes, more than twice the allotted time, have passed and though Greenberg has been a model of politeness, he is clearly getting busier. Trading activity is picking up.

I ask about his plans for retirement. In 1994, Greenberg relinquished the title of chief executive officer and day-to-day responsibility for the firm, but he retained the title of chairman and has never said when he plans to step down completely. "When it isn't fun, when I don't feel productive, then I won't do it anymore," he responds, and turns back to the business of the day.

His fast fingers put one call on hold—"Lisa, get on that," he barks—and pauses just for a split second before he dials another.

Lou Dobbs

LOU DOBBS, age 52, is the longtime anchor of CNN's "Moneyline," television's first nightly business broadcast, and executive vice president of CNN, where he is responsible for CNNfn, the company's financial news channel. Prior to joining CNN in 1980, Dobbs was a local news anchor and reporter in Yuma, Arizona. He has an economics degree from Harvard University, and has won the Emmy, CableAce, and George Foster Peabody awards. He and his wife have four children ranging in age from 9 to 26. In 1993, the National Father's Day Committee named him Father of the Year.

UNLIKE GREENBERG, LOU DOBBS IS MUCH MORE COMFORTABLE discussing other people's money than his own. On a recent Wednesday afternoon, the host of CNN's highly regarded "Moneyline with Lou Dobbs" and the top dog at the newer network CNNfn (short for CNN Financial Network), was sitting in his corner office at 5 Penn Plaza, overlooking the Hudson River on one side and Madison Square Garden on the other, and feeling distinctly uncomfortable. Dobbs had suddenly realized that working his way through a full hour's worth of questions about his investments and maintaining his unbiased perspective was going to be tougher than he thought. "I can't do this," he says more than once. "I just realized I can't do this." Then, gamely, he plows ahead.

Dobbs knows he's in the catbird seat. Except for economics correspondent Irving R. Levine, who hung up his game jersey a few years back, and "Wall Street Week"'s Louis Rukeyser, Dobbs has the longest tenure in this business of reporting on business—and with "Moneyline" running on a daily basis, compared to Rukeyser's weekly appearances, he has logged the most hours, no contest. Everyone who's anyone in the world of high finance, from Warren Buffett (who checked his sound levels in an interview with Dobbs to the count of "one million, two million, three million") to Michael Milken to Dobbs's own boss, Ted Turner, have found themselves seated at his mike. Every blip in every index since 1980 has been voiced in his calming tones. Clearly he has perspective that most journeymen lack.

IGNORING THE BUZZ

Yet Dobbs says the best thing he's done for his personal portfolio is to ignore most of those voices ringing in his ears. "The greatest danger for any financial journalist is to assume that you now have some specialized knowledge and that you should be able to make decisions as quickly and as ably as a Warren Buffett," he says. "Each day at the end of the day I wind up with a different impression of the market. One day I think we're doing fine, the next I'm convinced we're headed for a fall. This happens enough times and it tends to make a long-term investor out of you. Otherwise one day you're buying calls, the next day you're buying puts, and very soon you're broke. You have to be very careful."

For that reason Dobbs's portfolio doesn't change much day-to-day. He's got 30 percent in stocks, mostly traditional companies in the oil and banking sectors, and though he "loves" core technology stocks he carefully steers clear of the dish of the day. An "infinitesimal" piece of his stock portfolio is invested in purely speculative holdings, something he does for fun. Another 30 percent of his holdings is in bond funds, 30 percent is in real estate, and the remaining 10 percent is in cash and cashlike securities.

Dobbs says his buying strategy is very simple and straightforward. "The first thing I look at is the potential for return and price gains," he says. "You find that by looking at the strength of products, and markets." Since one lousy purchase in the early seventies, he has always done his own homework. "I remember my first bad investment. It was a company called New Idria Mining. They were mining for mercury and my friends said it was about to take off." Dobbs laid out $100 for 50 of the $2 shares—a hefty sum for a police-beat reporter at a small-market station—and then watched the shares fall lower, and lower, and lower until his entire investment was wiped out. "I didn't realize that it *could* go any lower than $2 a share," he chuckles.

Buying winners is just one side of the equation, however. Like Greenberg, Dobbs is convinced that it's his selling strategy that keeps him afloat. When a stock loses 10 percent of its price, he's out the door.

"I've always had a philosophy, and sometimes I've honored it, that you're better off letting profits run," he says. "But when an investment loses that much of its value, it becomes cheaper for me to sell and get back in later if it goes even lower. If it dips more than 10 percent, and I'm still holding, it's very difficult to make up any losses."

PAY ATTENTION TO THE PROS

More than any other fundamental, however, Dobbs wants to know who's running the show. "I think in all my investment strategies, I bet more on the jockeys than on the horses—the folks managing the investments more than the investments themselves. Mike Milken, years and years ago, said that the scarcest resource in American business is not capital. It's management. I think he was right on."

That was a lesson hammered home for Dobbs in the late 1970s. "Back in the days of tax shelters, a fellow approached me with an opal mine shelter," he remembers. "My wife and I listened. The fellow said the risk was minimal. It sounded intriguing. But before I did it, I went to a friend of mine, an accountant, and said, 'So, does this make sense to you?' I told him I had looked at the numbers; they seemed okay, and besides the fellow was very likable. And my friend said: 'Lou, if this guy is a con man, wouldn't you expect him to be likable?'" Dobbs shrugs. "He was right. It's important to judge people very, very carefully."

There are a handful of "Wall Street oracles" with whom Dobbs is quite comfortable hedging his bets. They include people like Buffett, Henry Kravis, and Wayne Huizenga, who have incredible track records as well as a history of creating great wealth in their businesses—or in Buffett's case, simply creating great wealth. "You spend five minutes with [Intel CEO] Andy Grove and you don't have to be a genius to know that you want to put your money with him whether he's building computer chips or widgets," says Dobbs.

Dobbs feels the same way about his real estate investments. He has a number of rental properties, as well as commercial properties, all brought to him by smart property managers with a solid handle on their particular markets. Most of Dobbs's commercial investments are in farmland, though he points out that he doesn't consider his primary residence, a working farm in New Jersey, an investment, and tries not to dwell on its rise in value. "The temptation when you do well is to try to make it serendipity," he says. "I'm just fortunate that the place I wanted to live happened to make sense to real estate investors at the time."

Farms are a market Dobbs understands, having grown up in Texas and Idaho. When he wasn't in school, he was hauling hay, picking potatoes, and doing the other chores needed to keep his parents' farm running. By the time he was in high school, he and a few friends had a bustling enterprise hauling hay for five cents a bale, not just for their families, but for the town at large. "We were making more money than most of the grown-ups in our small town," Dobbs remembers. His profits helped pay his way through Harvard, where he earned a bachelor's degree in economics, and he continued to make pocket change by carting cases of Coors beer from his home state to Massachusetts, where it wasn't on the market yet.

Such enterprises were inspired by his father, a small businessman and entrepreneur in the area of farm equipment, but Dobbs says his lessons about investing came from a different source: his Aunt Esther. Around the time of the Depression, she lent a friend $1,000. Her payback was 100 shares of treasury stock in Great Western Reserve Insurance, a company that was ultimately purchased by Mobil Oil and that made Aunt Esther a bundle. "Over the next 30 years, she invested in a lot of different companies," Dobbs remembers. "But she never matched the gain of those 100 shares. And I think my whole life I've been looking for the investment that is going to be my 100 shares of Western Reserve treasury stock."

ALMOST ALL NEWS HAS AN ECONOMIC BASE

He's ended up working for his paychecks instead. In 1980, when Ted Turner was launching CNN, Dobbs put together the first nightly business newscast. This was before the mutual fund craze, before junk bonds, but Turner believed that the national networks gave business reporting short shrift. "People now understand the relationship between policy in Washington and the money in their pocket," Dobbs explains. "Just look at the political process of the last 17 years. In 1980, it brought double-digit inflation. There was the recession of 1982, the crash of 1987 when investors saw one-third of their wealth wiped out in a week. In the 1990s, interest rates dropped precipitously. All along, there's been a rising sophistication on the part of the viewers and the television executives."

It didn't take much time before Dobbs, who spent years as a young reporter chasing fire engines and ambulances, found himself caught up in the activity of the market. By 1984, he was anchoring both

"Moneyline" and a nightly national report for CNN. Sensing he was overburdened, Turner told him one had to go. Dobbs stuck with the markets. "To me, financial journalism is the most engaging intellectually," he says. "It's fundamental to everything that happens. You can look at any story as a political story or an international story, but fundamentally every story is an economic story. The people one covers are the best and the brightest. They create wealth, jobs; they determine the future of this country."

There's no doubt in Dobbs's mind that he chose right. He vividly remembers covering the crash of 1987, now a full decade ago. "It awakened my consciousness as to how global the markets really are," he says. "We always said we were becoming a global economy, but until that point, I don't think I ever understood truly what it meant."

Today, in addition to "Moneyline," he anchors "Business Unusual" and "Managing with Lou Dobbs," a show focused on small business. In 1996, he was put in charge of Turner's multimillion-dollar launch of New York-based CNNfn. He has won practically every broadcasting award in the industry, including the Emmy and George Foster Peabody for his coverage of Black Monday, but they pale in Dobbs's mind next to the Father of the Year award he received from the National Father's Day Committee in 1993. Dobbs's four children range in age from 9 to 26 (his eldest is a producer at CNN).

Though he brings home a sizable salary each year, he still lives modestly. Aside from breeding horses, his primary splurge is his children—family vacations, college tuitions, and because he can afford to sock the money away, well-padded accounts for their futures. But Dobbs says he doesn't understand the rationale behind young parents who stuff their 401(k) or other retirement accounts with more money than they can actually afford. "I'd rather see them invest in themselves, their own education, their own careers, and a comfortable and warm environment in which to raise their children. I'm always running across young folks who are putting 25 percent of their income away for things like retirement and college, and I want to say to them, take some of this money and buy your child a book. *Buy a book!* That will yield much greater returns than putting it in zero coupon bonds."

STILL BULLISH ON THE MARKET

Dobbs is, of course, speaking strictly long-term. Today, the day after the market passed 6,700 for the first time, nothing looks more compelling than the market. That's why Dobbs isn't plunging any of his extra cash into real estate. He doesn't believe he can compete. And he doesn't expect stocks to slow anytime soon. "I hear everyone talking about how volatile this market is, how overdone it is. But from where I'm sitting, I personally believe we've got a way to go," he says.

His rationale? Dobbs can't find a single indicator that would lead him to think otherwise. He ticks them off: Earnings growth is keeping pace. Interest rates are now reasonable, with the long bond at $6^3/_4$ percent, and they're probably headed lower. He sees nothing in the economy's growth rate to suggest that inflation—which just logged its fifth year at around 3 percent—is a problem. In fact, Dobbs is among those who believe that inflation is probably overstated.

"Looking at the fundamentals, I don't see any reason why the market should turn," he says with confidence. "Then again, that's reason enough. When everything looks optimistic, when there is little anxiety, when everything looks perfect, that's the time the market's going to head the other way."

Charles Schwab

CHARLES SCHWAB, 60, is the chairman and founder of Charles Schwab & Company, the nation's largest discount brokerage firm. Prior to founding his company, Schwab ran a mutual fund with assets of $20 million and an investment newsletter. He is the author of the best-selling How to Be Your Own Stockbroker *(Dell, 1984) and an avid golfer and noted collector of modern art. He and his wife, Helen, have five children; they live near San Francisco, California.*

DOBBS'S LOGIC WOULD DEFINITELY APPEAL TO CHARLES SCHWAB. The king of the discount brokers considers himself many things: a topnotch golfer, a quality stock picker, *and* a contrarian. "You have to become a market psychologist as much as a market analyst," he wrote in his best-selling book, *How to Be Your Own Stockbroker* (Dell, 1984). "Sometimes the best time to act is when you find yourself throwing down your financial newspaper in total disgust. . . . Or you may be playing golf or tennis with a friend and you'll hear him saying, 'Ugh! The stock market is just awful, isn't it? It's all so depressing.' Those are the times to think about becoming more aggressive in your buying!"

We've just rolled into April 1997 and Chuck Schwab is about to make some of those buy-sell decisions for his own account: Around the corner is the annual day of reckoning for his portfolio. Once a year he'll sit down with his brokerage statement (from Schwab, of course) in his L-shaped office, high above the waters of the San Francisco Bay, to take stock of how well his investments have performed in the past 12 months.

It's time to put up or shut up. The one day of each year the disciplined investor allows himself to shift assets around. Say one of his funds is up 17 percent, he says. In 1996, that would mean it didn't quite keep pace with the Schwab 1000 index that is his gauge, but it's pretty good, so he'll keep it—especially if it did well in the prior few years. But, if a fund is up only 9 or 10 percent during a three-year period, it's a sign to Schwab that something's wrong with management, and he'll sell. "It's all relative," he explains. "Back in 1994, when the market was up only 5 percent [over] the year before, it was very different. Then if an investment was down 1 or 2 percent, I might have said it wasn't too bad in relative terms."

LONGER-TERM HOLDINGS

Once the day is over, Schwab files the statement and closes the book on his opportunity to get out for the next 12 months. In a broad sense, he'll pay attention to whether the market is soaring or tanking, but he makes a concerted effort not to turn his eye to the specific investments in his IRA. They get a longer honeymoon than many marriages these days: at least three years. "I used to be, in my youth, clairvoyant," Schwab jokes. "I had this perfect ability to call market turns. But as I got older I found that long-term investing is the way to go." He's found three years to be fairly typical of a market cycle. "I usually get a down market, coupled with an up market," he says. "I like to see how a [mutual fund] manager performs in a down market. That is, if the manager is still a manager."

Schwab's investments are largely in mutual funds. Of those, a good 60 to 70 percent are in index funds. He prefers them for their predictability. "They're also highly tax-efficient. Index funds have little to no capital gains distributions," he explains. "You get the benefits of compounding without having to worry about gains."

His largest position ("Of course, I'm biased," Schwab admits) is in the Schwab 1000, an index fund which includes not only the largest 500 companies like the S&P 500, but the next 500 as well, covering 90 percent of the market's total capitalization. "You get broader diversification in those second 500 companies," he explains. "They're not teeny companies, though. The smallest probably has a market capitalization of one billion dollars, so they're not little fly-by-nighters."

TAXES CAN BE A DRAG ON PERFORMANCE

As directed by Schwab, the fund's first and foremost goal is never to have to pay a capital gains distribution. The fund's managers try to offset a gain created by a corporate event by taking a loss in one of the index's holdings that has gone down in value. That might make it a bit more managed than other index funds, Schwab acknowledges, which is not always a good thing. Just look at 1996, when the S&P 500 index trounced the performance of United States equity funds on average. But since Schwab believes that "taxes happen to be the single largest drag on fund performance," it's a risk he's willing to take.

The remainder of Schwab's mutual fund portfolio is in managed funds, most of them growth funds from families including Twentieth Century, T. Rowe Price, Stein Rowe, and Federated. He believes it's worth paying managers who have a nose for finding just the right acquisitions in fast-evolving industries—like technology and communications—that are tough to comprehend. He prefers smaller no-load or low-load funds to behemoths because he believes they have greater flexibility, and he always reinvests dividends and capital gains. On the whole, Schwab says, those rules serve him well. Even in bull markets like 1995 and 1996, his managed funds averaged slightly better results than his index. But there has been the occasional off year as well, when fund managers somehow missed the movement of an entire industry.

CAREFULLY CHOSEN INDIVIDUAL STOCKS

The other 20 to 30 percent of Schwab's portfolio is in individual stocks, which he selects with the acumen of a seasoned analyst (coincidentally, one of the many jobs he held in his youth). Schwab won't buy a stock if he doesn't understand the industry, know the products firsthand, and believe customer service is up to par. Statistically, he thinks price/

earnings ratio comparisons are largely bunk. If a company is growing, with solid products and services in an industry that you believe has a future, that makes it a buy, and a p/e that seems out of whack is no reason to sell, he argues. Schwab also looks at how revenue per employee is trending (a gross measure of productivity). But to his mind no numbers are more important than the past five years of revenue and earnings per share growth.

Of course he doesn't expect every stock in his portfolio to measure up to some magic growth number. Based on his understanding of each of the companies he buys and their markets, he forms different expectations for each of his investments. Right now, for example, he serves on the board of directors of four publicly-traded companies—Gap, TransAmerica, Air Touch Cellular, and Siebel Systems, a recent hot IPO—and owns a sizable chunk of each. "TransAmerica has been around 100 years, it's probably a 15 percent grower, while Gap, which is expanding into new markets and new concepts, is a 20 percent grower," he explains. "Air Touch has a special problem; it came [public] at a high multiple—100 times earnings. It's probably a 30 percent grower but it had a tough performance in 1996. And Siebel is growing at 100 percent per annum." Then, of course, there's his own stock. "Schwab happens to be in the Gap category," he says. "We've had a pretty amazing 23 years, growing 30 percent per annum the whole time."

THE ADDED APPEAL OF INDIVIDUAL STOCKS

Although he runs the nation's largest mutual fund supermarket, Schwab believes that in some respects buying individual stocks is more fun than buying mutual fund shares. "You're a part owner in an individual company," he says. "If you like Home Depot, you feel really good when you shop there if people are happy and everything is in its place. And when the shelves are awful and disorganized and there are surly people working behind the counter, you can say, 'I'm out of here; I'm selling my stock.' With a mutual fund, you don't have that kind of personal experience. I've always felt that stocks *and* funds should be a part of your core holdings."

Schwab feels that way despite having, over the years, his fair share of clunkers. There was the law firm that was going to be the H&R Block of the legal business. Several bowling stocks he purchased tanked. And back in the 1960s, he bought a piece of a business called

Computer Time Sharing, which rented hours of computer time back before practically everyone could afford to own a PC. His shares cost him $5 apiece. When the company went public a year later, the shares jumped to $20, then quickly doubled. Unfortunately, Schwab was bound by a rule that required him to hold on for two years before selling. By the time two years had passed, his $40 stock had dropped to $1. Though worthless, the stock certificates serve Schwab as a priceless reminder of the market's whims; he used them as wallpaper in his house near San Francisco Bay.

AGGRESSIVE INVESTING STYLE

For most of his life, Schwab has been fairly aggressive with his money. The son of a California district attorney, he was bitten early by two goals: to earn a decent living and to work for himself. Schwab's first business venture was a farming enterprise. At age 12 he bought a few chickens and grew them into a booming poultry and egg operation. A few years later, he sold that business when he found that caddying on a local golf course was more lucrative.

After earning a bachelor's degree in economics and later an MBA from Stanford University, Schwab, with a few friends, started yet another business running an investment newsletter and mutual fund, both called Investment Indicators. But in 1974, when the SEC floated a trial balloon allowing brokerage firms to discount commissions on very small and very large trades, Schwab knew he'd hit on a business brainstorm with even bigger potential. He figured he could offer the buying and selling services of a brokerage firm without the costly research services, slash commissions by a good 25 percent, and still make a profit. Schwab didn't believe it was smart to buy a stock on a broker's say-so, anyway. After all, he points out, the last person to listen to about an investment is the one whose pocket you're padding when you make a trade.

By May 1975, when the SEC put a permanent end to fixed brokerage commissions, Schwab had a head start in the discount brokerage game. He took the company public in 1987 and today has more than 240 branch offices including an Asia-Pacific services center where brokers speak five Asian languages, and another for Spanish-speaking clients in Miami. There are more than two dozen major players in the business today, and his company is by far the largest.

ART AND REAL ESTATE FOR PLEASURE,
NOT AS INVESTMENTS

Schwab's job growing his company hasn't precluded him from trying his hand at the sorts of investments other people make work. For a while, he owned a piece of the San Francisco Giants baseball franchise. His office is a haven for modern art, though he doesn't consider the works part of his portfolio. "I buy art for pleasure; I buy it for enjoyment. Ultimately, [the collection] will probably go to a museum—I'm not going to sell it for a profit." He pauses thoughtfully. "Actually, I think [art is] inappropriate for core investments. It's illiquid. It's costly to insure. And the markets are very irregular—fads and fashions change very quickly over time."

Schwab ranks real estate one rung above his paintings. Properties are not investments to him. "I've always had serious questions about putting money into a building. It simply doesn't grow. The building always remains that size. It's not going to be 10,000 square feet in size today, and 50 years from now be 50,000 square feet in size. If you have two tenants here now, or four, then you're going to have two or four 50 years from now. Yeah, the rents may have gone up with inflation, but, unlike a company, the building didn't grow."

One area that does capture his interest is venture capital. That's how he first got involved with Siebel. Schwab bought a piece of the small developer of sales automation systems three years ago when it had just six or seven employees, because he thought they might someday produce a system his company could use. The company turned out to be a winner.

The biggest surprise for people who meet him for the first time is how unaffected he is by the fact he's now a billionaire. "I learned early on that it's always better to have more resources than less," he says, referring to the days when he had so little capital to start his mutual fund that he wrote the prospectus himself. "When you're a young entrepreneur, it's always difficult to have enough capital, enough staff, the right technical capabilities. I knew what I needed in my early days, but I didn't always have the resources to get it. Now, in 1997, I don't have those problems anymore. I feel much more comfortable, but I'm never complacent. As individuals we are much like companies. If we don't grow, we die. We're always at our best when we're finding ways to improve ourselves, do what we love, and serve others."

WHEN IT'S *YOUR* MONEY . . .

ONE THING YOU GET WHEN YOU'RE AMONG THE COUNTRY'S TOP financial minds—like Schwab, Dobbs, and Greenberg—is access to other financial resources. Greenberg has a topnotch research department at his disposal. Dobbs interviews scores of top-ranking executives and deal makers every week. And Schwab hits the links with other top CEOs. Along the way, they've learned to weed out market wisdom from clutter and junk.

That's much harder to do today, simply because there's so much more information available. "In mutual funds, there used to be just two sources for data, Weisenberger and Lipper. Fewer people had Weisenberger, so more read Lipper," explains Hrach Alexanian, of OneSource, a Cambridge-based financial information house. "Then Morningstar came into the fray. Then a bunch of other newsletters, and it became very difficult to separate a quality publication from one that someone was just putting together in his garage."

Radio and television only complicate matters. But, with discipline and a few simple rules, you can find sources that will work well in your situation. For example:

1. Print can be better than radio and television. If you're looking for a detailed picture, in-depth suggestions for what stocks to buy, which mutual funds to sell, or whether to shift the allocation of your assets, you're not going to get it in a two-minute sound bite. You need the sort of research that comes in articles, research reports, S&P tearsheets—information you can read, digest, and refer to if necessary.

2. Not all print is good print. Say a newsletter receives a letter from a reader that says: "I have $100,000, half in bonds and half in blue-chip stocks. What do you think of my asset allocation?" An analyst at that newsletter may actually spend a lot of time on a response, but whether you can learn something from it depends on how specific the printed material gets. If the answer reads: "You're not diversified enough. I would suggest adding X, Y, and Z mutual funds to your portfolio in these specific proportions," that newsletter belongs in the circular file. Why? Because reading the answer doesn't give you any indication of *why* those additions make sense. But if the answer goes on to explain that fund X has a solid track record in small-cap stocks, which are currently missing from your portfolio, while fund Y has been doing well over the past three to five years in emerging markets, which serves another of your needs, then go ahead and subscribe.

3. A track record is key. A recent article by Eric Moskowitz in *SmartMoney* magazine took a wry approach to the scads of stock market pundits preaching the gospel these days. The magazine analyzed everything these gurus said for the prior two years and awarded them batting averages. That's one way to approach the problem. If you're thinking of buying a stock or a fund on an analyst's or newsletter's recommendation, use the library or the Internet to track other calls this person or publication has made in the prior year or so. Some publications make a point of telling you when they've made bad calls as well as good ones.

4. Follow up by doing your homework. My former boss, a health-care industry analyst at Dean Witter Reynolds, used to say that in order to keep their jobs, stock analysts don't even have to be right 50 percent of the time—as long as their rights are bigger than their wrongs. That's why you need to follow up on any one source's recommendation by doing some research of your own. The annual and quarterly reports, 10Ks, and proxy statements of publicly-traded companies are now widely accessible on the Internet. If you're not hooked up, get them from each company's investor relations department. Call a mutual fund to request a prospectus; you'll usually get it within days. There's no substitute for reading these documents—not even a five-star rating from, say, Morningstar. "You can get star ratings just about anywhere today," says Alexanian. "To some extent they're even considered public domain." That's not to say the ratings and research services like Morningstar, Value Line, and Standard & Poor's should be ignored, but they're just one piece of the puzzle. Finally, though you don't want to purchase only stocks you know (that's one way to make sure you're not properly diversified, Alexanian notes, citing computer executives who hold primarily tech stocks and merchandising geniuses who have a tendency to buy retail), having firsthand knowledge of the company's product or service is beneficial. Even if getting that knowledge means an extra trip to the mall for you.

5. Knowing when to sell is important. Charles Schwab doesn't sell a mutual fund he's held for fewer than three years. Lou Dobbs and Ace Greenberg both dump a stock after it has lost 10 percent. Rules like this obviously run the gamut, and while you have to find one that works for you, having one is definitely a good idea. Especially when you buy a stock or mutual fund off a hot tip, you're going to feel emotionally invested in the purchase, says Alexanian. "There's an attachment and an inclination to say, 'No, I can't be wrong about this even though it's fallen 10 percent or so.'" A rule like this gives you an out. Of course, if you bought the stock after doing a considerable amount of research, fully expecting another quarter of bad earnings before turning the corner, you can always bend your rule. At least once in a while.

6. Knowing when to buy is also key. With the market now often described as "overblown," you may be tempted to steer clear of stocks and funds altogether, at least for a while. In this case, you could implement an acquisition strategy. You may have decided to buy and hold, which has proven to work well over the long term. But two other acquisition strategies have the advantage of taking the emotion out of purchase decisions because you make them routine. Using the first, dollar cost averaging, you put a set amount of money into your investments periodically, typically monthly. Value averaging is like a souped-up version of dollar cost averaging. Instead of fixing the amount you input each month, you fix the amount by which you want your investment to grow. Say you decide you want your stake in a stock to increase by $100 each month. You start with $1,000 worth on January 1. If by February 1 the value of your shares has dropped to $900, you have to buy $200 worth of additional stock. But if the value of your investment has grown to $1,150, you have to sell $50 worth. Notes Alexanian: "If you compare these strategies to simple buy-and-hold, you'll get a higher return with dollar cost averaging, but the highest return with value averaging." One big drawback to the latter: It's a record-keeping nightmare. "If you're doing this through an IRA where taxes don't matter, then okay," says Alexanian. "But if you try it in a regular account, your accountant is going to kill you."

LAST WORD: RAPID ACCESS

NO DOUBT WE'VE REACHED AN ERA OF INFORMATION OVER-load. On the Internet alone, you could read financial publications, scour stock-related Web sites, and swap messages with your fellow investors 24 hours a day, seven days a week, if you chose to spend your time that way. Assuming you'd rather be more selective, here are just a few truly topnotch on-line sources to consider:

- **Morningstar Reports** evaluating both stocks and mutual funds are available on America Online (keyword: Morningstar) as well as on the Internet at www.morningstar.net.

- **The Motley Fool** site on America Online (keyword: Fool) features message boards where individual investors congregate to discuss (and diss) thousands of stocks. You'll hear from neophytes who want to know what a p/e ratio is and why it's important, as well as unofficial experts who actually work inside the companies being discussed. This past spring, the Fool's Web site (www.fool.com) added message boards as well.

- **Zacks Investment Research** now provides Wall Street analysts' earnings estimates on the Internet at www.zacks.com. Zacks, which makes its money selling this information and more, isn't about to give away the store for free, but the site will let you know the ratio of bulls to bears on a particular stock as well as give you a detailed price history.

- **Streetnet** represents the other side of the coin. Where Zacks gives you a numbers perspective, www.streetnet.com gives you the verbiage: analyst reports on industries on the rise, in the spotlight, or headed for a fall.

Chapter 5

THE ENTREPRENEURS

Dave Thomas • Lillian Vernon
Charlie Trotter

"If you don't know the people involved, if you can't control it, you better not be in it."

—Wendy's International chairman Dave Thomas

WHAT MAKES AN ENTREPRENEUR? MOST ENTREPRENEURS ARE MARRIED men in their thirties who hold bachelor's degrees, are moderate risk takers, and, by the way, the oldest child in their respective families, according to *Entrepreneurship* (Irwin, 1993), by Boston College professor Michael P. Peters and University of Tulsa professor Robert D. Hisrich.

What makes an entrepreneur successful, however, is another question entirely. By the time they hit their teens, Wendy's founder Dave Thomas, catalog maven Lillian Vernon, and Chicago's top restaurateur Charlie Trotter each realized they had a calling. Thomas's favorite pastime was eating out. By the time he was eight he knew that he wanted to work in a restaurant. Vernon was a born shopper. When she was a young immigrant to America, the leather goods she selected for her father to copy in his manufacturing business were consistently his biggest sellers. And Trotter was drawn to the art of food. Even back in the 1970s—when prime rib and Yorkshire pudding pushed the culinary envelope—his birthday dinners were not complete unless they featured some impossible dish.

These three well-known entrepreneurs went into business for themselves when they realized *not* that no one else had the ability to do what they could do, but that few had the ability to do it better. They stayed in business because they quickly learned the one factor crucial to success—the ability to conform to a changing market. "People tend to start a business selling what they love," says Stephen Harper, professor of management at the University of North Carolina at Wilmington and the author of *The McGraw-Hill Guide to Starting Your Own Business* (McGraw-Hill, 1992). "But that's not the issue. The issue is offering what the market would like to buy. Entrepreneurs who succeed quickly learn that lesson and continue learning, finding new ways to do things and make money. "

In Thomas's case that meant abandoning breakfast menus that didn't draw a crowd, but sticking with a revolving door of chicken sandwiches that did. Mail-order queen Vernon lost a cool million trying to sell her middle-market customers upscale furniture, but found additional success in a spin-off catalog called Lilly's Kids, developed to meet the needs of her loyalists' children. And Trotter, strapped for space, found an added revenue stream by placing a table in the kitchen. It not only allows him to serve six extra patrons each evening, but also fulfills the fantasies of customers willing to pay up to watch him create their meals from no more than a few feet away. Notes Harper: "If you're flexible—if you can take a punch, dust yourself off, move on, and learn from it—you'll be okay."

In fact, you'll probably be more than okay. As Thomas, Vernon, and Trotter all report, once you've learned how to make a success in your own venture, it's easier to spot other investments that will rake in the bucks as well.

Dave Thomas

DAVE THOMAS, 65, is the founder and senior chairman of Wendy's International, the nation's third largest hamburger chain. Prior to starting Wendy's he was a Kentucky Fried Chicken franchisee and was a major stockholder in the corporate parent of Arthur Treacher's Fish & Chips. He is best known as a pitchman for Wendy's, having recently made his 500th commercial. Thomas, who was adopted as a child, is active in a number of adoption-related causes. He has five children and lives in Columbus, Ohio.

Ask Wendy's Dave Thomas about his most memorable investing experience and he doesn't need even a moment to recall it. It was that much of a doozy.

It was the late 1960s and Thomas, a father of five in his mid-thirties and the Midwest regional manager for a number of Kentucky Fried Chicken restaurants, had invested $50,000 in a privately-held firm called National Diversified Foods, best known for the Arthur Treacher's Fish & Chips restaurant chain. Over the years Arthur Treacher's expanded, National Diversified grew, and Thomas's moderate investment came to be worth $2 million. By this point, Thomas knew the managers at National quite well, and, noting some potential synergies, offered to introduce National's team to his bosses at KFC. His instincts were right on, and the companies started to talk about potential deals. But there was one sticking point: Thomas's stock.

As Thomas recounts in his autobiography, *Dave's Way* (Berkley Books, 1992), the KFC team (led by John Y. Brown, who would later be elected governor of Kentucky) sat him down and, claiming conflict of interest, asked Thomas to sell them his stock. But not for $2 million or anything close. They wanted to buy Thomas out at his original purchase price. Always a good company man, Thomas did as he was asked. But he soon came to regret it. Friends, relatives, and even his colleagues told him he'd been had. So Thomas went to the board of the company and asked to buy his stock back. He was given the cold shoulder.

Three months went by and Thomas got tired of being a nice guy. So fed up he couldn't think straight—much less concentrate on his work—he marched into Brown's office, quit his job, and threatened a lawsuit. And not just any lawsuit. Thomas had retained F. Lee Bailey, who had agreed to take on the case for 10 percent of any stock they recovered. A month later, without even entering a courtroom, Bailey prevailed.

Today, Thomas is still very much Mr. Nice Guy. The self-deprecating pitchman of Wendy's commercial fame is quite like Dave Thomas in person. Half Robert Fulghum, half Norman Vincent Peale, he's a trusting soul whose speech—peppered with plenty of "I guesses" and "I dunnos"—gives a clear indication that he believes there are plenty of people in the world smarter than he is. Except, perhaps, when it comes to his investments. There, Thomas draws a tough bottom line: "If you don't know the people involved, if you can't control it, you better not be in it," he says. "When I buy into a business, I have to know the management personally. And I have to take a big enough position so that I know what I say will be listened to. That's my overall strategy."

STAYING INVOLVED IN THE INVESTMENTS

As you might expect, the bulk of his fortune—more than 50 percent—is still tied up in Wendy's International. At present, Thomas owns 5 percent of the nation's third-largest burger chain, which he founded in 1969, then expanded throughout the world with the help of $50,000 from each of 20 investors, all of whom knew him personally.

He's also an investor in a number of strangely disparate businesses. There's a manufacturing company, for example, which does sewing work making leather seats and headrests for Honda and other companies. When Thomas bought his stake, the firm had 100 customers but was losing money on sales of $3 million a year. During his tenure as investor, the company slashed the number of customers to 10 and total sales to $1 million and turned a profit. Today, sales are back up to $25 million and profit margins have held.

There's his stake in the Woodlands Golf Course in Columbia, South Carolina. Thomas didn't pay cash for the club; he traded a 91-foot yacht for it. Whether he got a good deal was questionable for some time—even in his own mind. Woodlands had lost 70 members during the six months before the acquisition, the greens were in serious need of renovation, and the club restaurant on its last legs. Once Thomas got in, the club was tidied up a bit, the grill room expanded, and its menu updated. But what really brought the community back were the charity tournaments he planned. Still, he admits it took time. "Especially with real estate," he says, "you have to be prepared to make an investment for the long term."

For many years Thomas also had a lot of money invested in car dealerships selling everything from Hondas to Cadillacs. The manager, Thomas's partner, was a good friend. When the friend passed away a few years back, Thomas lost interest in the industry and got out of the business. "It was time for me to diversify some anyway," he rationalizes. And the list of deals goes on: from a crop insurance company to parking garages to a sizable stake in a local bank. "After 55 different deals," he laughs, "about the only thing I haven't been in in my lifetime are funeral homes."

GOING ON GUT INSTINCT

But for each time that Thomas has signed on the dotted line, there have been dozens of opportunities he's passed by. "There are tons of people out there who—if you have money—want you to invest," he explains. "The hard part is deciding who to trust. Reputation is part of it. And of course, I always do a background check. But mostly, for me, it's a gut feeling." The result, Thomas points out, is a comfortably diverse group of holdings. He may not have diversified in the classic way, by hiring a broker or financial adviser to pull together a broad assembly of individual stocks and bonds or mutual funds, but the large number of businesses he's in provide considerable reassurance that should one go belly-up—as an investment in Florida land did a few years back—his other ventures will insure a consistent return.

Which doesn't mean that losing money is an easy thing for Thomas to take. Despite his wealth, any loss—from a few thousand to a few hundred thousand—is difficult to swallow. Unlike most of the people in this book, who grew up if not in middle-class comfort then at least with family support, Thomas lost his adoptive mother when he was five, and his father, an auto mechanic, didn't bring home enough of a paycheck to provide Thomas with any extras. His only niceties came from his grandmother, Minnie, with whom Thomas spent his summer vacations. Somehow Grandma Minnie, who worked part-time in a restaurant and spent the rest of her time in her backyard gardening and tending to her chickens and pigs, always had an extra dollar in her pocket for her grandson. She was happy to hand it over to the cashier at the five-and-dime in exchange for a half-pound of orange slices or bridge mix. Her influence shaped Thomas into a spender as well as a saver. "I guess I never thought about people pinching pennies much," he says. "Sometimes people get so stingy, they save too much. To me, money is more a system of bartering; it's for buying products and having fun. I don't mean to say that you shouldn't save for a rainy day, but I never thought of myself just as being a saver. Me, I keep the economy going."

Still, during the school year Thomas was on his own. By the time he was 10, he'd learned that if he wanted to buy a new shirt, or a book for school, he would have to raise the funds. Fibbing about his age, he embarked on a long string of part-time jobs: gas station attendant, paper carrier, golf caddie, bowling pin setter, grocery deliverer.

For as long as he can remember, Thomas's favorite splurge was a meal in a restaurant. He swears he knew he wanted to work in the food world by the time he was 8. At 12, living in Knoxville, Tennessee, he got the first of what would become a long string of restaurant positions, working behind the counter at the local Walgreens making milk shakes. After being fired for lying about his age, Thomas signed on as a counterman at Regas Restaurant, where the meat loaf plate cost 40 cents, coffee was a nickel, and on a good day he could take home $5 in tips. And when his family relocated—to Fort Wayne, Indiana—Thomas joined the staff at the Hobby House, dropping out of high school in tenth grade so that he could work the 50-cents-an-hour job full-time.

He stuck with the Hobby House for more than a decade, coming back to the restaurant after a stint in the Army (where he boosted business at the enlisted men's club by adding shrimp cocktail and hamburgers to the menu) at a salary of $35 a week. Thomas's life revolved around the place. He worked 12-hour days, romanced a smart-mouthed waitress named Lorraine Buskirk (whom he later married), and borrowed $7,500 from his boss to buy his first home. Back then everything was "on payments," Thomas writes in *Dave's Way*, from his new home to his television set to his vacuum cleaner. He vividly remembers putting aside small change to buy a new living room suite.

The opportunity to boost his earnings came after Thomas's boss met Colonel Harland Sanders at a restaurant convention and struck up a working relationship. In an early franchising deal, Sanders allowed the Hobby House to make and sell his Kentucky Fried Chicken (they had to buy the spices and frying equipment and pay Sanders a nickel for every bird sold). The Hobby House soon had a thriving chicken business underway, but four Columbus, Ohio, franchises owned by the Hobby House group were floundering.

Thomas's boss begged him to save the restaurants. Thomas was reluctant to move his growing family, but the thought of advancing out of management and into ownership made it worth considering. His boss agreed if he could get the franchises out from under their total $250,000 debt he could buy 40 percent for just $65. So he went to work, quickly changing the names of the outposts to Kentucky Fried

Chicken. He developed the rotating bucket sign that later appeared on KFCs around the country, and bartered for publicity by taking tubs of his chicken around to radio stations just as the DJs were getting hungry for lunch. By 1967, he'd well earned his 40 percent. A few years later, when the company went public, Thomas borrowed enough to buy $10,000 in stock. His stake in the parent company plus his four franchises were worth close to $2 million, the same amount as his later ill-fated investment in National Diversified Foods. Lorraine celebrated by having a swimming pool in the shape of a chicken built in the family's backyard. Thomas celebrated by taking Lorraine out for dinner, and this time, he notes, there wasn't a bird in sight.

Thomas continued hawking chicken through the late sixties, up until the problem with his National Diversified stock. But it wasn't long before he had stirrings for a shop of his own. During lunch hour, when he couldn't find anyplace in downtown Columbus to buy a hamburger, he knew he'd not only found the right location but the right product. Wendy's (the nickname of Thomas's daughter Melinda Lou) opened in 1969 with five products, three employees, and one bright red sign. It turned a profit in six weeks.

To this day, Thomas is still his company's biggest cheerleader. "I'm not an expert on restaurant stocks, but I'd have to say we're the hot one," he boasts. He touts the franchises as well. "We stand 100 percent behind our franchisees," Thomas says proudly. "We hope we screen them enough to know that they're really willing to work—we don't want absentee owners—but once they're in we give them all the services they require to make a profit, from national advertising to operations assistance, the whole ball of wax."

Thomas, never an absentee owner himself, suffered a heart attack in late 1996 and has been forced to slow down a bit. As senior chairman of Wendy's, he's able to devote much of his time to charitable causes from St. Jude Children's Research Hospital in Memphis to the Children's Home Society of Florida to the Dave Thomas Foundation for Adoption. "I'm big on people who need help, not big on people who get help but don't need it," says Thomas. "There are thousands of children in foster care who need a permanent home and loving family. I'm committed to helping these children find the love they desperately need."

But whether he's working for the company or for a local cause, Thomas says he'll never really retire. "It seems to me," he explains, "I retired about 30 years ago when I took the apron off and wasn't working the grill every day."

Lillian Vernon

LILLIAN VERNON, age 70, got her start in the mail-order business at her kitchen table, when an advertisement she placed in Seventeen magazine for a monogrammed belt and handbag drew more than 6,000 orders. She published her first catalog in 1956. In the decades that followed, the Lillian Vernon catalog has spun off a number of other catalogs, including Lilly's Kids, Lillian Vernon's Kitchen, and Christmas Memories. Vernon serves as a director of more than a dozen organizations including Lincoln Center, Columbia University Business School, and her alma mater, New York University. Her company has been traded on the American Stock Exchange since 1987. Vernon, who resides in Greenwich, Connecticut, and New York City, has two sons, Fred and David.

L IKE THOMAS, CATALOG QUEEN LILLIAN VERNON ALSO KNOWS A thing or two about value. Take the little porcelain boxes featured on the back of a recent Lillian Vernon catalog. Each is around two inches long, in novelty shapes ranging from a baby in a cradle to a bottle of champagne on ice. They're obvious knockoffs of the popular Limoges boxes, right down to their little gold (in this case, painted) clasps. But at $12.98, they're about a tenth of the price.

"See," says Vernon, running her manicured hand across the page with the grace of Vanna White, "this is a value. It's not a bargain. It's a value. You could probably put the Limoges up next to it and say, 'Well, I don't see *that* much of a difference.' But unlike Limoges, if you want to buy a graduate a gift, if you have a little wedding trinket you want to buy, if you're going to a party and want to bring a bottle of champagne, these are great. They're not expensive and they're little. You can put it away if you don't like it."

This advice comes from one of America's consummate shoppers. Now 70 years old, Lillian Vernon has been at the business of buying for 46 years and she's still going strong, combing flea markets in Paris and factories in the Far East for products to import, taking the occasional stroll through Bergdorf Goodman for those she can imitate. "Something happens to me when I spot a hot product," Vernon writes in her autobiography, *An Eye for Winners* (Harper Business, 1996). "I feel it in my gut. I know."

She's had that feeling for everything from chefs' mitts to beach towels, jewelry boxes to brass bookmarks to Christmas ornaments. "I don't look for bargains," she explains. "A bargain to me is something cheap that somebody wants to get rid of. I look for value, which is different. It has a good price—but it also has to have a reason for being."

That's the same criterion Vernon imposes when selecting her investments, from collectibles to real estate to stocks and bonds. She glances around the living room of her Fifth Avenue pied-à-terre, elegantly appointed in beiges and pinks, until she fixes on a bust of Adonis. It's Greek, from the second century, with detailed folds of marble drawing the eye to the god's broad shoulders. "I could buy that statue—which I did, at Christie's [the New York City auction house]—and it was more than a dollar," she says. "But I had seen one like it, the same size, the same period, in London for four times as much. So I knew that it had enormous value compared to everything else at the sale."

AN ART-FILLED LIFE

In fact, Vernon's apartment—a few blocks from the Metropolitan Museum of Art—is filled with pieces from earlier centuries. "I won't buy foolishly," Vernon says. "I'm not going to pay $100,000 for a piece and then find out it's worth $20,000 just because I like it. I do my homework, because I know you have to be careful. You see that little bench?" she asks. "I bought it in Italy and it's a knockoff, a Giacometti knockoff. I had a restorer in here from the Metropolitan Museum of Art and he said, 'Your Giacometti bench needs repair.' And I said, 'Jeez, even the experts can be fooled.' "

SMART REAL ESTATE DEALS

She even looks for value in real estate. Her apartment was purchased without a broker after friends let her know a space in a sought-after building was opening up. And her residence in Greenwich, Connecticut—a sprawling home on four acres (she got a great deal) with a pond and pool—is, she says, the best investment she's ever made. A decade ago, she considered purchasing an "*òlio* and *vino* plantation" in Tuscany priced around $175,000. She came close to buying but then reconsidered; at the time she was keeping such long hours she would never have been able to visit the place. "Now," she says, "it's probably $1.7 million."

Knowing a bit about Vernon's history, you wouldn't necessarily think she'd have the confidence to plunk down hundreds of thousands for a piece of art, or more than a million for a piece of property. In fact, she admits, she's had to battle demons to get to this stage in her life. Vernon's father, Herman Menasche, was a very well-to-do lingerie manufacturer in Leipzig, Germany. But with the rise of the Nazi regime, Menasche and his family fled, first to Holland, then to America, and had to start from scratch each time. "It was tough. My parents were very wealthy and then they became not so wealthy. That's one of the reasons my mother became so careful with money. She saw it come and go through no fault of her own. She didn't squander it. My father didn't squander it. Hitler's Germany kind of made it go away."

As a teen, Vernon lived in fear that each dollar she spent might be her last. But as she entered adulthood, a gut feeling told her that even if she spent the last dollar in her pocket, she'd somehow be able to make more. "I'm an entrepreneur," she says. "You know what sets entrepreneurs apart. They never feel they're going to fail. They have this innate feeling that if they work hard at it, they will succeed."

That's not to say she doesn't panic. In fact, she says, when the going gets tough—when she got divorced from her first husband, when she faced the bills for her two sons' private school educations, when her business (as it has from time to time) hit a rough patch—panic is what she does best. "But that can be a very good motivator. I say, 'What am I panicking about?' And then I go about working it out. I work hard—just like I have for years."

STARTING FROM THE KITCHEN TABLE

In the early 1950s, Lillian Hochberg, a few years married and newly pregnant, needed to supplement the income her husband, Sam, was bringing home, in order to make life a little more comfortable for their impending baby. Back then pregnant women didn't work outside the house. So she decided to start a business from her kitchen table. She shopped the factories for a smart matching leather handbag and belt set, purchased an embosser to enable her to personalize the goods with her customers' initials, and placed an advertisement in *Seventeen* magazine.

The start-up expenses were a whopping $2,000—money she saved from wedding gifts—but Vernon (who changed her name to match that of her company) made it back in spades. She got 50 orders the first day, $32,000 worth in all. Soon that yellow Formica table was no longer large enough to house the business. Today, the Lillian Vernon Corporation is a publicly-traded entity with over $240 million in annual sales. And as founder and CEO, Lillian Vernon is a millionaire many times over.

Where did the knack for picking the merchandise come from? Vernon believes that, like her entrepreneurial spirit, it's something she was born with. "Where does Elizabeth Taylor's talent for acting come from?" she asks. "Or any actress's? Without an innate talent you can take all the lessons in the world and it won't help you. I have it in me, but I also practice my shopping everywhere I go."

LETTING THE PROS PICK STOCKS

Well, practically everywhere. One thing Vernon does not shop for are the stocks for her investment portfolio. She doesn't have the interest to select them, or the time to manage them. "I think you can only do one thing right at one time," she explains candidly. "I feel my energies have to be directed toward my business; that's my responsibility as a public company. I don't want to be distracted by worrying that AT&T took a dive because it got a new president. I don't want to have to worry about that."

Instead, Vernon concentrates on picking solid managers for her growth- and income-driven portfolio. She met one of her managers, Seth Glickenhouse, on a trip to Israel in 1979. Another, Mario Gabelli, came to her through connections in Westchester County, New York, where her company is based. Over the past decade, she says, he's done very well by her, particularly with his strategy of investing in "couch potato stocks"—entertainment stocks like Paramount and Time Warner—as well as in wireless communications and casinos. "I check the records of the people I'm considering using," Vernon explains. "I see how they've done over the long term."

Using two managers at the same time is one way Vernon keeps her investments diversified, though she gives both of them basically the same directive: Grow the funds. "I'm more of an aggressive investor than many people my age," she says, explaining that she recently got rid of one manager because he was too conservative for her liking. "At this point I don't need security. I don't have to worry about leaving my children a lot of money; they have a lot of money, so they have their own means of support. That's why I continue to go for growth."

As Vernon gained the confidence to build and invest her money over the years, she also gained the ability to enjoy it. Her first splurge, soon after she started her business, was a cleaning lady for five dollars a week. "My Germanic upbringing may have made me hardworking, but it did not turn me into the classic German do-it-all hausfrau," Vernon writes in her book. "Far from it. I'm too practical to ignore a sensible distribution of responsibility." Since then, her expenditures have become steadily more extravagant. There's first-class travel with overnights at the Ritz in Paris. There is a six-carat diamond necklace and her trademark oversized pearls.

A CAUTIOUS SPENDER

But there are times when Vernon's frugal roots rear up and she has to kick herself into making a purchase. "My parents taught me to be very careful," she remembers. "My father always felt that if I had an allowance, if I wanted something *extra* I could go out and get myself a job. So I did. I worked as a movie usherette. I worked in stores. And I always put something away. But although I'm very careful with my money, I won't deprive myself. I say, 'Can I afford it? Yes.'"

But not to the point of being frivolous. Like all passionate shoppers, Vernon loves a good auction. She happily attended the Jacqueline Kennedy Onassis auction at Sotheby's ("*That* was a shrewd piece of merchandising," she says) and the Pamela Harriman sale. But she didn't go alone. "I plan to spend $10,000 and I end up spending $100,000, so instead I go with an expert friend of mine and he bids for me. He doesn't go in right up front. He bides his time. It's a strategy he has and it works."

The only auctions where Vernon gives herself free rein are those for charity. She's on boards of organizations ranging from City Meals–on–Wheels to New York University to Lincoln Center to the Israel Philharmonic. And when she took her company public in 1987, she set up a charitable foundation to pass along much of her wealth to the causes she believes in—primarily education- and arts-related organizations. "You have to give back," she says, admonishing those who don't. "I'm busy, but you know what? I go to all the Lincoln Center board meetings; unless I'm out of town, I go. Some of them are a pain in the neck—they're down at Lincoln Center in the middle of the day and I'm up in Westchester, and for me to be down there takes three hours out of my day, so it's hard. But I really make an effort. And if I'm invited to a charity event as someone's guest, I send a donation, because I feel if someone invites you as their guest you do that. It's social etiquette that you do that. The trouble is very few people know that. A lot more people would do it if they knew it was the protocol."

One thing that keeps Vernon working as hard as she does is that the more money she makes, the more money she'll have to give away. Though she's passed along much of the day-to-day responsibility for operations to hired executives, she continues to be the face of her corporation. At a recent analyst meeting, it was Vernon who delivered both the bad news (high paper costs had been a drain on earnings) and the good (another new catalog had just debuted). She also continues to be chief shopper. "I just went to London for three days," she says. "I shopped, ate and shopped, shopped some more. And I went to a few museums. I always shop. That's really my job." Her desire to give something back is the reason she'll never *ever* retire.

"When I'm dead, I want people to say: 'That woman made a difference,'" Vernon says. "I don't want that to seem like a conceited remark because it's not meant that way. But I think we all have an obligation to make life a little better—and a little pleasanter—for others."

Charlie Trotter

CHARLIE TROTTER, 38, is the owner and chef of Charlie Trotter's, one of Chicago's top eateries and the most expensive restaurant in America. After graduating from college, he worked as a bartender and waiter, then moved into the kitchen where he trained in some of the country's finest restaurants, including San Francisco's Campton Place and Chicago's Gordon's. He is the author of books including Charlie Trotter's *(Ten Speed, 1994) and* Gourmet Cooking for Dummies *(IDG Books, 1997). He and his wife have one son, Dylan Thomas Trotter.*

LIKE THE OTHER ENTREPRENEURS IN THIS CHAPTER, CHARLIE Trotter doesn't do things in a small way. He doesn't jog around the block a few times a week; he goes four to six miles and he goes every day. He can pull 150 sit-ups at a shot. And when he quotes, he quotes Dostoyevsky. Charlie Trotter is, well, intense—just like a trip to his restaurant proves to be.

Venture to Charlie Trotter's, located in a renovated brownstone, circa 1908, in the Lincoln Park section of Chicago, and you're in for one of the country's greatest degustatory experiences. Your meal—composed of organic fruits and vegetables, the finest meat and game, and line-caught seafood less than 24 hours out of the water—will be served on fine bone china. The wine you select from his award-winning list is poured into Riedel stemware. Perhaps you'll finish the night with an ethereal warm chocolate cake with banana sorbet or a chocolate flan with macerated oranges. You'll pay an average $135 for the privilege, a tab higher than at any other restaurant in the country. But if you're like most of Trotter's customers you won't complain. You'll probably make another reservation before you walk out the door.

"We charge a lot of money because we can," Trotter says frankly. "It's what we feel the market will bear for the service and product we deliver. If people say it's expensive, that's true. If they say it's not a good value, then they're missing the mark completely."

Lest you think he's 100 percent ego, Trotter explains that it costs a great deal to provide the kind of experience he does week in and week out.

"We are on a high, high wire doing rather daring acrobatic maneuvers," says the former high school gymnast, who has a thing for sports metaphors. "We have an obligation not to miss the mark. We have zero margin to fall short. Basically, it has to be perfect. If we stumble it's a serious consequence. Meaning: If the customer says, 'This is too salty,' I may prepare a special extra course. But if we blow it with lousy service, with improperly cooked food, then they're my guest. I'm picking up checks. I'm paying for eight-hundred-dollar dinners."

SPLURGING ON FOOD

Next to his wife, Lynn, and young son, Dylan Thomas Trotter, food is priority number one in Trotter's life. When he splurges, it's on perfect black truffles and 1959 Veuve Clicquot. The first time Trotter remembers blowing a big chunk of change was in his early 20s, when he took himself to Europe—to eat. "It's fun for me, even though it's ridiculous in some ways," he says. It's also part of the job. "I study restaurants the way someone else might study paintings. Everything from the exterior to how the doorman opens your car door to everything in between. Material things don't interest me much. But when I travel, I don't cut any corners. If I fly, I fly first class. I stay in a nice hotel to see how their service operates. And of course, I eat."

Sometimes to the dismay of his family. Last Thanksgiving, Trotter and his friend the New Orleans restaurateur Emeril Lagasse (see page 191) jetted off to a little restaurant called Girardet—that some have called the finest restaurant in the world—in Crissier, Switzerland. The restaurant was closing for good, and Trotter and Lagasse were determined to sink their forks in one last time before that happened. "Sometimes people fly halfway around the world to come *here*," Trotter says.

Along the way, the friends got into a discussion of how misunderstood the restaurant business is. "People don't understand what it takes to run a successful restaurant," Trotter says. "The staff, the upkeep of the place. We plow everything that we make back into it." For example, Trotter purchased the building next door and turned it into a combination office and test kitchen. It was there he refined the recipes for his four books, *Charlie Trotter's* (Ten Speed, 1994), *Charlie Trotter's Vegetables* (Ten Speed, 1996), *Charlie Trotter's Seafood* (Ten Speed, 1997), and *Gourmet Cooking for Dummies* (IDG Books, 1997). He's also producing a line of packaged smoked salmon and sorbets, and has recently started developing a cooking show he hopes will air on PBS.

Many weeks, the operation takes over his life. Charlie Trotter's is open for dinner Tuesdays through Saturdays. On his days off, Trotter takes to the road, cooking at charity events, giving motivational speeches, promoting the latest of his ventures. "The main thing is, we have this restaurant," he says. "People can come to us, any of those five nights, for a once-in-a-lifetime experience. But it's not enough to merely be adept at sautéing a piece of fish and making a few sauces. To run a restaurant, you have to be a leader, a manager, a psychologist, a total entrepreneur."

NO NEED FOR A "QUICK KILL"

Trotter's restaurant has estimated annual revenues of close to $5 million—along with his other ventures, that gives him a sizable income, but very little time to manage it. For that job, Trotter turned to William Blair and Company, the Chicago firm that has managed his family's funds for decades. He told them he wasn't interested in a "quick kill" but had designs on "long-term growth." He doesn't have retirement on the brain yet, or college for his son. Trotter believes the latter, especially, will come out of his day-to-day expenses. He'll be satisfied if he sees his investment income grow at a steady rate of around 12 percent.

With stock selection, Trotter is generally hands-off. But there is one place he tells his money managers *not* to invest: restaurant stocks. Theme palaces and franchises driven by the bottom line are totally in opposition to Trotter's food-foremost philosophy. "Those places go against everything I believe in," he grimaces. "I don't want to support mediocrity and inferiority. Forget about investing. I don't even want people to eat at those kinds of places. It's better to buy fresh food and cook it yourself. Or to go to restaurants where they're working with fresh seasonal food."

Trotter is slightly more open-minded when it comes to investing in individual restaurants. As long as the food is fresh, he's not diametrically opposed to such investing. But he's not at all convinced he'd make money either. "There's no magic formula. I don't know that anyone has figured it out. You have to know going in that it's going to be pretty tough to get your money out," he explains. "One of these days, I might do it for fun, though."

Curiously, Trotter had none of those hesitations about putting his money—and several hundred thousand dollars in seed capital from his father, Robert Trotter—into his own place. It was 1986 and Trotter, fresh from stints in some of the country's other fine restaurants, including Gordon's in Chicago and Campton Place in San Francisco, was ready to try his own hand. "I never entertained the idea of failure," he says. "For better or for worse, I knew we were going to make it."

Despite his confidence, the road to success wasn't entirely smooth. The reviews, from publications like the *Chicago Tribune* and *Gourmet* magazine, were terrific. He was flooded with reservations. And yet, after nearly two years in business, the restaurant was still losing money. Trotter could see he was moving closer and closer to the black; he just wasn't hitting it. He had two alternatives: Get rid of the truffle oil and Osetra caviar or raise prices. Trotter chose the latter. "I knew we were underselling our product," he explains. "Other comparable restaurants were charging more. We just weren't charging enough."

The strategy worked. Diners from all over the country, indeed the world, continued to make their reservations weeks if not months in advance. No spot is more booked than the chef's table, a six-seat spot in the kitchen where diners can eat and watch Trotter's 16-member team in action at the same time. According to the *Chicago Tribune*, it represents $400,000 a year in revenue. In fact, by 1995 the restaurant was doing so well it could afford to close for two weeks to undergo a

$650,000 kitchen renovation. Among the improvements: brushed aluminum appliances and a theatrical lighting system.

EXPANSION DIFFICULTIES

Outside the Windy City, things haven't always gone so smoothly. Back in 1995, Trotter cut a deal with Larry Wolf, the CEO of the MGM Grand Hotel, to open a second restaurant within the Las Vegas showplace. Trotter was extremely excited about the deal. He signed a 10-year contract with just one stipulation: If management asked him to change his concept, he had the right to walk away. They got the restaurant up and running, at an average per-person tab of $150—even higher than Trotter's in Chicago—and within the first eight months, the restaurant turned a profit. But management wanted more. Trotter was asked to downscale his concept by adding 80 more seats and lowering his price point. Trotter and the MGM folks tried for four months to work out their differences. When they were still at an impasse, he closed up shop rather than depart from his philosophy.

The experience hasn't soured Trotter on the possibility of opening additional restaurants. "I wish I could make a deal like that once a year," Trotter laughs. "At the end of one year we shuttered the restaurant and MGM had to buy us out of the remaining nine years on the contract. We were paid for 10 years and my people all had a great experience." His next restaurant will likely be a second Chicago location, this time featuring a menu focusing on vegetables and grains, though not vegetarian. And he has, typically, five or six other ventures cooking at all times. Some, like the chocolates he sells each Valentine's Day, are a simple success. Others, like his ambitious plan to vacuum-pack and ship out his cuisine along with an instructional video telling customers how to prepare and plate it, went by the wayside.

HARD WORK LEADS TO SUCCESS

But Trotter—who professes a love of "impossible things"—is convinced if he works at anything hard enough he can turn it into a success. "I always had jobs, cleaning gutters, mowing lawns, delivering newspapers, even back in junior high," he says, remembering his childhood on Chicago's North Shore. "Sometimes I'd even have other kids working for me. I liked the sense that if you worked hard, you could make money. Not just for how big a paycheck you'd bring home, but the idea that your money was a symbol of what your efforts are. The money is not that important. If you love something you do, then the money will come."

Perhaps that's why he told the folks at William Blair not to worry too much about his retirement. He can't envision himself slowing down. "Dostoyevsky described a kind of purification and salvation through work," says Trotter. "I buy into that. I don't see myself retiring—ever. I see myself always working at something."

WHEN IT'S *YOUR* MONEY . . .

ACCORDING TO THE SMALL BUSINESS ADMINISTRATION, THERE has never been more interest in owning your own business. The 820,000 new businesses formed in 1995 marked a new record for the third year in a row. Some 22 million Americans have already taken the plunge, and even more are considering it. A whopping 85 percent of the people surveyed in Peters and Hisrich's *Entrepreneurship* said they'd like to have their own shop someday.

Unfortunately, the failure rates put a damper on the start-up statistics. The University of North Carolina's Stephen Harper predicts that of the 800,000 new businesses that will open their doors in 1997, more than half won't be around in five years, especially those run by first-time entrepreneurs. Some will go belly-up and some of these businesses will be sold, while other entrepreneurs will close successful shops. Still, a significant number won't have enough capital to stay in operation.

If you're interested in taking the plunge, you should understand exactly what you're getting yourself into and whether you have the temperament for the task ahead. Start by considering these four questions:

1. Do you have a tolerance for turbulence? If you're starting your own business in order to be your own boss, you'd be better off getting another corporate position. That way you only have to answer to one or two individuals. When you're running your own shop, you have to answer to hundreds, perhaps even thousands, from your suppliers to your customers. "If you are a control freak, starting your own

business may not be the way to go," says Harper. You have to be willing, he explains, to try to please your customers at all costs. A new
restaurateur who decides to open for breakfast at 9:00 A.M. in a town
that downs its coffee at 7:30 will quickly have to change the hours in
order to do any business, just as a shoe manufacturer has to conform
to the whims of teenagers who suddenly decide they want two-inch
platforms on their sneakers. "One big mistake many entrepreneurs
make is locating their business where they want to live," says Harper.
"Those who are in the right mind-set place their businesses where
people will come to buy."

   2. Are you filling a gap in the marketplace? Peter Drucker,
one of the nation's foremost authorities on entrepreneurs, often says
that a lot of people start businesses but very few are entrepreneurs.
What's the difference? An entrepreneur brings something new to the
marketplace, while a plain-vanilla business owner is content being a
clone. To be a true entrepreneur, you'll be a step ahead by starting a
business in a field that is expected to need a great deal of additional
manpower in the *coming* decade—not one that is hot today.

   3. Do you have the necessary capital? Running the numbers to
figure out not only whether you can actually afford to begin this business, but also if and when you'll make a profit, has to play an integral
role in your go/no go decision. "Most entrepreneurs are eternal opti-
mists," says Harper. "They believe that they'll open the door and the
customers will come. But you're much better off if you go in with
guarded optimism. Figure that your revenue will be half as much as
you expect and your cash expenses and outlays will be twice as high,
and you'll probably be on target."

   One loose but well-tried formula for estimating the start-up costs
for a new venture is to first add up all your one-time cash outlays—
grand opening advertising, fixtures, equipment, and the like—and then
add to that three or four months of ongoing cash outlays—salary, utili-
ties, regular advertising, rent, and wages. That'll give you a ballpark
idea of what it'll take to open your doors and stay in business for 100
days without seeing any revenue. Double those numbers, as Harper
suggests, and you can stay in business for 200 days. In most cases, of
course, you'll see at least some revenue, but you'll be happy you
banked an extra three months of operating expenses before getting

started. If you're weighing several business options, the start-up costs for each can give you a clearer indication of which one best suits your needs—and your wallet.

4. Do you love what you're doing? People become entrepreneurs for different reasons. In Lillian Vernon's case, working for herself was the only way to insure that she could take care of her financial needs and her young children simultaneously. That same need drives thousands of working mothers into their own ventures every year. Other people believe they can do what they're doing for their current employer better on their own—by offering a product or a service that takes what's available now and improves on it. "I find that the most successful entrepreneurs are the ones who keep driving forward," says Amy Millman, director of the National Women's Business Council. "Obviously they take input—they don't operate in a vacuum. But it doesn't dampen their enthusiasm. I think one business owner, a woman named Nina French said it best. 'In order to be an entrepreneur,' she said, 'you have to believe in your product and your service, almost like a religion. That's what's going to get you up and out—each and every day.' "

The *Occupational Outlook Handbook: 1996-97 Edition* from the U.S. Bureau of Labor Statistics sites areas that are expected to grow at an above-average rate through the next decade. In each of the following fields, you can hire yourself out as an independent consultant; or you can think bigger, perhaps opening an agency that finds employment for many practitioners. You may find that just reading about these growing industries triggers a slew of other related business ideas.

• Personal and home health aides: The need for individuals who assist the elderly, disabled or ill within their own homes is expected to more than double by the year 2005 due to the aging of the population and a move toward home health care.

• Physical therapists and physical therapy assistants: Physical therapy is expected to be one of the fastest growing fields well into the next century for two reasons: There is a growing number of elderly Americans needing such care. Second, aging baby boomers will need assistance to recover from heart attacks and strokes.

• Systems analysts/computer engineers: The market for these high-tech workers, who use computer technology to solve the problems of the companies they service (mainly by automating various tasks) is expected to rise 90 percent by the year 2005. The primary reason: new demand as businesses try to make use of the pricey systems they've installed.

• Paralegals: Over the past decade, law firms realized that skilled, well-trained paralegals can save them a lot of money by performing many of the same tasks a lawyer does, at a fraction of the cost. No wonder the field is expected to grow much faster than the average occupation for the next 10 years.

• Other above-average growth areas for the coming decade include: construction (building inspectors, site managers), education (adult and special education teachers, guidance counselors), engineering (civil and electrical engineers), financial services (branch managers, brokers, financial planners), health and health services (chiropractors, internists, geriatric specialists, physician assistants, registered nurses, respiratory therapists, emergency medical technicians), marketing and public relations (account managers), protective services (private investigators, police officers, guards), and social sciences (economists, psychologists, urban planners, social workers).

LAST WORD: IS A FRANCHISE YOUR ANSWER?

FOR MANY WOULD-BE BUSINESS OWNERS WHO SIMPLY LACK a great idea, buying a franchise would seem to be the perfect solution: You pay a fee and the franchiser antes up all the trade secrets you need to ensure success. But the truth is that three-quarters of all new franchisers fail over a 12-year period. Notes Robert Purvin, CEO of the American Association of Franchisees and Dealers and the author of *The Franchise Fraud: How to Protect Yourself Before and After You Invest* (Wiley, 1994): "Buying a franchise in a proven company can be a good move, but in an unproven company it's raw speculation." With 3,000 franchises to choose from, that's no easy feat. Here are a few of the important things you need to know—about the business and yourself—before making a move.

- **Opt for a franchise most concerned with serving customers.** As Purvin notes, this may sound obvious, but many franchisers are more interested in simply selling more franchises, not an objective compatible with franchisees who are interested in selling their product. Your franchising company should also freely provide sales and earnings projections that demonstrate an attractive return on investment, encourage you to ask questions and develop relationships with other franchisees, and serve an established market niche.

- **Choose one that fits your skills.** You may believe that a frozen yogurt shop in your neighborhood would do terrific business, but that won't do you any good if you can't stomach the idea of working there. Most franchisees are also managers, so you'll be best suited with a business that jibes with your resume—a tax-preparation shop for a downsized accountant, for example. Before you buy a franchise, get a part-time position (or volunteer) to work in a company's location near you to make sure the business fits.

- **Entrepreneurs make bad franchisees.** People who want to do business their way and don't want to play by established rules aren't going to do well running most franchises. "Good franchises work by a set of procedures just as defined as every office procedure manual you've ever seen," says Purvin. What sort of people make the best franchisees? Retired military personnel and managers who come from within a franchise system where they can now afford their own shop.

Chapter 6

THE VENTURE CAPITALISTS

Jim Clark • Walter Payton
David Brenner

*"Basically, I believe that business is just a
reflection of life and how you approach it. You can
approach it blindly and pay for it in the end. Or
you can be very cautious and methodical in your
approach. If you do things the right way, you find
that you can be very prosperous."*

—Walter Payton

ONE PART OF LIFE THAT THE RICH AND FAMOUS QUICKLY LEARN TO anticipate is that every day—without fail—someone will come asking for money. Occasionally, it's a friend or relative looking for a loan to buy a bigger house or put a child through college. More often than not, it's a stranger cold-calling with a business proposition. Someone looking for funds to open a restaurant, a mail-order computer business, or some other venture. Sometimes he wants more than money; he wants the celebrity to sign on to publicize the business or to attach his name. Many of the high-profile folks featured elsewhere in this book have highly protective business managers whose primary job it is to say no to such requests.

What sets football great Walter Payton, Netscape chairman Jim Clark, and comedian David Brenner apart is that they've found a way to say yes selectively. And they've been successful when doing so. Walter Payton's business manager Ginny Quirk says she receives three to four dozen proposals each week. Among those Payton has agreed to—an Indy car team, a construction equipment company, and, most recently, a restaurant/brew pub/cigar bar. All have turned a nice profit. Jim Clark—who views himself more as a venture capitalist than as an entrepreneur—has gone on after Netscape to help fund a health-care-related Internet business and a start-up using cable lines to speed Internet connections. And David Brenner got into the billiards business in New York City just as pool became a sensation in the late 1980s.

Along the way, each has learned a great deal about venture financing, business selection, and choosing responsible partners. But one lesson stands above the rest: When it comes to putting your money or your name behind someone else's business idea, it's not enough for the venture to look good on paper, it has to feel right in your gut. These three individuals have all learned how to separate the good from the bad. You'd be well advised to follow their lead.

Jim Clark

JIM CLARK, age 53, is chairman and cofounder of Netscape Communications, maker of the world's leading Internet software. Prior to forming Netscape, Clark worked as an associate professor of computer science and electrical engineering at Stanford University, a position he left to start another California-based highflier, Silicon Graphics, in 1981. He has launched another Internet venture, Healtheon.

IT WAS MAY 1995 AND NETSCAPE CHAIRMAN JIM CLARK, 53, WAS in Paris when he read in the *European Wall Street Journal* that Microsoft canceled its plans to buy Intuit, the maker of Quicken, because the Justice Department was holding up the deal. The market had immediately sided with Microsoft. Shares of Bill Gates's behemoth rose nearly $2 on the news as the overall market rallied. Not so Intuit. The stock fell $12.50 in a single day to close at $62.

Most Intuit shareholders may have been crying in their beers, but across the ocean Clark smelled opportunity. He picked up the phone and dialed his broker at Alex. Brown. "Buy $50,000 worth," he commanded. Click. Then he placed the same order with his broker at Morgan Stanley.

Smart move. Intuit quickly made the turn. By August, it hit $90 and split two-for-one. By November, it was in the mid-$80s and Clark had more than doubled his investment. "One of the things I've learned is that if you've got a fundamentally good company, the day there's negative news announced and the stock goes plummeting—you buy," he explained, when he talked to me for a profile in *SmartMoney* magazine back in early 1996. "Many times, I've made a lot of money that way."

TAKING A LITTLE EXTRA RISK

That kind of calculated risk is the sort of investment that appeals to Clark, 53. Rather than putting his money into five-star mutual funds or other broad-based investments, he's more comfortable buying individual tech stocks, or sinking $50,000 to $100,000 into a Silicon Valley start-up where he knows both the business and management intimately. "Rather than building a low-risk diversified portfolio, I've always taken a little more risk with my returns—but only in investments I understand."

The greater risk–greater reward maxim has held up in Clark's case. Some of his favorite holdings have been standout performers in the already stellar markets of 1996 and 1997. There's Cisco Systems, Ascend Communications, Intel, and Adobe Systems.

Clark finds his winners by picking minisectors within technology. He's a big believer in personal computers and Internet-related telecommunications, for example. But he's not a fan of systems companies. A few years ago he resigned as chairman of Silicon Graphics, the company he founded in 1981, which makes multimillion-dollar systems, including those used to produce special effects for *Jurassic Park*. Clark sold his position because he believes desktop machines will come to dominate. Plus, he said, he felt too distant from the company to keep tabs on his investment.

The other key to success in technology, Clark believes, is a massive installed-customer base, a trick he learned watching Bill Gates get rich by selling millions of copies of programs that consumers could just as easily have pilfered. "Installed base is far more important in the computer business than in any other industry," he explains. "In the automotive business, your installed base has a certain amount of loyalty. Once you've bought a General Motors car, you're more likely to buy another GM car, so it's worth something. But in the computer industry, you're wired to [your customers] in a much more intimate way."

The way Clark sees it, only a few companies in the desktop industry have a lock on installed base: Microsoft, Intel, and, of course, Netscape. Clark was first intrigued by Mosaic—the piece of software designed by Marc Andreessen and a group of students at the University of Illinois that eventually became the Netscape Navigator—because consumers downloading the program for free had achieved that sort of critical mass. The first day Netscape put a beta of Navigator up on its Web site, millions of copies were transferred to PCs around the globe. Recently, Netscape Navigator and the company's new Netscape communicator product held an estimated 70 percent market share according to analysts.

BETTING ON HIMSELF

"I figured, here's a network which is growing at this phenomenal rate," he explains. "If we can somehow capture that, we'll surely make money." Clark was using the royal "we." When he started Silicon Graphics, he had only thousands of his own money to put into the pot. When the company went public, Clark found himself worth a cool million, not pocket change, but much less than the hundreds of millions that his venture partners reaped. That's the way the game is played, he explained. Venture capitalists scour the globe for ill-funded entrepreneurs—they prefer rank beginners—because those people have no resources and can't invest in themselves. "That was me the last time," he said when we first spoke. "This time, I felt like if I'm going to make something happen, I'll make it happen, but I'm going to bet on myself rather than getting someone else to bet on me."

Clark dumped $4.5 million of his money into Netscape—a nerve-racking 25 percent of his net worth. By August of 1995, he had taken the company public in the highest-profile IPO in recent history, and within months that initial investment was worth just over a billion. More recently, due in part to competitive pressures from Microsoft, the stock has taken a tumble, but Clark's portion still nets him a place on the Forbes 400.

And he's ready to do it all over again. "I'm a venture capitalist at heart," he says. Not even a year after the Netscape IPO, he started a second Internet company called Healtheon, an on-line service to help consumers choose and manage their health-care benefit plans. Clark's initial $2 million investment bought him a 20 percent stake. He also has a small piece of @Home, a company he developed with Silicon Valley venture capitalist John Doerr, which speeds up a consumer's link to the Internet by using cable rather than telephone lines for access.

All this work hasn't left Clark much time to manage his money. He hasn't even had the opportunity to select a professional investment manager for his millions or develop a long-term plan. In part, that's because he still has limited liquidity. Clark wasn't allowed to sell shares of Netscape until months after the IPO. In November he sold a block for $15.5 million and has filed notice with the SEC that he may sell as many as 1.2 million of his remaining 18 million shares. Conscious of how investors look askance at insider selling, he notes that the move would be made solely for diversity's sake. "But," he says, "it's not like I have $100 million or $200 million to put into a new venture. Until I do, it's pointless to think about."

Besides, the thought of having so much cash at his disposal is a little hard to fathom. Talking in digits—about gains in the stock price, about his net worth—makes him clearly uncomfortable. He's made sure the Netscape offices are void of stock tickers and Quotrons; employees aren't allowed to discuss the stock price in the building. He'd much rather you look at his wealth on a posttax rather than a pretax basis, which shrinks the pie by a respectible chunk. And he admits that being able to buy not just any car he wants, but every car he wants, is a tough notion to get used to. Clark finds it even tougher to listen to cold calls from brokers and salespeople. They've made him reluctant to pick up his own phone.

"You've got to understand," he said when we spoke last year, "I'm just this poor boy from Texas who never had any money. I've been struggling all my life and I finally struck it rich. It's kind of like the Beverly Hillbillies," he smirked. "Just call me Jed."

Clark is only vaguely kidding. In the 1950s his mother, a nurse, supported Clark and his two siblings on a take-home salary of $300 a month. He got his first feel for a buck after he dropped out of high school to join the Navy at age 17. He was in training aboard a ship and in little need of cash, so he sent his modest paychecks home. But one weekend he borrowed $20 from the unit's slush fund to tide him over. A few days later, he owed $28 in return. He quickly determined the racket would be better if he were the one pulling the strings, and on his next assignment he started his own little loan-sharking business. In less than four months on the job, he took in enough interest to buy himself his first car.

Following graduate school at the University of Utah, Clark became an associate professor of computer science and electrical engineering. When he realized it would be impossible to afford a house "of any consequence" on his salary, he began consulting to a handful of Silicon Valley companies and substantially boosted his take-home pay. But even with the added income, he wasn't keeping up with the Joneses.

WITH MONEY COMES COMFORT

When Silicon Graphics finally paid off, Clark bought a five-bedroom house in the tony suburb of Atherton, California, a stunt plane he flies himself, and a 55-foot boat. He's since traded up to a 92-foot yacht (with what he calls "the world's most advanced audiovisual communications instrumentation system ever on a moving vehicle"), and the Royal Huisman shipyard in Holland was recently at work on a 155-foot masterpiece.

CHARITABLE PLANS

When he eventually gets his hands on a bigger piece of his Netscape payout, Clark plans to spend what he can and give the rest away, not leave a massive estate for his children. Besides, he notes, they've already been taken care of: Each received $15 million in Netscape common stock. One early gift went to National Public Radio's Garrison Keillor, who needed money to fund a Web site. "He's just a very special, neat guy," says Clark, an avid listener.

As he looks toward retirement a few years down the road, Clark is thinking that starting his own venture capital firm would be one pleasant—and profitable—way to ease the transition. "I'll be the only limited partner and I'll hire a couple of general partners and give them a carried interest to help manage this money." Then again, he may just sink his money into a few carefully selected stocks and head for Tahiti on his yacht.

But whichever road he chooses, the general public isn't likely to hear much about it. The wealthier you become, he explains, the more you need to protect your privacy. "Ten years from now, if all goes well, I can imagine myself having lots of interesting things to talk about," he says. "But by then, I probably won't."

Walter Payton

WALTER PAYTON, age 44, is the NFL's all-time leading rusher and a member of the 1987 Super Bowl–winning Chicago Bears. Since retiring from football in 1990, Payton has been involved in a number of ventures, including a construction equipment rental business, the Studebaker's nightclub chain, an Indy car team, and most recently, Walter Payton's Roundhouse, a restaurant/brew pub/cigar bar in Chicago. Payton, his wife, Connie, and two teenage children live in South Barrington, Illinois.

IT'S JUST PAST NOON ON A RECENT THURSDAY AFTERNOON, AND Walter Payton is on the phone to his Chicago office—just as he has been at least once an hour since early this morning. That's how often the former football great checks in. With his longtime business manager, Ginny Quirk, manning mission control, Payton runs through a checklist of his ventures.

"Has anyone called from the Roundhouse?" asks Payton about his recently opened restaurant, a brew pub, a cigar bar, and banquet facility.

"What's happening with Payton Power Equipment?"

"How about the health club?"

"The Indy car team?"

"Have any new speaking engagements come in?"

By the end of a five-minute phone call, it's clear that Walter Payton has his hands in more ventures simultaneously than many businessmen see in their lifetimes. It's also clear how seriously he takes each one.

"Basically, I believe that business is just a reflection of life and how you approach it," says Payton in his high-pitched voice, still a surprise after a two decades in the spotlight. "You can approach it blindly and pay for it in the end. Or you can be very cautious and methodical in your approach. If you do things the right way, you find that you can be very prosperous."

For Payton, doing things the right way means being—at least somewhat—in control. Unlike Jim Clark, who puts his money into businesses in exchange for an equity stake, Payton may fork over a small sum, but his greater contribution is his name. That doesn't seem to bother the folks that want to be his partners. Every week, he receives at least two dozen business proposals. Out of nearly 1,200 pitches each year, Payton accepts maybe two or three.

CHOOSING INVESTMENT OPPORTUNITIES CAREFULLY

How does he make the cut? Most, to be quite frank, don't make it through the first pass. Payton's not interested in franchising opportunities, is currently steering clear of real estate, and despite acting as pitchman for products from Kentucky Fried Chicken to Buick during his days on the field, now would rather preserve his name for his own ventures. When he does receive a tempting offer, the next step is to have his people meet their people.

"Walter can't close shop and open up the next day without all of America hearing about it," explains Quirk, who functions as Payton's right hand. "So we've learned to be very careful about how we choose our partners. Each time we take a meeting, I have to think: Are these people open-minded? Are they flexible? What type of relationship are we going to have with them? Are they going to uphold his image in the fashion that we want them to?"

Payton echoes the sentiment. "It's not fun to have something with your name on it. When I'm associated with a venture, I'm the headline and everyone else is John Q. Citizen. So when there's a problem, everybody looks at me."

His cautious stance is a result of one venture in particular. Back in 1982, when he was still rushing for the Chicago Bears, Payton got involved in a nightclub chain called Studebaker's. The eighties were terrific years for the nightclub business. But, the "moderation" lifestyle of the nineties hurt the clubs.

Payton and Quirk wanted to change Studebaker's into a family joint, but they were vetoed by their management partner. Management opted to stick with the concept, while cutting corners to keep profit margins high. It didn't work. "We were inundated with complaints," Payton remembers. "And since it was my name, of course I had to follow up, to find out what the problems were and try to remedy them."

A few years ago, he sold his stake in the nightclubs and has since put together his own management team to look for ventures rather than waiting for them to land on his desk. He sleeps better knowing that if a problem does come up, he can depend upon this same team to remedy the situation.

That strategy seems to be working. Consider Walter Payton's Roundhouse complex. Right after getting out of Studebaker's, Payton and his team decided they'd like to open a multidimensional restaurant facility that would reach that family niche—a place that could serve chateaubriand to sweethearts on Valentine's Day, but also do chicken fingers for the kids. Finding a site was not easy; the place they envisioned would seat hundreds and include a number of meeting rooms as well as outdoor space for concerts. Finally, one of Payton's partners found an old Chicago roundhouse—an end-of-the-line holding pen for a defunct railroad that was scheduled for the wrecking ball. Two years, an environmental feasibility study, and $10 million in building costs later, the restaurant complex opened its doors. In addition to dining space for 350, it contains the largest microbrewery in Illinois, a cigar and cognac bar, and a Walter Payton museum, where diners can get a look at his high school and college jerseys as well as his Lucite-encased Super Bowl ring. Payton joined forces with three investors who'd already opened two of the top 10 brew pubs in the nation. Now open more than a year, the Roundhouse is drawing crowds. On a weekend night, the cigar bar alone sells 125 to 150 cigars at $7 to $19 a pop. The homemade "Payton Pilsner" is also a big draw.

LENDING A NAME AND A PRESENCE TO HIS VENTURES

Big equipment is another important part of Payton's business mix. Four years ago, he invested his money and his name in Walter Payton Power Equipment, which sells and rents cranes, grade-alls, and other building equipment to builders and contractors in the Chicago area. He also has been involved in several auto racing ventures. Payton drove a race car for five years—moving through the Sport 2000 class and into the TransAm Series—before the opportunity arose in 1994 for him to purchase a stake in an Indy car team, with former race car driver Dale Coyne as his partner. It's a tough field to make money, Quirk explains. "Even if you have ample sponsorship for the year, you can't count on a certain profit because in the last race you may total a car and there goes the profit," she says. Their luck has held so far. Payton/Coyne has turned a profit in both of the last two years.

One thing the businesses share is Payton—in person. Most mornings, he starts his day at the Power Equipment yard, spray painting equipment that's been returned with assorted dings, even tuning the occasional engine. Many nights, especially when a headliner like Maynard Ferguson is entertaining the crowd, he's at the Roundhouse. And 12 to 14 long weekends each year, Payton works the racing pits.

All of which, believe it or not, leaves him with more time to spend with his family than he had when he was playing and working out or making appearances seven days a week. South Barrington, the tony suburb where Payton lives with his wife, Connie, and two children, Jarrett and Brittney, is a far cry from Columbia, Mississippi, where the football great was born and raised. His father, Peter, a custodian in a parachute factory, taught Walter and his siblings early on that money was not to be squandered. In his teens, Payton held many jobs, from hopping cars to driving diesel tractors to working with the Army Corps of Engineers. His most memorable profits were made, however, in the city dump. Payton and his friends would head to the dump to scrounge for copper wire, which they'd sell back to the town's factories for anywhere between 85 cents and $1.80 a pound. "Being a small kid in a rural town, it didn't take much to buy a soft drink—a big belly washer like a Toppa Cola—and a Stage Plank or a Moon Pie," Payton remembers fondly. "What!" he exclaims. "You've never heard of a Stage Plank? It's kind of like a long graham cracker cookie with strawberry icing on it. Sometimes we used to be able to sell scrap iron too, but copper was what we got the most for."

After college at Jackson State University, Payton immediately signed with the Bears. He sent his first big check to his parents, and he's tried to pass the same unselfish values on to his offspring. "I'm not into fanfares," he says. "You take care of your family not because you have to but because you want to. These days, a dollar is not always a dollar, but you can always be yourself."

That's one of the messages he tries to get across in the dozens of motivational speeches he gives each year. Payton's remarkable 13 injury-free years with one team earned him a reputation as a loyalist as well as a fitness and strength fanatic. That reputation, combined with his smooth transition into the business world, has made him a big hit on the speakers' circuit. He gives, on average, a speech a week for about $15,000 a pop—adding a nice $800,000 or so to his annual income. "There are more ways to choke a cat than on butter," audiences will often hear him say. "Meaning that choking a cat on butter is doing things the hard way. There are easier ways to solve your problems in business and in life. Then I tell them how I went about solving some of my own."

One of Payton's own business problems, for example, was not being able to fill all of his speaking engagement requests. He solved it by forming a new company, Celebrity Appearances Inc., a speakers bureau, event and sports marketing company that finds work for—you guessed it—current and former pro athletes.

Then there was the problem of finding a place that Payton felt was suitable for a workout. He wanted a health palace with strength coaches, one-on-one training, private workout rooms, nutritionists, and more. Payton put together a group of investors to open his own.

"The facility is going to be very plush," he says proudly. "And everything will be confidential. It's not a place where you're going to be intimidated by all the other guys pumping iron. But it'll be focused on the kind of conditioning that kept me in the game as long as it did."

LITTLE TIME TO FOCUS ON STOCKS

With a new venture on his mind practically every moment, Payton hasn't found much time to invest in the market. The few stocks he owns are mostly large technology and communications issues traded on the New York Stock Exchange, though he's currently very high on Columbia Healthcare. He also has a small piece of his wealth in mutual funds. The fact that he basically sat out the bull market drives Ginny Quirk—an avid investor—to distraction. "I'm always telling him, you have to get this or you have to get that, but he rarely listens," she says. "When I saw Humana's president bought $1 million of stock in his own company, I loaded up and I told Walter to do the same. I tripled my money. He snoozed."

"It's very hard to keep up with the market," Payton says a bit defensively. "Especially with stocks, if you don't have time to stay on top of the companies you're in every day, you may miss something important. But I'm in the process of developing a portfolio. I understand that I need to sit down with someone, map out where I want to be, and stick to that plan."

Real estate has captured more of his interest, but right now even less of his capital. Payton owns homes in Florida and designed his South Barrington residence himself. Though Payton is interested in doing some building, perhaps of high-end condominiums or golf-course apartments, Quirk is afraid of attracting lawsuits. "Sometimes it creates myriad problems if people think a celebrity owns a property," she says.

So for the most part, he keeps plowing his money back into his existing and new businesses. They spill off plenty of income to keep his family comfortable, and if there is ever a shortage, he still has his NFL money to draw from. Payton chose to have his final NFL contracts paid out as an annuity for life; he receives a solid $240,000 each year. That money, combined with Quirk's prowess at bartering (she traded a few personal appearances and speeches for cars as well as select clothing and computers), is more than enough to keep Payton in nice suits and new music. His only other splurge is luxury travel. And though he has a hankering for a Cessna plane, he's fairly resigned to the idea of not actually getting it.

"I remember when I was growing up, I must have been in sixth grade, and my friends were all getting ready to go to a movie," says Payton wistfully. "It was something with Tarzan, and I really wanted to go. But I had spent all my money, and my mom and dad weren't home, and because I wasn't wise about my decisions, I missed out on being with my friends.

"That stuck with me. It's something I learned early on, and a lot of pro athletes never learn today. Just because you have money, doesn't mean that you have to spend it."

David Brenner

DAVID BRENNER, 52, is one of the country's foremost comics, frequently appearing on "Late Night with David Letterman" and the "Tonight Show with Jay Leno" as well as in clubs throughout the nation. He is a partner in the Amsterdam Billiard Club, with two locations in Manhattan, and in David Brenner's Laugh House, a new comedy club that recently opened in Philadelphia. A Philadelphia native and the author of Soft Pretzels with Mustard *(Arbor House, 1983), he now resides in New York City. Brenner is the father of two.*

IF YOU'RE A SMALL BUSINESSMAN LOOKING FOR FUNDING, YOU'D be better off knocking on comedian David Brenner's door than Walter Payton's. Though Brenner has a business manager investigate all of his big-ticket investments, he'll occasionally hand over a few grand to an entrepreneur simply because he likes the product or idea.

That's what happened with Lip Chips, which Brenner says were undoubtedly the best potato chips of all time. "They came from Maui," he remembers. "They had this great logo—these big lips—and they were delicious." The comedian took a $5,000 piece of the company and promptly lost it all. Brenner has no regrets; "I'll invest in people every time," he says. "If I think someone has a terrific concept or a good idea and I have the money, I'm going to go for it."

Fortunately, the other businesses in which he's invested—like the Amsterdam Billiard Club—have been much more successful. Back in 1988, Brenner decided to open a billiard club in his hometown of Philadelphia. The son of a pool hustler and part-time bookie, he had watched and played the game since he was seven years old. "In those days the game was called pool and there were these nefarious characters. You didn't know when some of these guys left the pool hall if they were going to end up in jail or dead," he recalls. "It was like the movie *The Hustler*. But now it's called billiards and it's all clean and upscale and respectable." Brenner found a location in Philly's chic Society Hill section, bought 30 tables from Brunswick, loaded up on Centennial balls, and was ready to move in when the neighborhood's residents started giving him a hard time. The comic was up for a battle, but as it turned out he didn't have to fight.

At the same time, Greg and Ethan Hunt of New York had been scouting for a location to open their own club in Manhattan. They'd just signed a lease on the Upper West Side when they read an article about Brenner's situation. The three joined forces. "I had the tables; they had the location," says Brenner. "It was perfect." The Amsterdam Billiard Club opened to great fanfare, in large part because of Brenner's participation. "I'm a walking promotion machine," he shrugs. "I go on "Conan," I go on "Letterman"; sometimes we get into this stuff." The club turned a profit practically from day one. And the trio just opened a second location in Manhattan, this one on the Upper East Side, and is looking at sites in other cities. Philadelphia is once again on the list.

On a rare occasion, Brenner will put his name, instead of capital, behind a business. David Brenner's Laugh House opened this past spring on Philadelphia's South Street, and Brenner didn't put any cash into the deal but has a sizable equity stake.

SCORES OF OPPORTUNITIES

The businesses Brenner opts for have a few qualities in common: Young, smart, enterprising management teams. A fun quotient. And tangibility. "I get business proposals all the time," he says. "People propose a Dairy Queen; they propose chicken stores. I like chicken, but I don't want to be around chicken stores. To me, the point of money is to have fun. If it's not fun, I don't want to deal with it. I also like investments I can put my hands on. Instead of owning shares of some stock out there in the ether, I'd rather take my money and put it on a horse race and *watch that horse*. I like the billiard club because I love the sport. I mean, it's a great sport. You can come here and you can talk while you're doing it. With tennis, if you want to talk you gotta yell with a megaphone. What kind of sport is that? Or golf—you can talk, but you've got to walk for 12 miles. I come here and I actually see my investment and see that people are having a great time with my investment—that's the kind of investment I like."

Brenner has also learned, over time, to stick with investments he understands. His choices of tax shelters in computer chips and outdoor advertising in the 1980s were a disaster. "I'm going to be paying the government off for the rest of my life," he says. Likewise, his purchase of a Manhattan townhouse in the late 1970s was a debacle. Brenner bought at the bottom of the market, but poured in too much capital renovating the place to conform to his admittedly wild (think bright colors) taste. When he decided to sell in 1990, it took him four years to move the place and then—because of all the improvements—he took a loss. "Even worse," he says, "the realtor made me paint all the rooms white—how boring—and then I had to *live* in them. I'll never buy a house again unless I'm sure I'm going to die there."

STOCK PICKING FOR FUN

His investments in the market, a mixed bag, are too confusing for Brenner to take seriously. He'll pick up the occasional penny stock, but he approaches it more like a roll of the dice than as an investment. When it comes to researching companies, taking the time to figure out which businesses will be strong in the future, Brenner doesn't feel he has the skills. On the rare occasion that he purchases a stock—and he does own a handful of blue chips—his business manager does the picking.

"You've got to delegate in your life," Brenner explains. "You've gotta know your weaknesses and strengths, and get rid of what you're weak at. I'm not a good businessman. Otherwise, I would have majored in business and I would have been a businessman. What I *am* good at is making money. So I make the initial money. And then I take that money and I give it to a specialist to invest it."

Brenner has long understood these facts about himself. He's been making money since the ripe old age of nine, when he took a job as assistant to a butcher in his West Philadelphia neighborhood. He'd moved on to jobs as a grocery bagger, delivery boy, and bowling pin setter by the time they got around to teaching about bank accounts, checks, and balances in his sixth-grade math class.

WHAT'S MINE IS MINE . . .

Brenner wasn't much of a student, but when the assignment was to open a savings account at the neighborhood bank, he participated wholeheartedly. You see, by that point Brenner was earning a fairly decent wage. Much of the money went directly to his mother, but he held onto a dollar for spending money each week. That in itself was a risky proposition. Brenner's neighborhood was a bit rough and there was always the chance his pocket change would be stolen before he had time to spend it. The idea of a bank standing guard was quite appealing indeed.

"I put my dimes, my nickels, and my quarters in that bank and eventually I had $100 and I wanted to buy something—I don't remember what," Brenner recalls. "So I decided to go downtown to the bank to take out my $100. I explained to the woman behind the counter that I wanted to close out the account. She sized me up and finally agreed and then went about counting my money." The teller put Brenner's $100 in one pile. Then she counted out an additional $8.17.

"Wait a minute. I had $100 in the bank and you just gave me $108.17. You've made a mistake," Brenner corrected her, eyeing the second pile of bills.

"No," the teller explained. "That's your interest."

"Look," argued Brenner, who'd slept through the lesson on compounding. "I gave you $100. You held my $100 so no one would take my $100. You kept my $100 safe. That's all I wanted you to do. I don't want the other money. It's not my money. It's the bank's money." And with that, he put his $100 into his sock—so that it wouldn't get stolen on the way home—and left the bank, the $8.17 still sitting on the sill.

"And that," laughs Brenner, "is exactly why I have had a business manager for many years—I still don't get it. For me to open a news-

paper and look at the numbers on stock tables—I find that boring. But I can go out and make millions."

A ROUGH CAREER START

Well, he can now. But there were some rough periods. After being employed practically his entire life, Brenner found himself jobless upon his graduation from Temple University. His father handed him a quarter and told him to go to the corner and buy a newspaper. "It's your world now," Louis Brenner told his son. "Read about it. Then turn to the classifieds and find yourself a job." At the time, Brenner remembers being a bit peeved. "Other kids got a suit; some got a car. I got a newspaper. It wasn't until later that I realized he gave me the whole world."

Two months after graduation, Brenner was still unemployed, living above a laundry in Philadelphia, in a tiny apartment at the corner of 60th and Market, and—he recalls—surviving on lettuce and coffee, which he lifted from the small greengrocer on the block. Why lettuce? Displayed outside, it was the easiest thing to steal. "It was great, a great existence. Sometimes I'd chop it up, sometimes I'd eat it right off the head. Sometimes I'd sauté. I'd think: Oh, I think I'll have lettuce today," he quips. By the time Brenner finally landed a job writing documentaries for NBC, he had just 80 cents in his pocket. That same 80 cents is now framed in his home with an inscription that says "Lest We Forget."

When he decided to have a go at stand-up comedy in the seventies, he had a whopping $12,000 to his name. He invested $3,000 in the stock market to shore up his future—he promptly lost it. Then with the remaining $9,000, he tightened his belt and started hitting the clubs.

It didn't take long for Brenner to break into the big time. The late 1970s and early 1980s were his heyday. Brenner was headlining in Vegas, appearing regularly on the "Tonight Show," working a full 250 days a year. His autobiography, *Soft Pretzels with Mustard*, hit the *New York Times* best-seller list. And Brenner's annual income rocketed into seven figures. The comic went on a spending tear. He bought new cars for his father and siblings and a home for his parents; he carried some of his friends from the old neighborhood when they were a little down and out. "Money is the most fun when you see the power it has to make people happy," he says.

PERSONAL MONEY WOES

In more recent years, his financial picture has been a little rockier, primarily for personal reasons. Brenner's divorce a decade ago led to a $600,000 three-and-a-half-year battle for full custody of his son Cole. At the time Brenner was working five nights week. But in order to wage a serious fight, he had to reduce his hours dramatically or risk that a judge might deem him an absentee father. Brenner cut his nights to 50 a year and won his fight. Though he hasn't been able to regain the momentum in his career, he says he'd make the same choice today. "He's a great, great kid," says Brenner. "Without a doubt, the best investment I ever made."

Whether Brenner is feeling flush or on shaky financial grounds, he still spends like a millionaire. "I figure, if you worry about money, you have money worries," he says. "That's why if I have it, I spend it." He just returned from a trip to Bombay, Oman, Yemen, and Greece. He has set up a trust fund for Cole and purchased a good-sized life insurance policy for his younger son born two years ago to Brenner and his live-in companion, Elizabeth, an artist. He drops a bundle each year on summer camp and gifts for his children and he continues to take care of his siblings.

"They say you reach an age when you can't spend like this anymore," says Brenner, 52. "Maybe you do, but someone will have to tell me when I get there. I figure, you can't take it with you. You never see luggage tied on top of a hearse."

He smiles: "Let me tell you about my epitaph," he says. "I'm going to have a two-sided stone. On one side will be all the basic information, born, died, etc. On the other side, it's going to say: 'He lived. He died. But, man, did he live.' That's my philosophy—of business and of life."

WHEN IT'S *YOUR* MONEY . . .

MOST LIKELY, YOU DON'T HAVE A NAME—LIKE WALTER PAYTON OR David Brenner—that brings business suitors to your door. But that doesn't mean you can't invest a piece of your portfolio in up-and-coming ventures, just like Jim Clark (or Payton or Brenner) would. In fact, many of the celebrities profiled in this book, from Cincinnati

Bengals quarterback Jeff Blake (page 57) to David and Helen Gurley Brown (page 160) have done just that. Or perhaps you see yourself on the other side of the equation. If you're an entrepreneur looking to take a new business to the next level, venture funding is one way to get there.

If You're Looking to Invest . . .

In a nutshell, venture capitalists fund businesses they hope will be big winners later on. Their investments take on two basic forms: a venture pool or "angel financing."

The large, professionally managed venture funds are run by companies like Silicon Valley's Kleiner Perkins Caufield & Byers or Cleveland's Morganthaler Ventures. Although they are looking for stellar growth—10 times their money in 5 to 10 years—they also understand that only one business out of hundreds (maybe thousands) becomes the next Netscape or Intuit. That's why they pool investors' money and then divvy it up among 20 to 30 different fledgling businesses each year. Once they make an investment, professional venture firms take a very active role in the day-to-day management of the start-up; they often assume seats on the board, approve hiring and budget changes, and help develop a plan for making sure the company reaches its goals.

Firms like these make a total of 1,000 investments each year, for approximately $5 million each, making venture capital a $5-billion-a-year industry. With a sum that large, you'd think they'd be angling for capital, but in fact the price of admission is quite high—$2 to $10 million on average—and these operations have many pension fund managers and other institutional investors knocking at *their* doors, especially when the markets are soaring. So when it comes to individuals getting a piece of the action, only the very wealthy or extremely well-connected have access.

That's why investors with smaller balance sheets go the angel route. For chunks of change up to $100,000, angel financing is a less-structured, less-demanding type of investment. A doctor with a little extra cash may be out to dinner with a colleague who's trying to get a new business, say an outpatient surgery center, off the ground. If the flush physician decides to ante up some capital, he becomes an angel.

"Angels invest for a whole range of reasons," says Robert Pavey, general partner of Morgenthaler Ventures and the former president of the National Venture Capital Association. "Some may want to get involved in a company; others may want their kids to work there; still others want to be able to talk about it at the country club." Angels are looking for a return, typically of two to three times their money in five to 10 years, and they aren't generally as active in the day-to-day management of the companies in which they invest.

One thing a venture pool provides that the angel market does not is instant diversification. Is it smart to put all of your eggs in one basket with a fledgling operation? "It depends on how well you know the industry," says Pavey. "Diversification is one way to reduce risk; knowledge is another. If you know the industry very well, consolidating your investment in one firm may be the smarter way to go. Angels don't do this with a portfolio allocation mentality," he continues. "They're much more opportunity-driven. They tend to be entrepreneurs themselves in many cases. A lot of them also think they can't lose."

That, of course, is a big mistake. The new-business failure rate is even higher for ventures with a first-time entrepreneur at the helm. So while you may have high hopes, you have to be willing to go down with the ship. "You have to be wealthy enough that you can lose every nickel," says one California venture capitalist, "and not lose any sleep at night."

If You're Looking for Funding . . .

You're in luck. Driven by the roaring over-the-counter stock market, the exchange on which most venture-funded companies go public, the venture industry has reached a new, strong peak in the last couple of years. Explains Pavey: "Everybody's making money. More money means more activity."

If you need $1 to $10 million to get your business to the next level, you'll need to go to a venture firm. You'll have the most luck getting funding if your operation fits the description of the businesses venture capitalists look for: small firms in health-care, technology, or information services (the only industries that can grow rapidly enough to satisfy a venture firm's demands) that have seen some success, but now need a cash infusion to take it to the next level. One good thing about venture firms is that once they invest in a business, they're often willing to contribute additional money to make sure that their original dollars pay off. The bad news is that this may cost you your company. Venture firms will not only expect you to develop a business plan, they'll demand that you stick to it. If at the end of the time allotted to meet your goals, your venture partners feel you're not meeting expectations, you may be shown the door.

If you're not in one of those rapidly growing industries—or if you need less cash to move your business along—angel funding is your better option. But because the protocol is less structured, and in many cases your extra cash may be coming from a friend, relative, or businesses associate, it's very important that you lay the deal out on paper, and that the expectations you and your angel have for each other are clear. If you expect your angel to be a silent partner but your angel is looking to participate, you're in for trouble. Notes Pavey: "That's where most of the problems come in."

LAST WORD: IF YOU STRIKE OUT IN THE VENTURE ARENA

THERE ARE OTHER OPTIONS BEYOND ANGEL FINANCING AND venture capital, of course. One popular alternative is a loan approved and granted by a bank or other lender, but guaranteed by the Small Business Administration. These loans, which usually run from $100,000 to $750,000, come with preferential interest rates (for loans over $50,000 interest may not be more than 2.75 percent above the prime rate) and terms may extend anywhere from 10 to 25 years. The money from these loans may be used for expansion, equipment purchases, inventory, working capital, or even to acquire a new location. There are several different types of SBA-guaranteed loans that may work for you, including:

- **Low Documentation Loans** provide funding of up to $100,000 for people who haven't been able to find reasonable financing elsewhere. The paperwork for "low doc" loans is minimal (there is a one-page application), the turnaround is fast, and the SBA guarantees up to 80 percent of the loan.

- **Women's/Minority Prequalification Loans** allow the SBA to prequalify a woman or minority business owner before she approaches a lender. The SBA's approval is based not on collateral, but on charter, credit, and experience.

- **CapLines** is a short-term loan program that is designed to finance the cyclical working capital needs of small businesses. The amount of funding available depends on a business's accounts receivable and/or inventories.

- **Small Business Investment Companies** are the SBA's own angels. These are for-profit firms that make equity investments and long-term loans to small firms using their own capital supplemented with SBA-guaranteed debt or securities.

For more information on any of these programs, contact the Small Business Administration office nearest you.

Chapter 7

THE REBOUNDERS

Dennis Rodman
Olivia Goldsmith
Ivana Trump

"I'm telling you, I couldn't do it again. I couldn't start from scratch again. What I feel money does is give me a certain sense of security. It lets me get on with my life."

—Olivia Goldsmith

A RECENT *PEOPLE* MAGAZINE COVER STORY FLASHED THE HEAD-
line "Going Broke on $33 Million a Year." Inside, it detailed how
rap artist M. C. Hammer managed to blow through such a huge
chunk of change. It explained how two divorces, a custody battle,
and a business failure caused tennis star Bjorn Borg—whose fortune was once reported to be $60 million—to be "more or less
bankrupt" in 1992. And Burt and Loni? According to the magazine,
they both hit the skids following their divorce.

Why do such tales of financial woe get so much ink? In a
strange way, they make the rest of us feel better. When our Visa bills
come in higher than anticipated, when the payments on our mortgages are suddenly overwhelming, when the loss of a job has us
considering bankruptcy court, it somehow helps to know that even
the rich and famous occasionally face tough times.

Chicago Bulls rebounder Dennis Rodman, best-selling author
Olivia Goldsmith, and Ivana Trump (who these days prefers to be
called just Ivana) have all been there. Hefty alimony and car payments and a half-million-dollar house loan that had swelled with
interest put Rodman close to a million dollars in the hole.
Goldsmith's undoing was legal fees from a divorce in which her ex
seemed to get just about everything. Putting a halt to hefty spending and developing a smart investment strategy helped both of
them turn the corner. And while Ivana was not exactly in the poor-
house, her financial transformation following her divorce was on a
par with the other two.

Listening to these three individuals describe how they picked
themselves up is inspiring. If they can do it, you can certainly do it
too.

Dennis Rodman

DENNIS RODMAN, 36, is the NBA's leading rebounder. Rodman, who joined the NBA at the late age of 25, played for the two-time champion Detroit Pistons, before being traded to the San Antonio Spurs and then the Chicago Bulls, where he was instrumental in bringing home an NBA title in 1996. He is as well known for his antics—head-butting a referee—and technicolor hair, as for his playing. His autobiography, Bad As I Wanna Be *(Delacorte, 1996), hit the best-seller lists last year.*

IT WAS EARLY 1996, THE NBA WAS ON HIATUS FOR THE ALL STAR game, and forward Dennis Rodman—who never seems to make the coach-chosen team—had come to Las Vegas to soothe his bruised ego. Shortly after breakfast, the league's best rebounder headed down to the craps tables at the Mirage Hotel and Casino. To the delight of the growing crowd, the NBA's bad boy was on a roll. The shooter to his right threw double threes once, then again and again. A woman across the table hit three straight tens. Soon Rodman was up $1,500.

Elated, he wrapped his arms around his best friend and agent, Dwight Manley, who was gambling next to him. Rodman was still watching as Manley, a 31-year-old bespectacled coin dealer, took two $500 chips—his original stake—and put them in his pocket. Rodman raised his eyebrows. Sifting through his own rack of chips, he counted out his own $1,000 original investment, measuring the stack between his thumb and forefinger. Soon his luck began to turn, but Rodman held his ground. Instead of delving into his stash, he sauntered from the table, the tower of disks still in his massive grasp.

Is this the Dennis Rodman who came to Las Vegas for three days in 1993 and left five weeks later and $30,000 poorer? Who poured $40,000 of upgrades into a 1987 Ford Mustang? Who spends $100 to change his hair from blue to orange to white, or $400 for a new tattoo at the drop of a hat?

In fact, at 36, Rodman is something of a changed man. On the court, he may still tussle with the occasional cameraman, elbow an opposing player or head-butt a random referee, but financially Rodman is on a path toward the straight and narrow. After a couple of years of playing Eliza to Manley's Henry Higgins, he has a growing bank account and an investment portfolio, and is socking it away for retirement—all of which, quite clearly, are a source of newfound pride. On one appearance on the Howard Stern show, Rodman coyly changed the subject from his date with sidekick Robin Quivers to the growing balance in his mutual fund accounts. And as we sat down to talk in his suite at the Mirage for an article that appeared in *SmartMoney* magazine, Rodman stated frankly that one reason he agreed to discuss his finances with a reporter was to show the world he'd become a more prudent soul. He also likes to demonstrate how very far he's come.

Born in Dallas and deserted by his father at age three, Rodman was raised in a housing project by his mother, Shirley. At 20, he was working as a janitor at the Dallas Airport for $5 an hour, but a year later he was arrested there for stealing 50 watches; the charges were dropped when the authorities were able to recover the goods. (Rodman had given them to his friends.) Then, when he was 21, a local junior college scout suggested that Rodman, who had sprouted a good half foot since high school, try basketball. It seemed to be in his genes. After all, his two older sisters, Debra and Kim, had been standouts in college ball.

Rodman's first foray was an off-the-court disaster. In a matter of months, he flunked out. But on his second try, at Southeastern Oklahoma State, he made All-American and the grades required to stay in school. Rodman was 25—ancient for a rookie—when he finally landed in the NBA. His low $110,000 salary reflected the fact that as a late bloomer, he was something of a risk.

Though Rodman proved his talent as a pivotal member of the two-time champion Detroit Pistons, it took him a long time to catch up in the salary game. He has long been one of the league's best rebounders, grabbing an average 15 boards a game, but until 1997 he never earned more than $2.5 million in a single year. Still, you'd think he would have been able to live on that.

GETTING OUT OF FINANCIAL TROUBLE

During the 1995 playoffs, on a day off for the forward's team, the San Antonio Spurs, Rodman was sitting in his kitchen pondering his financial woes with Manley. His $3,800 Ferrari payment was more than a week late. A $9,000 alimony check to ex-wife Annie was looming. And to make matters worse, a half-million dollars he'd borrowed from the Pistons to buy his first house years earlier had gone unpaid for a half-decade and with interest had ballooned to $745,000. All told, Rodman was close to $1 million in debt. Turning to his friend, he said plainly, "I need you to make me some money, bro."

Manley was certainly up to the task. Something of a financial whiz, Manley had earned his first $100,000 the year he turned 18. "No problem," he told Rodman. "Fly out to my house in California after the playoffs are over and I'll set a few things up." Rodman arrived in early June planning to stay three days. He didn't leave for three months.

Manley's first move was to build up the cash in Rodman's bank account by having him sign autographs for $50 a pop. He negotiated with Rodman's creditors, telling them if they wanted to get paid in full they'd have to wait awhile, and if they wanted cash today, they could take a discount. And he put together a seven-figure deal to publish Rodman's autobiography, *Bad As I Wanna Be* (Delacorte, 1996), which became an instant best-seller.

BUDGETING AND PAYING OFF BILLS

Rodman, famous for his large tips and frivolous ways (at one time he had nearly a dozen vehicles) was surprisingly deferential about the program. "Before, if I had money I spent it or I gave it away," Rodman says. "I figured, I can't die and take it with me." Not any more. He agreed to go on a $1,000 weekly allowance (though he prefers to call it a budget). He exchanged his American Express card for a debit card, eliminating his ability to make a large purchase if he doesn't have the funds. And he gave Manley power of attorney on all of his accounts. What Rodman kept was signing power. As Manley explained, the point was to make sure he felt the pain of paying his bills. Otherwise, he wasn't going to learn. "I told him that if he kept spending the way he was spending, he'd be bankrupt before the end of the year," says Manley. "But if he straightened himself out, he'd not only be able to take care of his mother and his daughter, but his grandchildren."

In the midst of Rodman's financial makeover, another lucky break: Rodman was traded to the Chicago Bulls. At first, he balked. But Manley convinced Rodman that playing with Michael Jordan and Scottie Pippen was the best conceivable way to boost his marketing muscle. "If you do this," Manley pointed out, "you'll make more than a million dollars this year in endorsement deals alone."

DEALS TO BOOST HIS BANK ACCOUNT

That proved to be an understatement. Early deals with Nike and Viking Computers immediately boosted his bank balance. In an effort to keep that money in the bank, Manley bartered for a few necessities. He convinced a local Ford dealer to give him a truck. As payment, Rodman, who stored the rest of his vehicles in Texas, agreed to be seen behind the wheel. In return for allowing his likeness to be plastered on a billboard above Chicago's Expressway, a local retailer filled his closet with extra-tall clothes. His house, a three-bedroom in the suburb of Northbrook, was also on free loan. It's clearly no palace; the hot water was on the fritz for two months and Rodman showered at the gym—but he didn't mind. "It kept the guests away," he smirks.

By the end of the 1996 season, Rodman had $1 million in the bank, a chunk of it from the $150,000 per man bonus he earned for helping the Bulls make their way to the NBA championship. He was on track to hit $2 million by the end of the year. Plus, he now had a sizable investment portfolio that included not only the mutual funds he bragged about to Howard Stern but also some aggressive plays. There were tech stocks like Lam Research (purchased at $41.50 and sold five days later for $50) and Applied Materials (purchased at $36.50 and sold a week later at four dollars higher). He bought IPOs like Quintel Entertainment (purchase price $5, selling price $11) and also made a killing in Oakley—maker of the sunglasses he wears "every damn day." "Just call him Hillary Rodman Clinton," Manley quipped.

Rodman doesn't pay attention to every one of his holdings, but does closely follow Oakley as well as some of his larger positions. In his suite at the Mirage, his ears burned as Manley placed a call to his broker. He heard Manley tick off the prices of some of his holdings, and was quick with his reaction. "Safeway stock's up a point?" Rodman shouted. "How about Oakley? Is it still only 38½?"

Manley has also been hunting for nightclub sites in Vegas on his client's behalf. He keeps tabs on Rodman's controlling interest in a $10 million (sales) excavation company, for which he lent a friend's brother several hundred thousand dollars and his name a few years back. Rodman never expected he'd see anything in return, but helping out a friend was no big deal. "I don't mind sharing," he shrugs. One Las Vegas cabby offered confirmation that Rodman was indeed a generous guy. "He was one of my all-time best tippers," the driver said. "I took him to Red Lobster and he gave me $20 on a $10 fare."

INVESTING FOR LONG- AND SHORT-TERM GOALS

Rodman's long-term goal is to take care of his daughter, Alexis. His short-term goal is to take care of himself. He has endorsement deals with Kodak, Converse, and Carl's Jr., a California-based fast-food chain. He has a store of extracurricular projects, including a series with MTV, the movie *Double Team* with Jean Claude Van Damme, two more books in production, and more scripts than he can count.

And, for the first time in his career, Rodman's pay is coming up to par. Manley angled for a full $10 million for the 1997 season, arguing that his client should make at least as much as onetime Bull rebounder Horace Grant is getting from the Orlando Magic. Bulls owner Jerry Reinsdorf countered with a $6 million offer and according to the Chicago press they met in the middle.

Rodman is thoughtful on the subject. "I've got this image because I've been working my ass off all these years," he says. "Now all of a sudden people want a part of it. They're willing to pay for a part of it. Because right now, it's not so bad to be bad."

Well, most of the time. The kick of the cameraman cost Rodman an estimated $1.5 million in salary and incentives. But experience has taught him that he'll make it back somewhere else.

Like the Mirage, for example. When we left Rodman, he had sauntered from the table, his original $1,000 investment in chips still in his massive hand. A few minutes later, Rodman rejoined Manley underneath a neon MegaBucks sign. He held out an empty palm. The $1,000 had vanished at another table nearby. The pair looked at each other and sighed. Maybe they'd make it back tomorrow.

Olivia Goldsmith ════════════════

OLIVIA GOLDSMITH, 42, is the author of The First Wives Club *(Simon & Schuster, 1991), the top-selling send-up of divorce that became one of the highest grossing movies of 1996. A former marketing consultant to the computer industry, she is also the author of* Fashionably Late *(HarperCollins, 1994),* The Bestseller *(HarperCollins, 1996), and the recently released* Marrying Mom *(HarperCollins, 1996). A* First Wives *sequel—for both the page and the screen—is in the offing. A New York native, Goldsmith splits her time between New York and Vermont.*

WRITER OLIVIA GOLDSMITH, THANKFULLY, HAS NEVER BEEN CLOSE to $1 million in arrears. But the $40,000 she owed a few years back caused her even more anxiety than Rodman's debt caused him. She wasn't sure she had the ability to make it back.

Back in the summer of 1991, Olivia Goldsmith was up every morning at 3:15. She wandered into the kitchen, sat down at the table, and—as she had done yesterday, and the day before that—devoured an entire Sara Lee pound cake.

Goldsmith tried to shrug it off. After all, she asked herself, what sane person could sleep with $40,000 of debt on one's mind? She already owed that much, a combination of credit card bills, loans from friends and business associates, and, oh yes, outstanding legal bills. Seven years in divorce court had transformed her from a successful marketing consultant with a Manhattan apartment, a home in the Hamptons, and a fat IRA into a fiction-writing insomniac with a pile of rejection slips for her manuscript—a send-up of divorce called *The First Wives Club*—that was 27 pages high and growing.

Then Goldsmith got the call that would change her life.

"This is Todd Harris," said the voice on the other end of the line. "I'm an agent at Triad. And I thought you should know that Sherry Lansing at Paramount, Paula Weinstein at Warner, and Dawn Steele at Touchstone are all in a bidding war over this book of yours."

Goldsmith thought it was a joke. "Who are you?" she asked. "C'mon, get off this. Who is this really? Is it [my friend] Brendan?"

"No, this is Todd Harris at Triad," he said patiently, asking which of the three bidders Goldsmith felt most closely shared her vision of the book.

"Whose check is going to clear first?" Goldsmith wanted to know.

"Well," he said, "Sherry Lansing at Paramount will have the best chance of getting the picture made."

"So, sell to her," Goldsmith directed. "By the way, what's the bid?"

"They're up to $100,000," Harris said.

"So it's really, really sold?" she asked again.

"Definitely."

Goldsmith and her boyfriend, an audio technician, didn't waste any time heading out to the Polo Lounge to celebrate. A bottle of champagne and several hours later, she returned to her apartment and fell into bed. The next morning, she awoke to a nasty hangover and a red blinking light on her answering machine. There were six calls, all from Harris.

Beep. "Listen, Olivia, the bidding has gone up to $150,000 and I don't know what to do. What do you think? Please call me back."

Beep. "The bidding has gone even higher and Dawn Steele's dropped out. Please call back."

Beep. Beep. Beep. After not hearing back from Goldsmith, Harris finally made the deal on his own. "I haven't been able to reach you, and I didn't know what to do to," his final message said. "So, I took Sherry Lansing's offer. And Olivia, I just want to say, you're a *very* wealthy woman."

In fact, she was a good half million dollars wealthier. "At that point, I was pretty much drained by the cost of living in New York," Goldsmith remembers. "I was trying to be frugal, but I was watching my account go down and down and down. Even my agent had lent me money. And I knew that very soon, it was either go back to the straight world and get a job, or sell this thing. It was only because Sherry Lansing decided that it would make a great movie that I got that offer at all—and essentially my life changed. Then all the publishers who'd said 'No' said 'We'd like to take another look at that.' And I got to say, 'Nah—nah—nah—nah—nah!' "

Now, some seven years later, Goldsmith, age 42, has around $5 million to her name. The books she wrote after *First Wives*, including *Fashionably Late* (about victims of the fashion industry) and *The Best-seller* (about the publishing industry) brought substantial advances and sold well. *First Wives*, of course, became one of the top-grossing movies of 1996, and paved the way for another Goldsmith novel, *Marrying Mom* (about grown children trying to marry off their mother), to head into pre-production. A *First Wives* sequel—for both the page and the screen—is in the offing.

STILL WORKING AND NOT OVERSPENDING

But Goldsmith is still too financially wary to sit on her laurels. She puts in long hours, sometimes logging 8- and 10-hour days at the computer. And she lives on a lot less than her income. "I don't have a place on the West Coast," she says. "When I'm out there, I don't stay in the Hotel Bel Air. I don't need a lot of things. I don't care about jewelry. I don't even want very, very expensive clothes, because I just wind up spilling things on them." To Goldsmith, having money gives her three things: security, freedom, and insurance for comfort. "I'm telling you, I couldn't do it again," she says firmly. "I couldn't start from scratch again. What I feel money does is give me a certain sense of security. It lets me get on with my life."

NO TOLERANCE FOR LOSSES

Not wanting to lose even another penny has made her relentlessly conservative about investing. She doesn't have hundreds of thousands sitting in a coffee can or in an interest-free checking account. ("I'm not nuts," she says.) But the bulk of her portfolio, around $1 million, is in AAA municipal bonds, invested by her broker, a woman named Chris Olsen at Tucker Anthony. Another half million is in a tax-deferred pension fund that Goldsmith set up after she formed a company several years back to house her writing enterprises, and to which she contributes the maximum allowed by law. The final, much smaller piece is to be invested in the market at the broker's discretion. The deal is that Olsen doesn't regularly tell her client when she's lost money in a stock. "It's so hard to earn money that I can't stand to lose any," Goldsmith says. "Chris also doesn't tell me when a stock has gone up and she's sold it. Because if it then makes more money, I feel like I've lost that. I'm so neurotic. Four times a year, I go through my statements, and as long as my net worth increases, that's fine."

Although Goldsmith isn't constantly on the prowl for stock tips, when a company catches her eye, she will bring it to her broker's attention. After all, she points out, she did once work on Wall Street. In fact, she was a young superstar. Born in the Bronx and raised in Manhattan, Goldsmith earned a BA in education from New York University. Out of college, she opted not to teach, and instead joined a large consulting firm, where she soon broke the $100,000 salary barrier. Her investment haul provided nice padding. She got into Microsoft and Apple early on, as well as Toys "Я" Us, which she purchased in anticipation of the eighties' baby boomlet. More recently, her decision to invest in a company that was marketing a self-administered drug test paid off in spades.

As her income rises, Goldsmith says she's trying to be a bit bolder. "I feel like this year, 1997, I'm going to have more money that I can afford to be more speculative with," she says. "But I'll still leave most of the decision-making to Chris. I worked on Wall Street long enough to know that if you're not following the market full-time, you have no idea what's happening."

AN EYE FOR REAL ESTATE

She has more confidence in her ability to buy real estate. Over the past two decades Goldsmith has been in and out of a number of properties—from the two homes she owned with her ex-husband to the half dozen places she owns today—and has never sold at a loss, even at the end of the 1980s when the market was dodgy at best. "I think I have a really good aesthetic," she says. "If a place appeals to me, it's going to appeal to a lot of people." What does she look for? "I know it sounds stupid, because everyone knows it, but location, location, location. Plus potential in the house."

A townhouse in Florida, purchased in 1992 and sold at a 400 percent gain in 1995, was just 300 feet from the ocean. Her country home in Chester, Vermont, a 150-year-old structure right in the middle of Stone Village, has historic significance. "The Scots came over in the 1830s to prove to the people of Vermont that it was very much like Scotland. They built a school, a church, a store, and five spec houses. It's a beautiful little enclave." And her most recent purchase, a Georgian mansion on the Hudson River in upstate New York, is situated on two acres of property with "drop-dead water views." Goldsmith has put $500,000 into the renovations alone, and she's still not finished. "Everything that could go wrong did go wrong," she says. "But I feel like I'm preserving something for history."

NO DEBTS

In an effort to maintain her sanity—and her sleep—she doesn't have a mortgage on any of her properties or a loan on her car. In fact, aside from her monthly credit card bills, which usually get paid in full as soon as they come in, she has no debt at all.

She has also sworn off marriage. Her boyfriend has been a part of her life now for eight years and Goldsmith says she trusts him completely. "If he said he needed $500,000 I'd probably give it to him," she says. What she doesn't trust are the courts. "It's a male-created and -dominated world. Most of the lawyers, most of the judges. During my divorce, I felt like I was being totally controlled by other people. You know, people don't understand. You get into a marriage and it seems easy. Then you head for divorce court and someone else is saying: 'Hey, you're responsible for half his debts. Hey, he can take half your money. Sometimes he can take more than half.' I'm not willing to let the court be involved in my private life anymore."

PICKING UP THE PIECES

Since *First Wives* became a sensation, Goldsmith has become a sort of patron saint to the divorced. She's received thousands of letters from women reeling from their own horrible experiences. One woman, who had a lot of inherited wealth, was convinced by her husband to buy major paintings as investments. They were going to appreciate, he said. He put them in the back of their BMW and drove to Canada. Another woman wrote that her husband embezzled money and signed her name to the damning documents. Now she's in prison and he's living in Mexico with the money. Goldsmith answers every one, with patience and, wherever possible, humor.

If you're in the same boat, she offers this piece of advice: Get a woman attorney—a good one—but a woman nonetheless. It's no accident that Goldsmith's broker is a woman, as are her lawyer, her doctor, her publisher, and the head of the movie studio where she's found a home. (Lest you think she's man-bashing, she quickly points out that her accountant, with whom she's worked for 20 years, happens to be a man. "I'm not going to dump him just because he's not a girl," she quips. "I'm not *that* unreasonable.") Once you find a lawyer, Goldsmith says, there are three other things to do. "One, you have to separate the damage to your psyche from who you really are, 'cause you're going to feel like second-class goods. Then what you have to do is be very, very honest with yourself. Say, 'Yes, I've made some mistakes with my life, but what do I want? What can I do?' Don't fall into the Zelda Fitzgerald syndrome. Don't decide at thirty-eight that you want to be a ballerina; that's not going to happen. But aside from that, realistically, anything you want. Thirdly, decide that you can prevail."

All it takes, she firmly believes, is a lot of hard work, direction, and a pinch of good luck. Back when Goldsmith was nine years old, she rode her bicycle to Central Park at twilight, which you could still do back then without fearing for your life. There were a number of kids hanging around, watching baseball games and eating ice cream and drinking sodas from the refreshment stand. Goldsmith wanted desperately to buy a candy bar, but she had left the house without any money. She kicked her foot in the surrounding gravel and there, to her disbelief, was a quarter. "It was magic," she says. "It just seemed like I wished for it so hard that it appeared. Now, I don't believe wishing makes things happen. But I wished for it, and I kicked the gravel. It was really good luck. And that was a lot of money for a little kid. I got a drink—*and* a candy bar."

Wouldn't you know, it was a Payday.

Ivana Trump

IVANA TRUMP is the founder and CEO of the House of Ivana, a clothing and jewelry manufacturer that sells its merchandise via the Home Shopping Network, and the author of three books, The Best Is Yet to Come: Coping with Divorce and Enjoying Life Again *(Pocket Books, 1995) and two novels,* For Love Alone *(Pocket Books, 1994) and* Free to Love *(Pocket Books, 1994). During her 14-year marriage to real estate developer Donald Trump, she ran New York's Plaza Hotel. She has three children, Donny, Ivanka, and Eric.*

IVANA TRUMP WENT THROUGH A DIFFERENT KIND OF TURNAROUND than both Dennis Rodman and Olivia Goldsmith. Having enough money at her disposal was never a problem. Still, after years of being taken care of financially, first by her parents, then by husband Donald Trump, she had to learn to take responsibility for her own money matters. Perhaps that's why there seem to be two Ivanas. One whirls through the social scene, from London to Prague, Manhattan to Palm Beach, and favors Cristal champagne over Dom Perignon. The other shops the Price Club, her teenagers in tow. But there's no doubt which one has shown up today to talk about her personal finances. She's wearing a $49 Bermuda-shorted jumpsuit. And she's proud of it.

Ivana? Shopping off the rack? Don't be fooled. Though she candidly admits that the "billions and trillions" she had at her disposal while married have been reduced to the mere millions in her own account, Ivana is doing just fine, thank you.

She has taken firm control of her financial assets, a conservative cocktail of stocks, bonds, and real estate. And with the help of her advisers she has already reaped a sizable gain on her $25 million divorce settlement—which included $14 million in cash and a mortgage-free mansion in tony Greenwich, Connecticut (now on the market for more than $18 million, a bundle even by Greenwich standards). She put much of the original cash in trust for her three children, telling friends she was perfectly capable of earning her own money, and then went about proving it. Income from her investments and her businesses are responsible for the $5-million mansion called Concha Marina she purchased in Palm Beach, a townhouse on Manhattan's East Side, and a 180-foot yacht appropriately named *M-Y Ivana*.

Her 1995 book, *The Best Is Yet to Come: Coping with Divorce and Enjoying Life Again* (Pocket Books)—Ivana's thank-you to the tens of thousands of women who wrote her letters of support as she was going through her toughest time—even includes a chapter on investment and money management. She may have a good deal more wealth than her readers, but she has a similar attitude. Ivana says her financial advice comes from her own risk-averse heart. "I am not a gambler and other women shouldn't be either," she says. "You have to take whatever you have coming in and think about your life. First you make a budget—say, 'Here's how much I want to spend on the household, on travel, on a new car.' Then you can decide how you want to invest."

Ivana's helpful hints include separating your bills into categorized envelopes to make things easier at tax time, a warning for all readers that prenuptial agreements are an absolute must (unless he's nearing

100 and chained to a walker), and a plea to stay away from risky investments and high rollers. "I tell women to make sure they have a conservative banker," she says. "I had a friend who gave a million dollars to one hot new guy. The next thing, she gets a phone call: He's lost it. It took her two years and a lawsuit to get it back."

Ivana, of course, can afford to take risks that would be wildly speculative to most of her readers. "But why should I?" she asks. "What's an extra $1,000 if I can't sleep at night?"

Her portfolio consists of 60 percent individual bonds and bond mutual funds and 40 percent stocks, largely blue chips. Alongside her friends' birthdays in the pages of her date book, Ivana tracks the maturities of her bonds, which stretch from two years to nine. When they come due, typically twice a year, she sits down with her broker, Bear, Stearns chairman Alan "Ace" Greenberg (see page 70), to plot out a strategy of rollovers and reinvestments that will maintain a comfortably diversified mix.

As for stocks, Ivana weighs in when it comes to sectors, but she allows Greenberg to select the individual companies. "They don't call him Ace for nothing," she says. Though she struggles for the word, Ivana justifies playing the "how-do-you-say" pharmaceutical sector, despite its uncertainties. "There are some drugs people will always need," she laughs. "I don't care what happens. Johnson & Johnson are always going to be very strong."

Though Greenberg has been a longtime friend, as well as one of Donald Trump's advisers during the couple's 14-year marriage, Ivana wasn't quick to put her portfolio in his hands. "I did my homework," she insists. "I picked up a lot of articles, spoke to a lot of friends, asked them how they invest, what they do, who they use." She's had no regrets about signing on with Greenberg, least of all for the personal service she receives. In addition to the twice-a-year bond-strategy sessions, each time Ivana finishes a business deal and lands a large check, they sit down to decide where to put it. And they speak on the phone every time Greenberg buys or sells a stock, as well as when Ivana has an investment idea or concern.

During one trip to Vienna a few years back, Ivana nearly had a heart attack when a Friday *Herald Tribune* ran headlines predicting "The Next Black Monday." She was on the phone with Greenberg's office immediately and again when the market opened on Monday. Her preference was to be reassured that she wasn't going to be worth far less when she returned to American soil, but she was willing to discuss pulling out of the market altogether. As it turned out, it was a false alarm.

Greenberg also manages the portfolios of Donald and Ivana's three children, Donny, Ivanka, and Eric, but even more conservatively. Any gains on the younger Trumps' portfolios are quickly reinvested, while Ivana considers at least some of hers play money. "I can go and spend and blow it on whatever," she says with a wave of her hand, dismissing six-figure expenditures like most people shrug off a trip to the Gap.

But try as she might to seem cavalier, Ivana doesn't buy anything without thinking about what it does to her bottom line, and, more importantly, what it will be worth tomorrow. Concha Marina, for example. First, Ivana says she decided to buy it at the last minute. Then she launches into an analysis of the house, the Palm Beach real estate market, and why she expects both to appreciate. On the heels of the riots and fires and earthquakes in California, "80 percent" of her friends are bowing out for the sunny Florida skies. Where else would they go but Palm Beach? "Besides," she points out, "I improve on places with my name. If I live there even one, two years, it will have a certain value."

At around $25 million in estimated value, Ivana's real estate portfolio is now even larger than her investment portfolio—probably too large. The sale of the 40-room house in Greenwich would restore a comfortable balance, leaving her with a townhouse on the East Side of Manhattan, which she purchased when she moved out of Trump Tower, and another on Cadogan Square in London—all debt-free.

But in a few years, when the children leave the nest, Ivana says she'll trade the townhouse for a spectacular penthouse, and put the money into other vehicles that look attractive at the time. "No matter what kind of investment you have, you cannot just sit on something constantly," she says. "I have a friend of mine, she buys a home. It's a $100,000 home. She goes there, she lives there, she improves on it. She sells it for a quarter million dollars. She takes the quarter million, she buys a new home. She improves on it. She sells it for $400,000. She doesn't sit." Ivana shrugs. "I do the same, slightly differently. As I make money in my businesses, I take it and invest it, in the stocks, in the bonds, in the real estate. I move my money around like that."

While Ivana is expounding on real estate, her soft-spoken, unassuming, brunette mother is puttering around in the background, a nudging reminder that her bombshell of a daughter didn't grow up with gilt walls and tea service. In Communist Czechoslovakia, where Ivana spent her youth, everyone was middle-class and the Zelniceks were only slightly more middle-class than most. It wasn't until Ivana left home in her late teens to work as a runway model in Montreal that she began earning enough to sock a few extra dollars away. As always, she did her homework, asking the owners of the agency that represented her what investments they'd recommend for a young girl. On their say-so, she plunked her pennies into CDs.

During her 14-year marriage to Trump, Donald and his advisers managed the family finances. But since their separation in 1990, Ivana has taken over the reins with an unexpectedly sharp eye for detail. A few years back, she noted that the bills for Donny's phone card had tripled from one month to the next. She knew he wasn't calling home more than the usual three times a week. Something else must be up. When questioned, Donny admitted he had a girlfriend who lived in another state. "I'll pay it this month," Ivana told him sternly. "But you've been warned. Next time, it comes out of your allowance." (She admits his allowance was a few dollars higher than the $25 the school suggests.)

If that firm hand and watchful eye surprises you, get this: Not only does Ivana shop at the Price Club, she actually likes it. Three or four times a year, she loads the kids into the car and heads to an outpost in Connecticut to load up on soap, paper towels, and toilet paper. And since she's shopping for more than one home, Ivana returns with a trunkful. "It is an incredible invention," she raves. "You really can save a lot of money, it is fast, painless, and you can't do much damage. Of course, I wouldn't want to do it every day," she admits. "But the kids have a ball."

Courtesy of Donny she also had her first fast-food experience. On one trip back to school, he requested a stop at Taco Bell. Though she was slightly put off when her request for a glass of Chablis met with giggles from behind the counter, Ivana recovered sufficiently to enjoy her burrito as well as the bill: $16 for lunch for five. The cashier was dumbfounded when she tried to pay with a $100 bill.

All of this bargain shopping was research as far as Ivana is concerned. In 1992, she cut a multiyear deal with the Home Shopping

Network to appear once a month selling a line of clothing and jewelry. Although she originally intended to appear as a celebrity endorser, Ivana got wind of the volume of merchandise she was moving—$3 million to $5 million a weekend—and quickly became a vendor. The House of Ivana now has factories in Hong Kong, India, Rumania, and Spain, as well as the United States. The $49 jumpsuit, the $29 faux pearl watch, and the $19 gold-plated bracelet she's wearing are from her own collection. Stylish business suits in soft grays and taupes are $180 to $280. Even evening gowns don't break the bank. Ivana has had such success she's been asked about opening a boutique. Her response has always been "Why? How many suits do you think Chanel sells in a season? Two thousand? I sell 10,000 in an hour." But lately she's begun to think twice and is putting out feelers about renting space in Manhattan. She's already selling her cosmetics line and fragrance (called Ivana, of course) at 1,500 J. C. Penney counters across the country, as well as on the shopping channel in Canada and QVC in London and Germany.

And that's not the last of it. Ivana has a second company, Ivana Inc., which is a holding pen for her media ventures. In addition to her self-help book, she has written two romance novels, *For Love Alone* (a CBS made-for-TV movie in 1996) and its sequel *Free to Love* (now in production). There's the "Dear Ivana" advice column she writes for *The Globe*, her Pizza Hut commercial (much of the money went to charity), and her hysterical cameo in *The First Wives Club*. Laid out on a dining table are Polaroids for an upcoming coffee-table book on table settings, complete with menu suggestions. "Many women don't understand if you're serving shrimp for the appetizer, you can't have fish for the entrée," she confides. Lest she sound like she's aiming out of the realm of her mass audience, Ivana insists: "If you don't have much money you can still entertain. You can have a fabulous blini party with lots of blini and all kinds of toppings."

Ivana is this matter-of-fact about all her ventures and successes. You would think each new project would be a bit of a reach, but she's had a long history of triumphs, starting as vice president of design of the Trump Organization, working her way up to the Plaza Hotel and a position as CEO of Trump Castle and Casino, and now building an empire that bears her name alone. Ivana, clearly, is now strong enough to handle just about anything. "You either have it or you don't," she says. "You can go to the Wharton School of Finance and all of that. If you don't have it you're never going to learn it. I was always very good at business, but I had no training."

So just who is Ivana training herself to be? One *Vanity Fair* profile suggested that in the coming decade she could emerge as the next Margaret Thatcher, Martha Stewart, Brooke Astor, or Estée Lauder, depending on how she charted her course. In the last five years, Ivana has shown that it's her intention to go after every one. "I'd like to be all of them," she says with such determination you believe she very well might.

WHEN IT'S *YOUR* MONEY . . .

WHETHER YOUR FINANCIAL SETBACK IS THE RESULT OF A divorce, a job loss, or just pulling out that nasty credit card too many times, the strategies for getting back on track are very much the same. "The most important thing is to be realistic about your problem—and ultrarealistic about your spending needs," says Howard Rothwell, a financial planner in Media, Pennsylvania. "The people who get themselves into difficulty first go into denial mode. But once they get themselves to address the problem—usually by putting on paper, 'this is how much I owe Visa, this is my mortgage, this is my home equity loan, and this is what I need to live on'—they find it's much easier to manage. Frequently, they find the situation wasn't as bad as they were afraid it was."

Step One: Set Goals. Your first move is to develop your personal balance sheet—basically a snapshot of your financial picture. That means figuring out how much you have in cash, in investments, and of course, in debt. You also want to track your cash flow month-to-month to recognize how much you're saving and spending. This can be done with pencil and paper, though computer programs like Intuit's Quicken and Microsoft Money make the task much easier.

Once you have a grasp of your financial picture, ask yourself: How much money do I need to accomplish my goals? Do I want to go buy a new car in six months, put a down payment on a house in five years, or retire when I'm 50? And how much do I need to save/invest each month to get there?

Then go about trying to make it happen. To sock away $150 to $200 a month, trade in your morning cappuccino for a cup of office-provided coffee (a savings of $2.50 a day). You'll be one-third of the way there. Give up one restaurant meal each month and that's another $40 to $60. Fewer taxis each week in favor of the bus or subway and you've made up the difference. Or, put your gym membership on hold for a few summer months in favor of outdoor exercise to get you on track. It's a matter of what makes sense for you.

Step Two: Pay Down Debt. Now that you've got some substantial savings, you need to decide what to do with it. Forget about stashing the money in your bank savings account where it might earn three percent in interest, or even a money market where it would earn five percent. "The best investment you can make is to pay off your credit card debt," says Gary Schatsky, a fee-only financial planner and attorney in New York City. "If that credit card interest rate is 18 percent, you'll get an immediate 18 percent return, and that's before you consider the effect of inflation and taxes." (The one exception to this rule, Schatsky notes, is if you have an employer matching 50 to 100 percent of your contributions into a 401(k). Since that return *does* exceed what you'll earn by paying off your credit card debt, it's best to try to do both simultaneously. Try putting half of your excess cash into your retirement account, and sending the other half to your credit card company.)

The best trick to paying off a credit card balance is to break the minimum payment habit. If you make the smallest acceptable payment each month, it can take decades to pay off your balance. By the time you're through, the interest component of your payment often exceeds what you've paid in principal. If you've been paying the minimum, break the pattern by paying an additional $10 each month, then $20, then $50. You'll be out of debt much sooner than you imagined.

You can also slash your cumulative interest payments by transferring or consolidating your balance to a lower-rate credit card.

According to Robert McKinley, publisher of *CardTrak*, the average credit card interest rate was nearly 18 percent in early 1997 and—due to the expiration of many 1996 teaser rates—edging up. But there are still low-rate cards available. The best of these offer variable, but not teaser, rates in the 10 to 11 percent range, but these programs are often so small and so selective that if you have even one blemish on your credit report (and if you've experienced a financial setback, you probably have several) you'll likely be rejected. Instead, apply for a card in the 12 to 14 percent range with no annual fee. You can get a list of the country's lowest-rate cards by sending a check or money order for $4 payable to the not-for-profit consumer group Bankcard Holders of America, 524 Branch Drive, Salem, VA 24153. (Note to repeat offenders: Consider cutting up all of your credit cards in favor of a debit card. This newfangled piece of plastic works much like an ATM card. Money for purchases comes out of checking automatically, which means you can't spend what you don't have.)

If you're burdened by student loans instead of credit card debt, you may also want to consider consolidating. Since 1994, a government program called the Federal Direct Consolidation Program can help you consolidate multiple higher-rate student loans into one lower-rate one. (For information call 800-4FED-AID.)

Finally, if you can't come up with the necessary cash to even start getting out of debt, consider a few other sources. You can borrow from your 401(k) plan. The rates are lower than credit card rates, and the interest goes to you, rather than an institutional lender. And because your payments come directly out of your paycheck, it's easy to stick with the program. Your home can be another source of funds. A home equity loan or line of credit typically comes at a lower interest rate than a credit card, and the interest is usually tax-deductible. Finally, there's family funding. If you have a friend or family member willing to lend you the money at a reasonable rate, it may be time to take them up on it. Of course, just like a bank loan, the transaction should be fully documented, complete with an amortization schedule. Some personal finance software packages have easy-to-use amortization schedules built in.

Step Three: Start Saving. Once you're out of the hole, it's time to begin saving and investing. Try setting aside 10 percent of your salary at first. When that becomes routine, bump your savings component to 15 percent, then 20. Your first goal should be to accumulate an emergency cushion of about three months of living expenses. Many financial advisers believe six months is necessary, but too much time spent simply saving wastes powerful investing years. "I don't recommend my clients maintain huge cash reserves," says Howard Rothwell. "Instead, you want to make sure that at least a portion of your investments are in instruments which can be counted on not to fluctuate wildly—like balanced mutual funds or GNMA funds. There they'll earn a much better return than in the bank but can also be immediately liquidated if something goes wrong."

Once you've got your emergency cushion, it's time to start investing. Although it would be terrific to be able to fund your 401(k) to the government's limit of $9,500 in year one, you'll be better off keeping at least some of your investments where you can get to them without penalty. Start by socking half into your 401(k), and the rest into mutual funds or individual stocks. As the dollars you have to invest rise over time, you'll want to boost your 401(k) contribution to take full advantage of your employer's matching offers as well as the tax advantages. If your employer doesn't offer a 401(k), you'll want to put 50 percent of your investment dollars (up to $2,000) each year into an IRA. (For more on how to allocate your investment dollars, see page 44.)

If you get to the end of each month and find that somehow you've spent the money you should be saving or investing, consider a forced saving or investment plan. Ask your employer to deposit part of your paycheck into savings each month and the rest into checking. Alternately, you can arrange with your bank to automatically transfer funds from checking to savings once or twice each month. To boost your investment holdings, you can also arrange for a mutual fund company or a discount brokerage to automatically deduct money from your checking account each month. Financial planner Gary Schatsky notes that automatic investment plans have one drawback: They don't allow you to take care of hot investment opportunities that might arise. But if you're stuck in the starting gate, they may at least make sense short-term.

LAST WORD: BACK IN BUSINESS

YOU'VE DONE A SOLID JOB OF GETTING BACK ON YOUR FEET again after a financial crisis. Finally, there's money in the bank; you're even putting a bit away for retirement. Now there's just one lingering problem: No one seems willing to give you a credit card.

Don't worry. A "secured" credit card can help you rebuild your credit rating without embarrassment. Here's how secured cards work: You deposit a certain sum, typically $500 to $1,500, with the bank that issues the card (which looks just like a regular Visa or MasterCard). That sum becomes your credit line. Although you're still required to pay your bills each month without delay, should you miss a payment the bank already has enough of your money to pay itself. The best programs also pay you an above-average rate of interest on your card, and convert to a regular card once you've paid all your bills on time for a period of, say, 18 months to two years. Here, courtesy of *CardTrak*, are a list of some of the country's best secured cards, the deposit they require and interest paid on them, and phone numbers to apply. All rates and annual fees are as of June 1997:

- **Community Bank of Parker's** Spirit Visa is a secured card with an interest rate fixed at a reasonable 15.9 percent and a $29 annual fee. The trade-off is that the bank pays 1.5 percent interest on your $300 minimum ($3,000 maximum) deposit, which is lower than the rate you'll earn from other cards on this list. To apply: 800-779-8472.

- **Amalgamated Bank's** secured MasterCard has a 16.5 percent variable rate (8 percent over prime) and a $50 annual fee. Your $500 minimum deposit earns interest at a rate of 3.75 percent. Maintain a blemish-free payment record for one to two years and you may qualify for an unsecured card. To apply: 800-365-6464.

- **Chase Manhattan's** secured MasterCard is fixed at an interest rate of 17.9 percent with a $20 annual fee and 4 percent paid on deposits (minimum $300). Pay on time for 18 months and you may qualify for an unsecured card. To apply: 800-482-4273.

- **Orchard Bank** of Portland, Oregon offers a secured Visa and MasterCard with a variable interest rate of 18.9 percent (10.4 percent over prime). The annual fee on the card is $35, and deposits (minimum $400) earn 2 percent annually. After 18 months of on-time payment, you'll typically qualify for one of Orchard's unsecured cards. To apply: 800-873-7307.

Chapter 8

THE PARTNERS

Helen Gurley and David Brown
Ken and Daria Dolan
Susan Feniger and
Mary Sue Milliken

"Other married people, they say: 'This is my money. This is her money.' But not us. We trust each other financially and unconditionally. We've never had a moment's anxiety about it."

—David Brown, on his relationship with wife
Helen Gurley Brown

I F YOU'VE EVER BEEN HALF OF A COUPLE, WHETHER IN A ROMANTIC or a business partnership, you know that money can muck up the works at the least opportune time. Dr. Joy Browne, one of the country's most prominent radio psychologists, likes to tell her listeners that money is responsible for more divorces than sex is. Her logic? "Sex, if you think about it, really doesn't take up much time. It takes up a lot of emotional space, but that's it," says Browne. "Money, on the other hand, is policy. It's power. It's a determining factor in your lifestyle, in who's in charge, what you do, when you do it."

One mitigating factor is that people who spend frivolously are often wildly attracted to compulsive savers, just as a gregarious man is likely to be drawn to a woman he thinks is a good listener. "Opposites always attract," Browne says matter-of-factly. "Then they aggravate the daylights out of each other."

The pairs profiled in this chapter are definitely financial opposites. Movie producer David Brown is a notoriously big tipper, for example, which drives his Cosmo Girl wife Helen Gurley Brown crazy. "You don't even know this [waiter]," she'll chide him for leaving a 30 or 40 percent tip on the table. "Maybe not," Brown will answer. "But he'll always remember me." And radio talk show host Daria Dolan is practically compulsive about investment management—a chore she handles for herself and her husband and cohost Ken. He on the other hand can't be bothered with the details. Likewise, Susan Feniger—the brunette half of "Too Hot Tamales"—is free-spending, while her partner Mary Sue Milliken has trouble forking over $25 for a pair of jeans.

What these couples have learned is how to make these differences work *for* them, rather than *against* them. In some cases that's meant compromise, in others a division of labor. The solutions that they've hit on may work just as well for you.

Helen Gurley and David Brown

HELEN GURLEY AND DAVID BROWN, ages 75 and 80 respectively, are one of New York's power couples. Until last year, Helen Gurley Brown—author of the best-selling Sex and the Single Girl—*was the editor-in-chief of* Cosmopolitan, *a position she held for 30 years. She is now editor-in-chief of the magazine's international editons. David Brown, producer of* The Sting, Jaws, The Verdict, A Few Good Men, The Player, *and more recently* The Saint, *is the author of* Brown's Guide to Growing Gray *(Delacorte Press,1987). Prior to meeting his wife, he was managing editor of* Cosmopolitan. *The couple lives on Central Park West.*

M OVIE PRODUCER DAVID BROWN CAME FROM A FAMILY THAT LOST everything during the Depression. Before the Crash, his mother had her share of fine jewelry, and his father knew the value of a good cigar. The disappearance of that wealth and subsequent reappearance of money in Brown's life taught the producer of *The Sting* and *Jaws* one important lesson: Save it while you make it.

Helen Gurley Brown's family didn't have much money after the Depression, either. But that wasn't anything new. They were from Green Forest, Arkansas, and her father died in an accident when she was a child. In later years, she has earned just as much (and sometimes more) than her husband. But she still reacts to money as though her life depended on it. Helen would sooner take New York's Number 10 bus downtown than she would pay for a taxi. When she visits her sister in Oklahoma City, she purchases a coach ticket and takes her chance on an upgrade. Perhaps Helen's friend Barbara Walters put it best when she said: "Helen is cheap." "Barbara meant that with all affection," says David Brown. "Besides, Helen prefers the word 'careful.'"

How have these disparate souls remained happily married for more than three decades? Their well-documented sex life definitely had something to do with it. Second on the list is that they have complete and total trust. Since the day they married, all the couple's assets—their stocks and bonds, their Central Park West apartment,

their cash in the bank—have been in joint name. What this arrangement means is that Helen could turn around, sell everything tomorrow, and flee to Mexico without telling her husband. Likewise, he
could unload the apartment or clear out the checking account without breathing word one to her. "We trust each other unconditionally,"
says Brown. "We've never had a moment's anxiety about it."

THE SIMPLEST WAY TO PICK STOCKS—
UNDERSTAND THE BUSINESSES

Of course, it's easier to trust your partner with money when that person just happens to have a knack for making it. David Brown has a
strong interest in the stock market, but also a Midas touch. That's
why nearly all of the couple's investment decisions land in his able
hands.

Late last year, he sat down with a visitor in his Manhattan office
on the fourth floor of the *Newsweek* building to explain how he invests
and how it affects his relationship with his wife. Tellingly, the television
set in one corner was tuned not to the E! Entertainment Network but to
CNBC's Financial News Network.

His stock-picking strategy is basic Warren Buffett: "I pick stocks in
businesses that I understand," he explains. These range from senti-
mental favorites like Pan American Airways, in which Brown lost a fair
amount ("I let my affection for the airline get the best of my judgment,"
he says now) to a long list of blue chip winners like IBM, AT&T, Colgate
Palmolive, and J. P. Morgan. "I bought my own bank stock, the Bank of
New York, because I think it's a terrific company," Brown explains. "And
I love GE. I think Jack Welch is doing a great job."

Now 80, Brown looks for dividends, a fairly clean balance sheet,
a price/earnings ratio that's reasonable compared to other stocks in
the sector, and directors and managers who have an equity stake.
How great an equity state varies with the company. Obviously, he explains, individual managers in a company like IBM aren't going to be
able to hang onto as large a share as they would in a small company
that has just recently gone public. "All I want to know is that they
have a strong, personal rooting interest," he says. "So if they have
more stock than I have, say 100,000 shares or 200,000 shares, that's

a plus for me. If I see companies where the managers and directors don't own stock, or where they have token shares, I'm wary because I don't think they can represent the shareholders with any passion or commitment."

REALLOCATING INVESTMENTS WITH AGE

Stocks represented the lion's share of the Browns' investments when they were younger. But once he and his wife reached 60, David started to rejigger the mix to lessen the risk. "Very early in life, I was in a yacht off the coast of Mexico. A very rich man approached me and I asked him his philosophy of investing," he remembers. "He said one-third of your money should be in bomb shelter investments that are very low-risk, where you're guaranteed a minimal income and the safety of your investment. One-third of your money should be in moderately aggressive investments. And one-third should be in companies that represent outright speculation where you can make a big score. That worked for me until I was 55 or 60, at which point I eliminated the outright speculation and concentrated on the first two principles."

The Browns' current investment goals are income and preservation of capital. That's why 65 to 70 percent of their investments are in fixed income securities, largely U.S. Treasuries and tax-free bonds. Twenty to 25 percent are in blue chips. These investments are doing quite well on paper, though Brown doesn't believe you count your gains "until you've sold the stock, deposited the money, and paid the taxes." (He has hardly sold a share of late because of the tax consequences.) The remaining slim slice of the pie—what Brown calls his "gambling or speculation money"—is represented by positions in venture capital partnerships.

UNIMPRESSED BY MUTUAL FUND MANAGERS

The couple's portfolio is devoid of mutual funds. Brown says he likes to look at the individual issues he purchases as a fund of sorts. And he doesn't feel he's missing out on any great advice by avoiding contact with fund managers. "I'm totally unimpressed by so-called experts," says Brown. That includes fund managers. "I noted that the *Wall Street Journal* said Friday: Don't look for the stock market to advance again. But the Dow went up 52 points on Friday. Then it went up 74 points again on Monday. Well, maybe the *Wall Street Journal* might have been right for Tuesday."

Many people consider Brown somewhat of a guru himself. Years back, he was profiled in *Forbes* magazine for his investment expertise. His book, *Brown's Guide to Growing Gray* (Delacorte Press, 1987), includes an entire chapter devoted to his methods of stock selection. But ask the movie-maker-cum-stock-guru how he got so smart and the answer might surprise you. Brown owes all of his knowledge, he says, to the woman he married. Before they got together in 1958, he says he was an "economic illiterate."

Twice married and twice divorced, Brown was "suffering from long-term alimony" that had dragged him into debt. Not Helen Gurley. On her secretary's salary, she had somehow stockpiled a bank balance of $8,000. "When I met Helen, I was struck by her sense of caution and prudence," he says fondly. And she was struck by his lack of it. At the time, Brown, like all up-and-coming Hollywood executives, had a business manager on his personal payroll. She was blonde and quite beautiful, he remembers, and she was also getting a full five percent of his income simply for writing his monthly checks. "I'll write the checks," Helen said, sending the business manager packing. From that day on, the couple's partnership was sealed.

Their financial successes followed their marriage in 1959. In 1964, Brown was named head of the New American Library, part of the Times Mirror Corporation and publisher of Ian Fleming's wildly successful James Bond series. His new position came with stock options, which of course he didn't have the money to exercise. He remembers wandering into his local bank one afternoon and borrowing enough money to buy the $200,000 of stock under option. "That was the first big money we ever had," he remembers. A few years later, Helen Gurley Brown sold the film rights to *Sex and the Single Girl* for $200,000. "We were one-third millionaires," Brown remembers. "Fabulous."

KEEPING TABS ON THE FAMILY FINANCES

Though David Brown soon assumed the lead in managing the couple's finances, he always made certain his wife knew exactly what was going on. For decades, she has combed through reports from their accountant that detail their spending. Every month for as long as she can remember, she has pored over monthly statements from the Bank of New York that chart their income. And every day for years she has sifted through the pages of the *Wall Street Journal*—where she, not her husband, was the recent subject of a story on page one.

As the money continued to roll in, both Browns began to develop a strong interest in the market. David's forte was traditional analysis. He'd gather analyst reports, scour the popular press, talk through the issues with his friends on Wall Street, and then watch the stock for a year or more before making his move. Helen was considerably more daring. She was once seated at dinner next to MCA founder Jule Styne. "Jule," she asked coyly, "where would you invest $100,000?"

"Do you have $100,000?" Styne replied.

"Yes," she said. "Yes, I do."

"Well then, I'd put it into a CD paying 6 or 7 percent." Though disappointed (Gurley had expected a hot tip), she followed his advice to the letter and reaped the 6 to 7 percent gain (although had she invested in his company's stock she would have made far more). Another dinner party suggestion didn't fare nearly as well. She sank a million dollars into a stock without doing any research and lost almost all of it.

David shrugged it off. Living through the Depression had taught him that better times could be counted on ahead. But *his* regrettable investment decisions were tougher for Helen to bear. Once he bought 200 acres of real estate only to discover that the entire parcel sat on wetlands. On another occasion he followed Bing Crosby into an investment that went down the tubes. Both times, it was a struggle for Helen to hold her tongue. Still, in their many years together, the couple had only one knock-down-drag-out stock-related battle, and it was recent. David bought Philip Morris in 1996, after it took a dive following a lawsuit by a former smoker and held on as it continued to fall.

"The tobacco industry is completely changing," Helen argued. "How can you be sure you know what's really happening?"

"Philip Morris is a great company," he shot back. "But if it makes you that unhappy, I'll sell when we get even."

The upshot: Although the stock later soared, they're now even and Helen has mellowed. Now she accepts a convincing argument to hold.

RISKY BUSINESS: INVESTING IN HOLLYWOOD

There were other investments as well, many of them quite speculative. Real estate deals, oil, cattle, and a slew of limited partnerships—mostly as tax shelters—during the seventies. One thing that's notably absent from the couple's portfolio, however, are Hollywood investments. Brown doesn't like investing in movies because he's seen the waste of today's movie studios firsthand. Back when he and his partner, Richard Zanuck, made their seed money doing *Jaws* and *The Sting*, Hollywood wasn't given to such excesses. But now with budgets topping the $100-million level he wouldn't consider putting his money into a single picture and would advise others to steer clear as well. "You, as an individual investor and an outsider, are the low end of the food chain," he explains. "The first people who make money in the movies are the talent and the distributors, because the distributors take the gross off the top. If you're really desperate to invest in a movie, I would choose a company that has motion picture studios as a part of its mix—for example, Polygram, Viacom, Time Warner, or Disney. You'll do better because most of their money is *not* made from movies, but from music, television stations, and other sources. The Disney and Warner Brothers retail stores probably return more money than most of their pictures."

They also have no real estate, save the Central Park West apartment that Brown said is one of the best investments he ever made. "When I was a young man, we owned acres and parcels, but we were looking ahead five, 10, or 15 years. Helen and I don't want anything that long-term anymore. After all, as Lord Keynes once said: 'In the long term, we are all dead.'"

LITTLE ESTATE TAX PLANNING MEANS PAYING UNCLE SAM

The Browns have also chosen to steer clear of fancy estate-tax devices like charitable partnerships and living trusts. In the long term, that means that more of their money than is necessary will go to Uncle Sam. By having all their assets in both names they immediately lose a deduction worth more than $250,000 when the first of them passes away. It doesn't bother them in the slightest.

"We don't care about estate planning," says Brown. "We have no one to leave [our money] to. All of our philanthropies will just get a little less, but they'll be fine; they'll get lots of money." One of Brown's advisers once suggested that he and Helen form a charitable remainder trust, which could save them hundreds of thousands annually in income taxes. Brown couldn't be bothered. "You know something," he says confidentially. "I like paying taxes. I have no problem with it. I'm not interested in surrendering my capital for a 5 percent lifetime income. When I die and pay this huge tax, all of these institutions will still get substantial endowments. Saving a quarter of a million dollars a year in income taxes means nothing to me. I don't need the money. I have enough left to give me a happy affluent life."

Perhaps, but Helen Gurley Brown has said many times that she has a great fear of being left alone. Her husband pooh-poohs her apprehension. Her bank would continue to handle their bond account, consulting Helen about each decision. Her longtime brokerage firm would handle her stocks, but never receive discretionary powers. Helen—at least financially—would do just fine.

On the other hand, David Brown isn't so sure that *he'd* be able to stand on his own two financial feet. Forget about GE and IBM and J. P. Morgan. They pale in comparison to the best investment he ever made, he says. "That, of course, was Helen."

Ken and Daria Dolan

KEN AND DARIA DOLAN (he's 54, she's not telling) are the cohosts of "The Dolans," a daily talk show about money, syndicated to more than 100 stations over the WOR Radio Network. Married 26 years, both worked on Wall Street before hitting the airwaves. Residents of Connecticut, they spend a good portion of each summer in Maine. They are the parents of one daughter, Meredith.

L IKE THE BROWNS, KEN AND DARIA DOLAN COME FROM VERY DIF-
ferent financial backgrounds. But through their 26-year marriage, they've found they agree on most money issues. Good thing, too.
Their job depends on it.

Ken Dolan punches line three, putting Laurie, 28, on the air at the
WOR studios in midtown Manhattan. "I just got married!" the caller
from Queens tells Ken and his wife Daria, hosts of one of the country's
most successful financial talk shows. Unfortunately, Laurie tells them,
her new husband has cancer. He's been receiving Social Security disability income for some time and Medicaid takes care of his prescrip-
tions, which run about $900 to $1,000 a month.

Daria and Ken know what's coming before Laurie can even voice
the question. "Now that we're married," she asks, "are the disability
payments going to stop?"

"It isn't the disability payments I'm worried about," says Daria.
"He worked for those. He earned the right to collect. The problem is
Medicaid. The state is going to see that you have income and take a
much harder look at whether he has a right to that support."

As they go to commercial, Daria turns to her husband of 26 years:
"I certainly wasn't going to ask her this on the air," she says. "But I
wonder what they were thinking when they got married."

The Dolans face questions like this one every day. A transsexual
wanted to know what to do about keeping his credit report in order,
since it was under *her* former name. ("Not to worry," Ken reassured
him. "The true identifying factor is your social security number.") A
tax cheat wanted to know how to invest the $30,000 he'd saved by
not paying Uncle Sam. ("I wish I had caller ID," Daria fumed. "I'd
turn you over to the IRS right now.") And dozens of people each week
want to know whether they should keep money in their name or their
child's, what kind of life insurance to buy, and whether vending machines are a good business opportunity.

DON'T INVEST WHAT YOU CAN'T AFFORD TO LOSE

The advice they get from this couple, whose years of marriage are
matched by their years working on Wall Street, is conservative up and
down the line. The Dolans would no sooner encourage their readers to
speculate than they would do it themselves. "Our whole investment

philosophy is that if you can't afford to lose it, you shouldn't be in it in the first place," says Daria, who is about as bearish as they come. "I think we've fostered a false sense of security over the past number of years with stock prices. People think that they can only go higher. And consequently, everybody thinks that they can put all of their money into mutual funds that invest in stocks and they'll be fine. And to a degree, I'm furious with Wall Street for not giving them some of the warnings that really should be out there. Even a package of cigarettes comes with a health warning from the Surgeon General."

Daria has been expecting a turn in the market since 1994 and heartily admits that she's been about "as wrong as wrong can be." But she hasn't changed her tune. And since she takes day-to-day responsibility for the couple's personal portfolio, it's very conservatively invested—evenly split between carefully selected stocks and fixed-income securities. "I've found some good places to be, in particular," she says of her stock component. "But I don't think you should be broadly invested in stocks at this point. I see nothing wrong in paying some taxes and taking some winnings off the payroll."

In November of 1995, for example, tired of hearing her sources and colleagues bemoaning how dead retail was going to be that Christmas, she bought stock in the Gap for her Keogh account. After all, she walked past a Gap store on her way to work every morning. The stuff in the window didn't look half bad, and the place was always crowded. "It went nuts and ended up splitting," says Daria, who got out after reaping a 30 percent gain. "[Those kinds of plays] are one reason I think individuals need to do a little more individual stock investing, and place a little less faith in the infallibility of mutual fund managers."

LOOKING TO THE SECTORS

When it comes to sectors, REITs (real estate investment trusts; see page 63), mainly those that invest in hotels and certain health-care facilities, are a current favorite. "When I start reading in the newspaper that the Japanese are selling off all their United States properties, and that people who are buying houses are buying them knowing full well that they're never going to see a profit but they need a roof over their heads, that sounds like a pretty good market bottom to me," she explains. She also sees potential in oil and energy, due to ever-looming problems in the Middle East. "We never learned from our mistakes in 1973 as to oil production in this country," she says. "[In early fall Energy Secretary] Hazel O'Leary was talking about the possibility of dipping into the strategic oil reserves to sell a couple hundred million dollars worth of oil because it's not there in supplies. What are we going to do come January if we're falling down on strategic oil supplies now?"

And though she doesn't have much company of late, she's a bit of a gold bug. "I think that the entire threat to the international monetary fund—that Russia is going to unload all of this gold onto the world just to keep the price depressed—is overblown," she says. "I think you can manipulate the market, particularly in something like gold, for a degree of time because it's so small. But I think eventually the price is going to rise because it just isn't coming out of the ground fast enough to meet the demand."

The couple's fixed-income holdings are currently fairly short-term, a mix of 13-week Treasuries and two- to ten-year bonds, many of them municipal bonds, rated AA or better. Daria explains: "I think a lot of people avoided muni bonds because they were absolutely certain we were going to have a flat tax. And I think they made a disastrous mistake. Here they are still paying taxes on their income, when they could have been invested tax-free." As the Dolans advise their listeners, they fund their retirement plans to the maximum, they don't take fliers into venture capital, and aside from their two homes—their primary residence in Connecticut and a summer house in Maine—they're not currently invested in real estate. "I've just learned that I'm better at stocks and bonds," Daria says.

Daria's prowess in the market is largely due to the many mornings and evenings she spends poring over proxy statements and annual reports, while her spouse turns his hand to managing their other ventures—a successful newsletter, speaking engagements, and weekly appearances on "CBS This Morning." Most of these are joint ventures, funded by the media operation involved in exchange for a slice of the profits. Ken no more wants to weigh in on the buying and selling of individual stocks for their retirement account than Daria wants to pore over contracts for their new television show on the Nostalgia Channel. "I'm very detail oriented and not terribly creative, I'm sort of the drone," she says. "Ken dreams up all these wonderful partnerships for us. He figures out the marketing, and he's so busy he doesn't care to do detail work. I think that's the secret to our success."

The Dolans met on a blind date in 1970. They were introduced, serendipitously, by a prominent local radio personality who worked at a station on Long Island. Daria was a musical comedy actress. She'd played Miss Adelaide in a regional touring company of *Guys and Dolls* and later opened her own dinner theater in Sarasota, Florida. Ken, fresh out of the Navy, was a broker at Merrill Lynch.

Daria's parents hammered home two financial lessons: One, always save something. And two, never go into debt for something that you can't afford. "When I was working as a broker, I never bought stocks for them, only good quality bonds, because I knew they couldn't track the price on a daily basis in the paper," she recalls. "If I purchased a stock and it went down fifty cents, I knew I'd never hear the end of it."

Ken never had much of a home life. His mother died when he was seven, and his father remarried. He left his home in Dorchester, Massachusetts, at 15 and moved into a boardinghouse, paying his rent with jobs as a short-order cook and later as a sales clerk at a local department store. Some days all he could afford for lunch (and then again for dinner) was a dollar plate of cheese and crackers at a local bar. A diploma from Boston College followed by Officer's Candidate School should have helped him get his financial footing. Yet when he met Daria he was $3,000 in debt. A year later, when the couple married, Daria's father lent him the money to pay it off.

By the time their daughter was born in 1972, Ken was no longer racking up a balance on his MasterCard. It was 1984 when Ken had an opportunity to fill in as host of a financial radio call-in show on a small local station in Florida, where they were living at the time. A local talent agent happened to catch the broadcast and was impressed by Ken's breezy style. He called for a tape, which several handoffs later landed on a desk at NBC Radio Network. New York station WOR hired him to do a show every day in 1985, and a year later Daria joined him on WMCA. Today, the WOR Radio Network syndicates the Dolans' two-hour show to more than 160 stations around the country. *Newsweek* called them "the Fred and Ginger of the airwaves."

A MODEST LIFESTYLE

Success hasn't changed the couple much. They still take Metro North Railroad and the subway to work. Their idea of a vacation is a couple of weeks at their home in Maine. And when their daughter Meredith, a college admissions counselor at a Boston College, recently paid off her credit card balance, they boasted about it in their newsletter as some other proud parents might a new grandchild. Daria is most comfortable in leggings and sweatshirts. And while Ken admits to paying a pretty penny for custom-made suits, he's not putting on airs. At six foot four inches, 265 pounds, he just has a tough time buying off the rack.

In the opening two minutes of a recent broadcast, Ken used the phrases "Darn it all" and "Guess who's gonna learn stuff—me." A bit hokey, they admit. But Daria says there's a bigger point. "If we can get people to listen, really listen, by explaining complicated financial issues in two-syllable words, that's what we're going to do. There's too much lingo out there." Even consumer tips, given Dolan-style, seem somehow easier to stomach. Witness the following, from a 1996 issue of their newsletter: "[One] rotten credit deal to avoid comes from banks and finance companies," Daria writes. "You open your mailbox and out pops an unsolicited check in your name. Free money? Hardly. Cash it and watch the check turn into an installment loan right before your eyes. I've told my Visa issuer I'm closing my account if they ever send me one again. You should do the same."

Not surprisingly, their media partners play up their down-home image in their advertising campaigns. One print ad fairly sighed, "Finally. A husband and wife who agree about money." Strictly speaking, that's not entirely true. About 10 years ago, Daria admits, she wouldn't dream of making an investment without getting "an absolute gilt-edged guarantee" that her husband agreed with what she wanted to do. Due to his hesitations, she missed buying United Airlines at $41 as well as a couple of others. So from that point on, she's forged ahead on her own intuition. "If he absolutely looks me in the eye and says, 'not with my money you don't,' then of course I wouldn't," she says. "But he knows I'm not going to go off on some IPO that has no earnings and a president who's been indicted for god knows what."

Avid listeners have come to expect them to contradict each other on the air. Daria says it only happens once in a while. Ken says it happens more like once every other day or so. Every day is more like it. "What do you expect?" he asks. "We're husband and wife. We bicker. We talk—it's like being home."

"Once in a while I may be saying something and Ken comes in and goes off in another direction and I realize that what he's basically, very kindly, doing is correcting an error that I made on the air," says Daria. "I'm smart enough to keep my mouth shut and just let him do it."

Always the protector, Ken's guard goes up. "She's not wrong. She just misheard the question or I misheard the question. If it's anything we think is important enough to correct the other we will. But it's just between friends, between us and our audience."

Echoes his wife: "There's no prima donna here."

Susan Feniger and Mary Sue Milliken

SUSAN FENIGER AND MARY SUE MILLIKEN, ages 44 and 39 respectively, are the cohosts of the "Too Hot Tamales" show on the Television Food Network and the co-owners and chefs of Santa Monica's Border Grill. Both born and raised in the Midwest, Feniger and Milliken met in the kitchen of Chicago's Le Perroquet. Later each trained in France before joining forces to open City Cafe in Los Angeles. Milliken and her husband, an architect, have one son; Feniger lives in Santa Monica with her partner who is a professional singer/songwriter.

EXPERTS SAY MARRIAGE—AT ITS ROOTS—IS A FINANCIAL partnership. If that's true, business partners Susan Feniger and Mary Sue Milliken, hosts of the "Too Hot Tamales" show on the Television Food Network, are quite happily wed—despite their very different money styles.

As she sits down to take a break between tapings at the Television Food Network in Manhattan, celebrity chef Susan Feniger, 44, looks like she might have walked out of Woodstock. Her arms bedecked in bangles, she is wearing nine rings in her ears, another in her nose. Her charmingly raspy voice—still overwhelmed with the flat Midwestern tones of her youth—is the vehicle for strong opinions about everything from politics to movies to money, of course.

Her partner, Mary Sue Milliken, age 39, looks like she just stepped out of a salon, in her pastel chef's jacket and neat-as-a-pin bob. Even the wave of nausea that's swept over her after hours of cooking and tasting doesn't show in her Donna Reed composure. Unlike the blustery Feniger, Milliken fills her sentences with modest remarks. And she avoids wearing black at all costs.

So which of this dynamic team of not only television hosts but also the owners of California's successful Border Grill is more fiscally conservative? Say Feniger and you'd be right. She's got her IRA and Keogh money in an array of low-risk mutual funds selected by her financial planner at IDS. She wouldn't dare venture into individual stocks. And she's big on products like disability insurance and whole life.

"I have life insurance," Milliken chimes in a bit defensively.

"There's life insurance, and then there's *life insurance*," Feniger quibbles.

Milliken shrugs. She can't really take issue with that. "I'm not big on worrying about not being able to make money, so I don't have disability insurance or any of that kind of stuff. I always figure I can make more," says Milliken, whose investments are substantially more aggressive. Unlike her partner, she has an avid interest in the market. Since the money started flowing in a couple of years ago, she's spent some of her free time scouring for individual stocks to fill her portfolio. It helped that the first stock she bought was tech highflier Iomega. Her $500 investment was worth a cool $7,200 when she sold it nine months later. She's been watching Seattle Filmworks, a company that processes film from digital disk cameras, and also recently invested in the initial public offering of a hip, Southern California–based clothing company for which her husband, an architect, had done some work. Milliken held her stock less than a full year, but nearly tripled her money.

"I got inspired by the Beardstown Ladies thing," explains Milliken. "I started paying attention as a way to relax. I would sign onto America Online and check all the stocks that I might be following or watching and then—weirdly, I never thought this would happen to me—I started reading the business section. Well, not really reading it, but looking at it. And I started getting a feeling for companies that I believed in, or that I thought had interesting concepts. Like Seattle Filmworks. I think that's a real forward kind of company with a vision for the future. I'd invest in that before I'd invest in Ford—until they release the affordable electric car, that is."

DISPARATE SPENDING HABITS

Feniger, who'd rather spend her free time examining new business opportunities, believes investing is too much work for an uncertain reward. "I think about investing in things that are going to be safe and give me a return," says Feniger. About 65 percent of her assets are invested in the markets—with a sizable chunk in fixed income, the remainder in stocks and stock funds. "I'm really interested in making money through our business. But watching and researching investments, to figure out how to turn my money into more, is too much trouble."

Milliken also recently decided to sink much of her free cash into a real estate partnership with her sister, a real estate broker about an hour north of Los Angeles. They bought three houses this year, all in foreclosure. Milliken provides much of the capital, while her sister manages the properties, handles maintenance, and finds tenants; they each own 50 percent. "These are the kind of things I really like being able to do," Milliken explains. "I feel like I had the extra cash around and she had a lot of expertise. It's a 20-year investment that will end up paying me a few thousand dollars a month just when I need it."

No such speculation for Feniger. The money that isn't in her retirement funds or in the markets is in liquid money market accounts, where she can get at it to bankroll future restaurant opportunities. She's also much freer than her partner when it comes to spending, be it on travel, entertainment, or a lavish gift. Milliken admittedly has trouble parting with a buck.

"It takes major, major pushing to get her to spend $25 for a pair of jeans," Feniger smiles.

"I have been consciously trying to ease up and enjoy my money more, but it's a struggle for me," says Milliken. When they travel, Feniger is inclined to splurge on a drop-dead hotel where she can indulge in a manicure, massage, and a great meal at the end of the day. Milliken happily jets off to Singapore, London, or Chile, but she flies coach and shops for bargain hotels.

DIFFERENT LIFESTYLES

The gap in their spending styles is undoubtedly a result of the fact that Feniger grew up wealthy, Milliken middle-class. Both women traveled to work in France in the mid-1970s, but they couldn't have had more different experiences. To afford her stay abroad, Milliken sold her car for $4,000 and went to work at a restaurant in Paris. Her $250 monthly salary barely made the rent, so she kept a lid on expenses to make certain that $4,000 would cover a yearlong stay. When she left 12 months later, she had budgeted so tightly she still had $2,000 in the bank. Feniger didn't have to find a job that paid. She lived on her savings and found the hospitality of the French people overwhelming. It felt like she never had to pay for anything, she remembers.

Though her parents' money came in handy at times, Feniger—always something of a rebel—went to great lengths to make sure her parents couldn't hold it over her head. During her first year at Goddard College in Vermont, she dropped out of school, went to work for a cabinet maker, and moved in with her boyfriend, then called home with the news. Her parents let her know in no uncertain terms that they were less than thrilled. At the time being distanced from her family was painful, but Feniger believes it helped make her more independent financially. "It always seemed important to me never to allow my parents to control me because I needed their money. In reality, I've had a stronger relationship with them on many levels because of that," she explains.

"It's all relative," Milliken agrees. "You know, my mother thinks I spend like crazy. It's everybody's perspective."

So how do a miser and a free spender—a conservative investor and one who likes to take a risk—manage as business partners? Very successfully, it turns out. Milliken and Feniger each returned to the States from France in the early 1980s, landing in Los Angeles and opening a tiny hole-in-the-wall called City Cafe. In the early years, the partners used to disagree about expenses. Feniger wanted to pay bus-boys $5 an hour, Milliken slightly less. Feniger believed the partners should take home more of the profits at the end of each week than Milliken believed they should. Usually, they compromised.

It didn't take long to discover that their similarities were a lot more important to the business than their differences. For one, their common work ethic. The Tamales met more than 19 years ago at Chicago's Le Perroquet; they were the first women to land jobs in the well-regarded French kitchen, and they put in longer hours than most of the men. "In my first job," Feniger remembers, "the owner would be in at seven in the morning and I would go in and meet him because I wanted to learn and just be there. I probably didn't go on the clock until around four. But I don't feel like that's ever been any different for either of us. I feel like that's why we were so drawn to each other."

It was their hard work and their ability to manufacture a fabulous duck confit on a stove just one step up from a hot plate that made City Cafe a hit with LA's critics. Within a few years, they'd expanded into City Restaurant, a former carpet warehouse that was massive by comparison. They turned the original space into Border Grill and later moved to larger quarters in Santa Monica where it was named one of the best restaurants in America by *Gourmet* magazine. Other accolades followed. The California Restaurant Writers Association named the duo Chefs of the Year in 1988. *Cook's* magazine nominated their first cookbook, *City Cuisine* (Hearst, 1989) for Cookbook of the Year. And the *Los Angeles Times* named Border Grill one of the 40 best restaurants in the city.

TIGHTENING UP THE BUSINESS TO SURVIVE

Then came the nineties, an onslaught of earthquakes and brush fires, and Southern California's economy screeched to a halt. The recession hit the real estate industry and small businessmen first, but soon even Hollywood executives were tightening their belts. The establishments they favored—the aerobics palaces and beauty salons, the water bars and chic eateries—began wondering how long they'd be able to remain in business.

City Restaurant and Border Grill suffered along with the pack. The film industry executives who had flocked to the hip eateries for roast black cod and soft crab tacos, began doing business over lattes instead of full meals. Within months, the restaurants were operating in the red for the first time. Milliken and Feniger's first move was to stop drawing a salary. Then they obtained credit with their purveyors. Then, when those moves didn't solve the problem, they quickly went on a search for other solutions.

"It scared the hell out of us," Milliken remembers. One smart decision they made was to get on the phone to their colleagues and associates who had restaurants and pick their brains. Calls for advice went out across town and across the country, to Wolfgang Puck at Spago, Bob Spivak at the Daily Grill, and Rich Mehlman at Chicago's Lettuce Entertain You empire. It was Mehlman to the rescue. He put his controller and his chief negotiator on a plane for California. Over the next three days, the two executives helped Milliken and Feniger renegotiate their leases, they explained which staff members were expendable, and they suggested that Border Grill close for lunch, which was—when they looked closely at the numbers—a huge drain.

"It was brilliant," Milliken says. "All of a sudden, we saw the break-even point again."

"It got us back on track," Feniger agrees. "We just kept looking at our financial statements and we kept tightening in a way that we had never thought about before. All of a sudden, we saw how tight we could run. It was mind-boggling."

Months later, however, still in debt to their vendors, the duo realized that one final move was necessary. They put City Restaurant on the block. The buyer came through with enough cash to pay them all of their back salaries and to get them out of hock. Finally, the chefs were able to breathe.

They took a break. Border Grill, open for dinner seven nights a week, was nicely profitable and self-sustaining. Milliken spent some much-needed time with her husband and young son. Feniger began to think about new business opportunities. Their classes, taught in the kitchen of their restaurant, were drawing crowds. But it was the publication of their second cookbook, *Mesa Mexicana* (William Morrow, 1994) that launched them into the limelight—a pair of Julia Childs for the twenty-first century.

"Whenever we finished a class, people would always say to us: 'You're so good. You should get yourselves a TV show,'" Milliken remembers.

"So we said to ourselves, that's a good idea, let's do that," Feniger jumps in.

"But pretty soon, after a few years, we realized, we don't know how to get a television show. We don't even know how to take the first step. We couldn't figure out why no one was discovering us."

As luck would have it, a savvy publisher brought their book to the attention of the fledgling Television Food Network. A half-hour program they hosted about the book was so well received that TVFN's producers asked them back for a second shot, then offered them a series.

"Too Hot Tamales," which now airs up to four times a day, saw its television debut in 1995. TV viewers, many of whom don't even cook, tune in to watch Milliken and Feniger finish each other's sentences, offer hints on how to get the most juice out of a lemon half (stick a fork in it and twist), and cut the heat of a jalapeno (remove the seeds). The success of the program—*TV Guide* recently called it one of the 50 Great Things about Television Now, citing the chefs' "special chemistry"—has opened up a host of other opportunities for the team. They've just written another book, *Cooking with Too Hot Tamales* (William Morrow, 1997), and they now market a line of chiles under their own label. They even turned down lucrative deals—like the offer to consult to a major Mexican restaurant chain—when they feel the chemistry isn't right. A weekly radio show on NPR, which has actually been around for a couple of years, has done well also, quietly supplementing the success of the TV show: its audience has grown by thousands and it was nominated for a 1997 James Beard Foundation Award, the culinary world's equivalent of the Oscar.

Feniger, who says she always believed she'd make a ton of money, is eagerly looking ahead. "We're looking at expanding a Latin American concept that would range through [the cuisines of] Spain and Brazil, all of Latin America," she says excitedly, explaining that initial plans call for four or five locations in Southern California with another in Las Vegas. They're also looking at locations for another City Restaurant in the Los Angeles area. Financing, she says, will likely come 100 percent from investors, with the Tamales receiving a cut for providing their concept and their name.

Will it be a good investment? The success of the original City Restaurant is one good benchmark; it returned investors' money in less than two years. "You have to look really good and hard at the people who are running a restaurant, not only how well they run it, but what kind of charisma they have and what kind of passion they have for serving people and creating something really new and different in the way of either the food or service experience," Milliken says.

"People who are successful that way are the people that investors should try to key into," Feniger chimes in. "I think about Bob Spivak and how passionate he is. And Rich Mehlman. And Doug Cavanaugh who owns Ruby's Diners. They're all really passionate, honest, charismatic leaders. That's how I look at all of my investments," she continues. "For example, my advisor at IDS—I'm looking more at him than I'm looking at what each investment is. I'm looking at whether I trust him and if he's smart."

Her partner was shaking her blonde head in agreement. "Absolutely. Someone straightforward. Someone honest. Someone you can believe in," says Milliken. "You want to look for the next Wolfgang Puck."

Feniger stops and faces her. "Let's hope we *are* the next Wolfgang Puck," she says emphatically.

Milliken rolls her eyes. "I know," she says, as if she's gotten this pep talk 100 times before. "I know."

WHEN IT'S *YOUR* MONEY . . .

ONE BIG PROBLEM WITH MONEY SPATS IN A RELATIONSHIP, NOTES radio psychologist Dr. Joy Browne, is that the fights really aren't about money at all. They're about different styles and different power issues that aren't money-related at their roots. That's why if you can remove money from the mix by coming to easy-to-follow terms about how financial matters get sorted out, you'll go a long way toward solving your real problems.

For many years, couples believed that opening a joint bank account was logical after a trip to the altar. But with women in the workforce and 50 percent of marriages ending in divorce, experts agree pooling all of your assets isn't the best idea anymore, especially if you have dissimilar spending or investment styles.

Instead, try three different accounts—yours, mine, and ours. Into the common pot goes enough to cover the household expenses, like the mortgage, your child's summer camp fees, and food. After the bills are paid, another chunk goes into a short-term investment account, to cover next summer's vacation or the private school tuition looming a few years out, and the final piece goes into long-term saving. Discrepancies in income can be handled by dividing all of the contributions proportionally. If one partner brings home four times as much as the other, all bills get divided into five pieces, with the higher earner paying four-fifths and the person making less paying one-fifth. Anything left stays in the yours or mine accounts as discretionary funds. "If you're a strict saver and you want to use your play money to buy zero coupon bonds, that's fine," explains Browne. "If the other person wants to buy a Porsche, that's fine too."

One oft-cited advantage to a three-account plan is that it makes it much easier to buy your partner a surprise gift. But there are other more substantial benefits, the first being in estate planning. The government gives each individual what's called a "unified credit," a tax credit that allows each person to pass along $600,000 in assets to someone else during one's lifetime or at death without having to pay hefty estate or gift taxes on the transfer. That means that a married couple is allowed to pass along a full $1.2 million in assets. But because many married couples keep all assets in joint name, the assets move to the surviving spouse at the first death, and half of that generous gift from Uncle Sam is lost forever. Keeping a substantial chunk of assets in the name of each spouse is a fairly simple maneuver that can save your heirs hundreds of thousands of dollars.

Having money in your name alone will also make it easier to get a credit card issued just to you, if you divorce or your spouse passes away. Many financial advisers, however, believe it's a mistake to wait for one of those two things to happen. "Just as with bank accounts, you should have a card in your own name, for which you get your own bills and pay them out of your own checking account," says Dee Lee, a Massachusetts financial adviser. "This is not something you need to be thinking about when you're under the stress of a divorce or death. It's much easier to handle beforehand."

Couples who have different spending styles will also likely have dissimilar investing styles. Fortunately, because IRAs, Keoghs, and 401(k) accounts are by their nature individual accounts, the easiest way to handle dissimilar philosophies is for each person to invest as that individual sees fit, says Lee. "It's very simple to agree that you invest yours, I'll invest mine, and we'll compromise on the dollars we invest together," she says, explaining that sometimes simply starting to talk about investing results in a shift in perspective. "A lot of people start out not wanting to take any risk. Either they didn't grow up with money, or they just want to accumulate, accumulate, accumulate. The more I can educate them, usually the more risk they're willing to take."

An easy way to get the dialogue started is by tracking both your spending and your investing with the help of a computer program like Intuit's Quicken or Microsoft Money. These are both easy to use, don't require a lot of time each month, and enable both people in a relationship to keep their eyes on the financial ball.

Once the conversation is rolling, experts say that keeping it going is crucial to maintaining a healthy relationship. Financial planner Lee says that quite often clients enter a marriage with similar money styles but over time, as they decide that the woman will stay home to raise the children or that they'll downshift to improve their lifestyle, one becomes the spender and the other becomes the saver. Then former nonissues such as how much to spend on the in-laws at Christmas become a big deal. When people get to the point where they're no longer discussing the money issues—when they're sitting in the car with their shoulders square and their eyes straight ahead—it's time to find some professional help.

"I tell my clients, 'I am not only your financial adviser. I am your financial mediator. If you need me to be, I'll be your financial nag,'" says Lee. "But these are big issues that can't be ignored, because you end up covering up other problems. Again, people who are either too tight with money or generous to a fault sometimes have another problem and it's not just the money. They're using money as a cry for attention for some other thing."

LAST WORD: LIVING IN SIN

THOUGH THE DIVORCE LAWS ARE FAR FROM PERFECT, THE piece of paper governing a married couple's relationship goes at least part of the way toward assuring that should a husband and wife part company, they'll each get a fair share. (Your license at least gives you credibility to battle it out in court.) If you're simply cohabitating, you're on shakier ground. Ralph Warner, founder of Nolo Press and coauthor of *The Living Together Kit* (Nolo Press, 1997), suggests you pay particular attention to the following sticky areas:

- **Household finance.** Before you buy a house together, you need to decide who's going to own it, says Warner. Some couples may want to own the property 50–50 because each contributed half the down payment and they're splitting the mortgage. Others may agree on a 60–40 or 75–25 split. In still other couples, one person has ready cash and the other has the skill to fix it up, so they set up a system where over time the laborer's sweat equity buys actual equity. Most important is to put the agreement down on paper in the form of a contract, Warner says. Decide if you want to own the property as joint tenants (in which case if one dies, the other receives the entire thing) or as tenants in common (if one dies, the estate receives the value of the decedent's share).

- **Income disparity.** While you're getting along, it may not seem to matter that you're supporting your significant other through law school. If you split, however, you may be sorry you didn't put a financial agreement down on paper, especially if the graduate decides to take the new six-figure salary and hit the road. For two situations Warner suggests some sort of written agreement, even if it's simply to say what's mine is mine, what's yours is yours. First, if one person gives up a job and moves to be with the other. And second, if one person is putting the other through school or vice versa. "It helps to have on paper, 'I'll go to school first, then you'll go,'" says Warner. "Just in case the relationship falls apart before the second tuition is paid."

- **Joint accounts and credit cards.** Steer clear, Warner says. Everything is so legally simple if you keep your money separate, he explains; there is no legal obligation of one to pay the debts of the other.

- **A will.** If you want your companion to receive any of your assets, you'll need to specify that in your will. Although each state has laws that pass assets along to a spouse if you die intestate, a significant other isn't similarly protected.

Chapter 9

THE COLLECTORS

Raoul Felder • Emeril Lagasse

"The best time to buy is at the end of the auction, when everyone is tired or leaving, particularly on a rainy weekday night."

—*Raoul Felder*

For Andy Warhol, it was cookie jars. For Jacqueline Kennedy Onassis, jewelry. And, as you've read, modern art for Charles Schwab and sports memorabilia for Walter Payton.

Some collectors consider their pieces a major portion of their investment portfolio. Divorce attorney Raoul Felder, for example. His office is littered with his collections—fine works of art, antique pens by the dozen, small sculptures. He's had better luck growing his money by purchasing smart pieces than he has, say, stocks or real estate. Celebrity chef Emeril Lagasse invests in wine because it's something he understands far better than the machinations of the market. It's not unusual for him to reap a 30 percent gain on a single case.

You can't count on such returns, however. That's why financial planners are decidedly against collecting as an investment. "Buy what you love," advises Massachusetts financial planner Dee Lee. "And don't count on being able to get your money out." Then if you do happen to make money—as both Felder and Lagasse have—she says: "It'll come as a welcome surprise."

Raoul Felder

RAOUL FELDER, 63, is one of the country's foremost matrimonial attorneys. Over the years, his clients have included Robin Givens, Larry Fortensky, Iolanda Quinn (the former Mrs. Anthony), and Jody Carson (Johnny's first wife). He is the author (or coauthor) of a number of books and articles including Getting Away with Murder *(Simon & Schuster, 1996), an examination of spousal abuse, and* Jackie Mason and Raoul Felder's Guide to New York and Los Angeles Restaurants *(Dove, 1996). He collects art, watches, and antique cars.*

OVER THE YEARS, DIVORCE ATTORNEY RAOUL FELDER HAS HAD A love-hate relationship with traditional investments. Twenty-five years ago, one of his clients, a professional investor, advised him to put his money into petroleum stocks. Felder took a look at some charts his client put together to indicate where the oil was expected to flow next, and invested $25,000. Three weeks later when the value of his shares hit $40,000, he sold. He was overjoyed until about a week later when he got a subpoena from the SEC. His large gain and short time horizon had raised a red flag in the commission's computer. "I had to explain to them that they needed to call my client, that he makes these charts for a living, and that I invested on a tip," Felder says, shuddering at the thought. "It wasn't worth the money I made. Now, not a week goes by that I don't get five tips from clients. I would never take one."

Then there was the time he bought an investment product from a broker who was extremely persistent in his cold calling. From the moment Felder purchased it, the value plummeted. And the phone-friendly broker stopped returning his calls. "At one point he refused to tell me what I had in the account," Felder remembers. "Of course I had him on tape by then." Felder sued the broker and agreed to an arbitration hearing to settle the case. Though it's still unbelievable to him, he lost. "An arbitration is basically a weighted proceeding," he says. "You've got arbitrators who are being paid for—and want to be reappointed by—brokerage houses. And you've got a limited number of brokerage houses. So the cast of characters remains the same, but yet the poor guy who got suckered is the one who loses." Felder smiles wickedly. "At least this broker was subsequently indicted over something else."

UNPLEASANT EXPERIENCES LEAVE HIM SKEPTICAL ABOUT THE MARKET

The experiences have left him with a bad taste in his mouth. He believes that if he pays close attention to trends and follows up with some homework, he could do just fine in stocks. But he's busy. He gets distracted. Besides, he says, who wants to bother in a world where you never know exactly what sort of business a company is running. "It's a morality question," he explains. "Very often, you're investing money over the broken backs of other people, because the heads of companies—of American companies—are money-oriented to the degree that they don't care what happens to anybody else. At one end is Kathie Lee Gifford. Somebody unknown to her may be exploiting somebody else."

Unfortunately, for Felder, his luck with stocks may have been bad, but his luck with real estate has been even worse. "I have exquisitely bad taste in real estate," he chuckles. For many years, he lived in a Manhattan apartment at 750 Park Avenue, on the corner of 72nd Street. The year after he moved, it went co-op. The same thing happened with his new apartment, at 123 East 75th; Felder moved and the building converted. "You must appreciate," he explains, "each time that happened, I lost hundreds of thousands of dollars because, no longer being a tenant, I couldn't buy at the insider price." He moved from 75th to a much bigger place, an entire floor at 815 Fifth Avenue. But lousy elevator service drove him nuts, so he didn't stay. When this building went co-op, again only a few months later, Felder vowed never to move again. "There I really lost money," he says shaking his head. "God, I probably lost $750,000 to a million dollars."

THE SAFETY OF T-BILLS

That's why these days the flamboyant attorney is taking most of the hefty fees he earns representing high-profile clients like Robin Givens,

Larry Fortensky, Iolanda Quinn, and Jody Carson and putting them where he knows they'll not only be safe, but above government scrutiny: in Treasury bills. "Everybody makes fun of that," Felder shrugs. "These days, probably, I'm losing money every year. But who cares? I've got plenty of money. I buy whatever I want. And I didn't have heart attacks when the market went down in 1987."

The rest of his money—and there's plenty to spare—he puts into collectibles. Before you even enter Felder's Madison Avenue office, you know you're with someone who has a thing for memorabilia. One door is emblazoned with Sam Spade's moniker; the other with Philip Marlowe's. In the colorful waiting room is an amusement park "Love Tester" to "Measure Your Sex Appeal," and one of the hot dish carousels from the original Horn & Hardart's Automat. A Botero painting hangs on the wall, near an Al Hirschfeld caricature of Felder and articles on the lawyer from *Forbes*, *GQ*, and *Vanity Fair*.

IF YOU INVEST IN ART, BUY WHAT YOU LIKE

Felder's L-shaped inner sanctum, with a working fireplace in one wall, plays host to one collection of more than 100 pens, another of two dozen eagle figurines, a StairMaster, and—oh, yes—a Picasso. The latter piece is representative of several of Felder's rules for investing in art. "First," he says, "buy what you like. After all, you have to look at it." Rule number two is to buy the lesser works of greater artists. In addition to the Picasso, Felder has acquired similarly "lesser" paintings by Willem de Kooning and George Grosz. "Picasso can't go off the radar screen," he explains. "You can say, he painted that. There's not much of a painting to it, but it's still worth X dollars." His best investment was a painting by Jean Michel Basquiat that he purchased for $3,000. "It was an angry, crazy thing," he recalls. "And I had the good fortune to have him die right after I bought it. I sold it for 20 times what I paid for it: $60,000."

His strategy for buying classic cars is similar. "The car has to be something you'd use," says Felder of his purchases, including a 1953 Plymouth convertible ("a big, growling car"), several old Thunderbirds, and, once, a hearse. He has amassed a collection of 120 antique watches, and says he's never lost money on one. "In fact," he says, pondering his luck, "I've never lost money on any of my collectibles. I buy expensive suits, and lose money on those." (Maybe not for long, however. Posing recently in an ad for Manhattan clothier Paul Stuart netted him a freebie.)

A CAREFULLY-HONED AUCTION STRATEGY

Many of Felder's purchases are made at auction houses. When the New York press reports on who showed up at a Sotheby's or Christie's opening, Felder's name often makes the list. His auction buying methodology boils down to a few simple rules: Get the catalog early. Go see the merchandise in person; you can't get a perfect idea of size or color from a photograph. Don't bid on the telephone. ("It's an abstraction, all those people shouting numbers," he says.) And remember that, especially in a state like New York, tax and commissions are going to add 20 percent to your purchase price. "The best time to buy is at the end of the auction, when everyone is tired or leaving, particularly on a rainy weekday night."

Felder was at Christie's, paddle in hand, as an estate of movie memorabilia made it to the block in 1997. "It was all fourth-rate stuff," he shrugs. Nonetheless, when the bidding started for *The Maltese Falcon*, one of four original copies in existence, Felder sprang into action. As the price rose from $100,000 to $150,000, then $200,000 and $300,000, he stuck with it. He raised his paddle again to bid $400,000, then was hit with an overwhelming case of buyer's remorse. "What if I end up buying it?" he thought to himself. "Thank goodness, Harry Winston got it."

Felder's desire to spend his days surrounded by beautiful things stems from a childhood with next to nothing. He grew up in the Williamsburg section of Brooklyn, in an area that is now overwhelmed by housing projects and shuttered buildings. In the 1940s and 1950s, he explains, there wasn't the sort of polarization between rich and poor that you find today. Being poor didn't mean a dangerous life; it meant eating provolone sandwiches when he wanted a piece of meat. And it has left its mark. "Money has always been a central theme in my life," he says. "I knew that a life without money was nothing."

Felder worked his way through college, then New York University law school, before taking a government job with the U.S. Department of Justice. But it wasn't until he went into practice for himself that he saw his income leapfrog. Today, he hosts a weekly television show with comedian Jackie Mason.

His writing career has also taken off. Felder has two new books on the market, an examination of spousal abuse called *Getting Away with Murder* (Simon & Schuster, 1996) and a volume of restaurant reviews called *Jackie Mason and Raoul Felder's Guide to New York and Los Angeles Restaurants* (Dove, 1996). And his reference manual called *The Encyclopedia of Matrimonial Clauses* (New York Law Publishing, 1990) is a perennial legal bestseller. Most of his pay, Felder says, comes from lucrative advances and an occasional article; *Penthouse* recently purchased one for $10,000. "If I didn't buy any new shirts or eat well, I could live on the writing," he quips.

A DEBT-FREE EXISTENCE

In fact, Felder could easily retire. He has no debt. There is no mortgage on his Sutton Place apartment or vacation home in East Hampton. No credit card debt or car loans. The pleasure of a debt-free existence is one lesson he's tried to pass along to his two children. His daughter, director of artists and repertoire at Sony Music, has taken the message to heart. "She's analytical, because she deals with money in her job," Felder says. His son, a freelance comic book writer, formerly with Marvel Comics, seems to have ignored Papa's advice. "My son is going to have to be very rich someday," Felder says. "He's nonmaterialistic to such a degree that it suffocates any other feeling about money. That's terrific if you're Picasso. And I hope he turns out to be that way. But I think he's going to have to find a balance." He stops. "Funny. I got more *his* way as I got older."

ESTATE TAXES TAKE AWAY THE BENEFITS OF WEALTH

Unfortunately, the kids aren't going to get much of a leg up financially from their old man. Felder says he plans on leaving each a relatively small sum, enough to purchase a two-bedroom apartment and to live comfortably, but not more than that. The reason? Estate taxes. "It's not enough that they tax money when you earn it?" Felder questions.

"They have to tax it again at death? There's something that doesn't make sense about that. There's no justification for it." That's why, he believes, America's wealthiest dynasties are falling apart. "In England, you own the duchy of this or the duchy of that. Take Marlboro—the Duke of Marlboro owns the whole thing. In America the wealth dissipates. Within two or three generations, you just have thirty-five rich people.

"That's why if something makes me feel good, I do it," Felder says. "I tell my children to marry a wealthy person who will work too, and that's it. There won't be anything left. I'm going to spend it all."

Emeril Lagasse

EMERIL LAGASSE, 40, host of the Television Food Network's "Essence of Emeril," is New Orleans's preeminent chef. Lagasse, who trained under Commander's Palace matriarch Ella Brennan, has two restaurants in the city's warehouse district: Emeril's and NOLA. Originally from Massachusetts, he attended culinary school at Johnson & Wales University, and is a skilled percussionist. He is also an avid collector of wines.

PERHAPS A DECADE OR TWO DOWN THE ROAD, RESTAURATEUR AND television chef Emeril Lagasse will share Felder's devil-may-care attitude when it comes to making or losing a buck. Today he's much more serious, much less confident. "I probably am one of the *worst* people you're going to interview," says Lagasse, normally quite a smooth talker. He's won rave reviews for "The Essence of Emeril," his show on the Television Food Network, which 25 million loyalists tune to each week. *Time* magazine named it one of TV's 10 Best for 1996. And his catchphrases— "Bam!" and "Kick it up a notch!"—have become so much a part of the vernacular that fans shout them to him on crowded streets.

But over coffee at New York's Waldorf-Astoria hotel, Lagasse is decidedly flustered about discussing his money. You see, he doesn't really believe in the markets. Save for a few token dollars stashed in an IRA, he has no stocks, no bonds, no mutual funds. He has no CDs, no tax shelters, no fancy trusts. He doesn't believe in handing his money over to a professional for management. "I have a bit of a different philosophy about money," he explains.

INVEST IN SOMETHING YOU KNOW

Philosophy number one is investing in the familiar. "My tax attorney and my CPA are always saying, 'Emeril, why don't you take X number of dollars and go with the big boys?' " he says. "I'm not really educated in that area. I'd rather buy what I know."

For example, he has bought New Orleans real estate. Since moving to the Big Easy, Lagasse has lived and worked in what is known as the Warehouse District. Today his two New Orleans–based restaurants, Emeril's and NOLA, are a slim eight blocks from each other within that district, with Lagasse's residence in between. Four years ago, the chef and his wife, Tari, a restaurant designer, purchased a former law firm's headquarters built in the late 1800s that had been foreclosed on by a local bank. They cut a deal for a fraction of its value, moved in, and have been restoring the place—paycheck by paycheck—to its former elegance. Since then, the couple has purchased three other historic Warehouse properties—one home and two warehouses which are home to the restaurant business. Lagasse believes the investments will take time to show a considerable profit, but that they'll come around. "I'm very silent," he says. "I'm not a visible landlord and this is not an income-driven investment, at least for right now. I'm doing it because I believe, in this neighborhood, the value of the property will appreciate."

INVESTING IN WINE

He's also made a sizable investment in wine. In his home cellar, Lagasse has a very reasonable 500 bottles, in his cellar at Emeril's there are another 1,600, but in storage throughout the city, he has another 40,000. "I'm a nut about wine," he says. "My CPA thinks I'm crazy because instead of taking $25,000 or $50,000 and writing a check to put it in the market, I'll go and invest it in wine. But to me, wine is not a hobby. It's a very serious love of mine. The art of food and wine—the pairing of food and wine—is about as infectious in me as it can get in anybody."

And as profitable. Lagasse purchased around 100 cases of 1982 Bordeaux, some as futures, some when they were released in 1990. It was a $30,000 investment and Lagasse made it without blinking. When the reviews came out raving about the exceptional wines of that year,

Lagasse sold them all at an average profit of 30 percent, slightly less when you deduct his costs—storage, maintenance, a caretaker to turn the bottles. That's not to say he *always* beats most mutual funds with his purchases. "It can be very tricky," he admits. "You never know who you're buying from. Let's say you buy at an auction; there are no returns. But I have, over the years, acquired some really good knowledge, and I have some outstanding people in my organization—including one master sommelier—who really know wine. When we go to shop for wine, whether it's at an auction, whether it's at a buying in France, whether it's at a wholesaler, or whether it's somebody's private collection, we do a tremendous amount of research, as much as we can, to cut the risk. And if I get back 10 percent or 20 percent or 30 percent, to me it's a better return than if I had given somebody a chunk of money and said, 'Put me in some sort of fund or stock,' because I understand it better."

PUTTING MONEY BACK INTO THE BUSINESS

The rest of Lagasse's money is in something he knows even better than real estate and wine. It's in his businesses. "I'm comfortable and educated in my business," he explains. "That's why I keep taking all of my money and putting it right back in."

Lagasse was born with a passion for food. At age 10, he was working after school and on weekends at a Portuguese bakery in his Massachusetts neighborhood, washing pots and pans for a dollar an hour. He turned down a college scholarship in music (Lagasse is a skilled percussionist) to pay his way through culinary school at Johnson & Wales University. After graduation, he floated around for four years, stopping briefly at restaurants in Boston, New York, and Philadelphia before landing in 1984 at the famed Commander's Palace in New Orleans.

Ella Brennan, Commander's beloved matriarch, had more than 40 years in the restaurant business at the time she hired Lagasse. Spending more than seven years in her kitchen, Lagasse got her sage advice for free. "She and her brother Dick really paved the way to my understanding that we're in business. We're not running a hobby. If we really wanted to run a hobby, then we should go and build airplanes or puzzles or railroad trains," says Lagasse, who believes that the reason that most restaurants fail is that their owners don't take the business end seriously enough. "They don't understand how to balance the food, the service, the decor, the personality of running a staff, and the whole aspect of what it takes to run a business, whether it's as simple as paying taxes or setting up a great health insurance program."

This was the philosophy Lagasse took with him when he decided to open his own shop in New Orleans. It wasn't a good time for the restaurant business, especially in that part of the country. Plagued by oil and gas woes, the local economy was suffering. According to Lagasse, not a single restaurant with staying power had opened its doors in the prior five years. He found himself turned down for funding by every bank in the city limits. Finally, Emeril wrote a business plan for his new restaurant, and got a personal introduction to the officers at Whitney Bank. They gave him $500,000 to open his restaurant providing he plunked down the remaining $250,000 himself. Lagasse went on a tear, selling everything he owned of value—including two Porsches—to hold up his end of the deal.

HANDS-ON MANAGEMENT STYLE

Lagasse opened the restaurant on a shoestring. He couldn't afford to pay people for the necessary market research and demographics, the menu analysis, or payroll analysis. So he did the work himself, from a one-room office inside his house. He tasted the complete 90-bottle wine list, hired the staff, and on the day before the restaurant opened its doors, composed the menu. "It was the easiest thing for me to do," he says. Emeril's opened in 1990 to rave reviews from local critics. By 1991, it had achieved national acclaim, including being named Restaurant of the Year by *Esquire* magazine.

In the restaurant industry, you're either a mainstay, like Commander's Palace in New Orleans or Peter Luger's in New York, or you're a flash in the pan—a place that opens to phenomenal reviews but can't keep the crowds coming back. Lagasse was determined that Emeril's would be the former, and he knew the key to achieving that goal was finding the right people to run the operation. So he hired carefully by asking his employees to recommend their former colleagues and friends. One teen came to Emeril asking for a job. Lagasse gave him an option—if he would stay in high school, Lagasse would teach him how to cook. Today, he's Emeril's head chef.

Through the years, he promoted from within, putting busboys who wanted to become waiters, or waiters who wished to become cooks, through a series of multiple-choice exams to prove they understood what the restaurant is all about. They were asked, "What is the house wine?" and "What was Emeril's before it became this restaurant?" He bought loyalty with IRA plans, health insurance, Sundays off, and paid vacations. And when he had more qualified employees at Emeril's than he could put to active use, he expanded, opening the more rustic NOLA, a few blocks away.

When the staff outgrew NOLA, he opened Emeril's New Orleans Fish House in the MGM Grand Hotel in Las Vegas, sending a few dozen of his most valuable players to Nevada, several with an equity stake, as he'll do when he opens a site at Universal Studios in Florida in early 1998. And just 13 months after opening the Las Vegas restaurant, he was readying for its first major overhaul. Why? Again to keep his staff. Lagasse's rationale is that if the customers stop coming, his well-trained staff will take their skills to a house that is more happening, where the tips are better, where the atmosphere is more fun. His goal is to provide that under his roof.

"When the staff squeaks, someone has to give it some oil," says Lagasse, who has clearly adopted some Southern expressions despite holding onto his Massachusetts accent. "Since day one, the growth of this business has been driven and directed by the staff. We opened NOLA because we could only have so many chefs, so many sous chefs, so many managers, so many general managers, so many waiters, so many chief cooks. So I had to make the decision that if I didn't want to put a revolving door in the front of the restaurant and start losing key people—which costs a lot of money—that we were going to grow. But you've got to drive it. We're not the automobile industry. Every year all of our costs are dragging up: rent, insurance, liabilities, payroll—they all get more expensive. There is nobody out there who is year after year doing 5 to 10 percent more business, particularly with all the competition, so you have to expand."

NO RAISES OR BONUSES FOR THE OWNER

Lagasse is putting so much back into his businesses, in fact, that he isn't padding his own pockets much. Though management in his organization took home bonuses of more than $100,000 total in 1996, he has yet to write himself a bonus check or to give himself a raise. He believes that there are better uses of the money. "It's funny," he says. "Charlie Trotter (see page 102) and I were just saying it's amazing how the general population thinks these restaurateurs are making tons and tons of money. They don't think of the investment. It takes a tremendous investment to keep evolving so that stagnation doesn't set in, whether it's the physical look, or the mentality in service of the kitchen or the dining room or whatever. To have people with you for five years or six years, it costs money to do that. I don't get anything back for having sixty place settings in the warehouse—in case the customer breaks one or the busman breaks one. I have no insurance on that stuff. There's nothing coming in for pilferage and breakage and loss."

And yet, come the fall of 1997, he'll be writing a check to Cornell University for his elder daughter's freshman year tuition. Where will that money come from? "Versatility," says Lagasse with a smile. Over the past couple of years, he has published two successful cookbooks and is working on a third, and he has taped more than 500 "Essence of Emeril" television shows for TVFN, cable's food network. "Essence" is the network's highest-rated show—last year its 20 million viewers actually registered on the Nielsen ratings, something few cable shows achieve—and was also named one of *Time* magazine's Top Ten Best television shows of 1996. All of these ventures pad his pocket. But they also keep people coming into his eateries. "Instead of doing 500 charity events a year to get the restaurant's name out, this is what I do for exposure."

So Lagasse, who just turned 40, will keep—as he likes to say—kicking it up a notch. He'll keep investing, as he's done to this point, in himself. There's a fifth restaurant in the planning stages, which he won't give details about just yet. A Christmas cookbook will be next. There may be packaged foods. And "The Essence of Emeril" has gone live, with plans to take the show on the road to Chicago, Philadelphia, and a few other cities.

"People say to me, 'Any day now, I know you're going to go through a midlife crisis and buy the fancy sports car and go through a bunch of other changes,'" says Lagasse. "I drive a truck. I'm a simple person. For years, I've been advised by people to buy stocks, to change my investing habits. But I haven't really met anyone that I've trusted enough to give them my money and to take some chances. For me, I'd rather open another restaurant. At least that way I'm controlling my destiny. So for the most part, I know where we're gonna go.

"But you know, that's the philosophy I live by. Today, when I got up, my only morning thought was: How am I going to do a little bit better than I did the day before?"

WHEN IT'S *YOUR* MONEY . . .

UNLESS YOU'VE GOT MORE MONEY THAN YOU KNOW WHAT TO DO with, collectibles—like venture capital investments—should account for no more than 5 to 10 percent of your portfolio. They may be fun, but they are also illiquid, difficult to sell, and if you or your estate needs the money, you'll likely have to go through a dealer or auctioneer to unload them—coughing up 20 percent of the selling price as a brokerage fee.

Collectibles are also subject to more of a roller-coaster ride in their markets than traditional investments, says Massachusetts financial planner Dee Lee. "During the eighties, for example, everyone wanted oriental rugs and antiques," she says. "Then the market for oriental rugs went way down and it's taken 15 years to come back. Likewise, a piece of jewelry that you thought was exquisite may be sold for its parts rather than for the whole." That's why Lee prefers to think of collectibles as a great hobby, but an inappropriate investment. "Everyone should have play money, and if you want to put that into collectibles, that's fine," she says.

Keeping those guidelines in mind, however, there's no harm in taking that 5 to 10 percent and hoping for a big score. A handful of experts helped us identify a few areas of collectibles that have had increased interest of late. The greater demand, of course, is driving at least some prices way up. Whether the pieces you buy will appreciate depends on how smart you are about your purchases.

Jewelry: Particularly if you believe you'll be buying at auction, jewelry is a hot item, and not just Jackie O's famous pearls. "We're seeing great growth in our jewelry sales across the spectrum of the market, from our lesser expensive 'arcade pieces' to the very top," says Matthew Weigman, senior vice president of Sotheby's, the New York auction house. One reason for the interest is that at many auction houses you can buy pieces from Tiffany, Van Cleef & Arpels, and David Webb under one roof; you can buy vintage pieces and new pieces. New York diamond merchant Jonathan Birnbach of Fullcut Manufacturers is more cautious, however. You're competing with professional buyers at nearly all jewelry auctions, he points out, and it's very difficult for the layman to get a good deal.

Photography: The market for collecting fine photography has been called a mile wide and an inch deep. More people are participating every year, which has been driving prices up faster than in just about any other segment of the art world, but they're only buying a few pieces each. Why? Photographs are affordable. "Photographs are works of art you can live with," Weigman points out. "They can enhance your lifestyle, they're not tremendously expensive—a few thousand dollars—and in the end they're still worth what you paid for them or more, assuming you bought wisely."

Celebrity Memorabilia: It seems that more and more celebrity-owned items are coming up for sale each year, most on the auction block. On the heels of the fabulously successful Jacqueline Kennedy Onassis auction, Sotheby planned to auction off Andrew Lloyd Webber's wine cellar, and the belongings—furniture, paintings, and, again, wine—from three of Pamela Harriman's residences. Competitor Christie's announced a sale of Princess Diana's gowns. Whether merchandise appreciates depends on the celebrity, and the hype around the sale. Andy Warhol's collection has done well in the aftermarket, but shortly after the Onassis sale the *New York Times* ran a story about how much of the merchandise wasn't worth the price paid.

Collectibles: Since the late 1800s, there has been a market for collectibles that are sold directly to the public—items like plates, dolls, figurines, and ornaments. According to Peggy Veltri, executive director of the Collectors Information Bureau, in Barrington, Illinois, buying smart means purchasing pieces that are only released in limited numbers. These are usually called "club pieces" by the manufacturers, Veltri explains. Only if you join the manufacturer's club are you allowed to purchase them. Then as the entire line becomes more popular and more collectors enroll, these new members go to the secondary market to purchase pieces that they missed—at a premium. Swarovski crystal has done very well on the secondary market, as have the lithographs of artist Thomas Kinkaid (one called "Beyond Autumn Gate," issued at $915 in 1993, now goes for $3,800), according to the CIB. The Walt Disney collection has had mixed success. But the secondary market for Franklin Mint merchandise—with the exception of the company's plates—is not well established, in Veltri's opinion, and the market for Danbury Mint merchandise is "not established at all."

LAST WORD: A FINE WINE

L IKE STOCKS, WINE IS IN THE MIDDLE OF A "BULL MARKET," says Sotheby's Matthew Weigman. In fact, there's practically no other collectible that has seen so much growth in interest over the past half decade. If you're considering opening a cellar in your basement, it's good to know that there are only a few keys to buying well. Mark Golodetz, a New York-based wine writer and consultant, set the record straight:

- **Get to Know Your Retailer.** You want to be on a first-name basis with the best retailer in town—in New York that might mean a salesperson at Zachy's, in Santa Ana, California, one at The Wine Shop, or in Chicago at Sam's. Look for a merchant who travels the globe to taste wine in person. You'll need to rely on this person's suggestions in order to stock your cellar successfully.

- **Place Your Bets with Parker.** "To a large extent wine writer Robert Parker (of "The Wine Advocate" newsletter) *is* the market these days," says Golodetz, pointing to Parker's rating of L'Evangile. "Most other critics rated the '89 and '90 equally. Parker gave a few less points to the '89. Now it's selling for $70 while the '90 is $150." When he publishes, you need to move fast, not only to get the bottles he's recommending, but to get them before the prices move.

- **For Investment Purposes, Buy French.** While the market for California wine is gaining interest among investors, Golodetz says Bordeaux remain blue-chip. The typical life span of Bordeaux is 25 to 30 years; California wines are only proven to last 15 years.

- **Try a Self-Financing Cellar.** If you're just getting started, consider something the English have been doing for years—a wine cellar designed to pay for itself. When the wines are released, you buy twice as much as you need. Keep it until the prices double, then sell half and with the proceeds purchase another parcel.

Index